Chronicle

of the year 1993

Chronicle
of the year 1993

Publisher: Jacques Legrand

Editor	**Andrew Hunt**
Picture Editor	Simon Danger, Xavier Rousseau (Sipa Press)
Writers	Christopher Dobson, Peter Gordon, Perry Leopard
Database	Frank Breyten
Proofreader and Indexer	Irina Zarb
Production	Henri Marganne
EDP	Catherine Balouet, Imprimerie Louis-Jean (Gap)
Artworks	Catherine Jambois

How to use this book

Chronicle of the Year 1993 reports the events of the year as though they had just happened.

The weekly chronology summaries do not aim to cover all the most important events since these are reported in greater detail in the reports adjoining the summaries. The summaries include less important events and those leading up to the main events reported elsewhere or their consequences. These chains of developments can be tracked through a system of cross-references which complements the index by pointing to the next link in the chain.

Arrows indicating the next link appear at the end of reports or summaries. They point only forward in time, but can lead to either an entry in the weekly summaries or one of the fuller reports. They work like this :

• If a cross-referenced event occurs in the same month, only the day of that month will appear after the arrow – for example: (→15).

• If the next linked event occurs in another month, then the month will also appear – for example: (→March 15).

Where an arrow appears by itself after a weekly summary entry it means that the event and its consequences are reported in greater detail in the adjoining pages. Only one cross-reference appears per entry or report so the index should be used to find earlier entries on an event or individual.

© Jacques Legrand s.a., International Publishing, for World English Rights, 1994

© Chronicle Communications Ltd., Farnborough, United Kingdom

ISBN: 1-872031-32-3

Color processing: Valois Photogravure, Angoulême, France
Printing: Maury Imprimeur s.a., Malesherbes, France
Binding: SIRC, Marigny le Châtel, France

Printed in France

USA:

JL International Publishing Inc.
244 West Mill Street
Liberty – Missouri
64068 USA
Tel. (1) 816 792 19 81
Fax: (1) 816 792 19 32

UK:

Chronicle Communications Ltd.
16 Invincible road
GU14 7QU Farnborough
Tel.: (0252) 378 000
Fax.: (0252) 373 222

Chronicle

of the year 1993

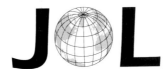

January

1993

Su	Mo	Tu	We	Th	Fr	Sa
					1	2
3	4	5	6	7	8	9
10	11	12	13	14	15	16
17	18	19	20	21	22	23
24	25	26	27	28	29	30
31						

Somalia, 1
President Bush bids farewell to U.S. troops in Mogadishu as he prepares to leave the White House. (→7)

London, 1
Premier John Major says Britain will see a steady recovery from recession in 1993. (→Feb. 18)

Dallas, 1
Notre Dame crushes Texas A&M, 28-3, in the Cotton Bowl.

Sydney, 3
Australia's cricket captain, Alan Border, becomes only the second batsman to score 10,000 runs in Test cricket.

Germany, 3
Finance Minister Jurgen Möllmann resigns.

Egypt, 4
Muslim fundamentalists kill two Coptic Christians. (→25)

U.K., 4
P&O European Ferries announces the closure of its passenger service between Dover and Boulogne after 170 years.

Washington, D.C., 5
Scientists announce the discovery of the world's most primitive dinosaur, a 225–million-year-old carnivore.

U.S., 5
For the first time since 1965, a convicted murderer is executed by hanging in Washington State.

Tokyo, 6
Japan announces the engagement of Crown Prince Naruhito to Masako Owada, a 29-year-old Harvard and Oxford graduate. (→June 9)

New York, 6
Reggie Jackson is elected to baseball's Hall of Fame.

London, 7
Ford unveils its new family car, the Mondeo.

New Delhi, 9
An Indian Airlines plane crashes on landing; all 163 people aboard survive.

DEATH

4. Danie Craven, South African rugby administrator (*Oct. 11, 1910).

AIDS criteria is redefined in U.S.

Atlanta, Friday 1
The U.S. Centers for Disease Control have broadened the definition of AIDS. The changes could raise the number of people diagnosed as having AIDS in the U.S. from 250,000 to 400,000. Activists have been pressuring the CDC to widen the definition so that more people would be eligible for public aid.

The first change in criteria is the addition of three diseases, pulmonary tuberculosis, recurring pneumonia and invasive cancer of the cervix, to the list of opportunistic diseases which are used in making the diagnosis. The second is that people with a T4-cell count of less than 200 will be considered as having AIDS.

Open borders make for booze bargains

Drinks are now cheaper in France.

Calais, Saturday 2
British shoppers have mounted an invasion of France today to take advantage of the arrival of the European Common Market with its relaxation on the amount of goods which may be imported free of duty for personal use. The main targets of the shoppers are alcohol and cigarettes. The shelves of the hypermarkets are being swept clean as each cross-Channel ferry disgorges a horde of booze-thirsty Brits who are loading up coaches and vans with drink. The recommended Customs and Excise limits of 10 cases of wine, 110 liters of beer, 10 liters of spirits and 800 cigarettes for each adult are pushed to the limit, to the delight of the French shopkeepers.

Bush, Yeltsin sign historic arms treaty

Reductions in superpower nuclear arsenals will take years to implement.

Moscow, Sunday 3
"Today the Cold War is over," declared U.S. President George Bush. He and Russian President Boris Yeltsin signed the START-2 treaty in the Grand Kremlin Palace today. Yeltsin called it "a major step toward fulfilling mankind's centuries-old dream of disarmament." START-2 calls for a 75% reduction of the countries' arsenals of nuclear warheads by the year 2003, inluding elimination of all multi-targetable land-based missiles.

Partition proposal for Bosnia is rejected

Only the Croats have accepted the Vance-Owen partition plan for Bosnia.

Geneva, Monday 4
The plan to end the war in Bosnia proposed by U.N. mediators Lord Owen and Cyrus Vance was left unsigned as peace talks closed for a one-week break. The belligerent parties in Bosnia – Serbs, Croats and Muslims – agreed in principle on a cease-fire agreement, but none of the three documents proposed – the cease-fire, a political agreement and a map for dividing Bosnia into 10 autonomous provinces – were signed by all three parties. (→8)

Jan. 1. Ben Silcock, a mentally disturbed man, is recovering in hospital after being mauled by a lion he had tried to feed in London Zoo.

Private school for First Daughter Chelsea

President-elect Clinton's 12-year-old daughter hopes to make friends here.

Little Rock, Tuesday 5
Hillary and Bill Clinton announced today that their daughter, Chelsea, will attend a private school when the family moves to Washington. "As parents we believe this decision is best for our daughter at this time," they explained. The decision is a controversial one for the first family. Clinton opposes voucher schemes which would divert public money to private schools by allowing parents to opt out of the public system.

Arap Moi wins free elections in Kenya

Nairobi, Monday 4
Daniel arap Moi was sworn in as Kenya's president today after being declared winner of the country's first multi-party elections for 26 years. At the State House ceremony Moi, 68, offered to put behind him the violence that marred the election. He swore to "serve all Kenyans, and I mean all Kenyans, with dedication and humility for the development and prosperity of our people."

However, he did not invite the three main opposition leaders to the ceremony because of their rejection of the vote, which they insist was rigged. Moi, they claim, completely lacks even the slightest commitment to the practice of democracy. Moi accuses them of pushing the country towards civil war. (→ 19)

A fourth term for Daniel arap Moi.

Russia reinstates price controls

Moscow, Tuesday 5
The government today reimposed price controls on basic foods and some consumer goods because soaring inflation has made the items "unaffordable for ordinary people." The move comes exactly a year after prices were freed from control by President Yeltsin, a decision presented as the basis of Russia's adoption of a market economy. Prime Minister Viktor Chernomydin, announcing the new regulations, said the first year of economic reform provided "no cause for euphoria."

AIDS claims ballet great Rudolf Nureyev

Paris, Wednesday 6
Rudolf Nureyev, who died today from cardiac complications brought on by AIDS, has been called the greatest dancer since Vaslav Nijinsky. Born in Siberia on March 17, 1938, he was in Paris with the Kirov Ballet when he defected in 1961. His intense and muscular style made him the most popular dancer of his day and helped to reassert the importance of the male dancer in ballet. He had a long partnership with Margot Fonteyn of London's Royal Ballet and was the director of the Paris Opera ballet company from 1983 to 1989.

Rudolf Nureyev, last year in Paris.

Plutonium ship arrives in Japan

Tokyo, Tuesday 5
The freighter *Akatsuki Maru*, carrying the largest cargo of plutonium ever to be transported by sea, docked near Tokyo today despite attempts by a yacht and five dinghies belonging to the Greenpeace environmental group to block its passage. More protests took place as the cargo was unloaded, with demonstrators screaming slogans and beating drums while Buddhist priests chanted prayers. The ship was guarded by 16 police helicopters and 69 boats.

Be-bop pioneer Dizzy Gillespie is dead

He recorded more than 100 albums.

Englewood, N.J., Wednesday 6
Jazz has lost its elder statesman. Born October 21, 1917, John Birks Gillespie died today of cancer of the pancreas.

Dizzy Gillespie will be remembered as one the most important innovators in jazz. He helped father modern jazz when he, along with Miles Davis, John Coltrane and Thelonius Monk, developed be-bop, a new style, quicker in tempo, more complex in composition, and more daring in improvisation, in the clubs of New York's 52nd Street. Gillespie also pioneered the use of Afro-Cuban rhythms in jazz.

Jan. Henry Ford, who established his company 90 years ago, sold his first Model A on July 23, 1903, to a Detroit physician for $850.

Tanker wreck threatens Shetlands

The tanker was carrying more than 84,000 tonnes of light crude when it ran aground in a 100-mph gale.

Sumburgh Head, Wednesday 6
Oil poured from the stricken tanker *Braer* throughout the night as she threatened to break up in the hurricane-force winds which drove her onto the rocks of this dangerous southern tip of the Shetland Isles. Pollution experts who have flown to the scene remain powerless to deal with more than 84,000 tonnes of light crude oil which has begun to foul the coastline of one of Britain's most precious wildlife sanctuaries, and it is feared that an ecological disaster is in the making. The best hope at the moment is that the stormy seas will break up the oil, causing it to evaporate. (→ 15)

U.N. peacekeepers reach Macedonia

Macedonia, Thursday 7
The arrival of the first contingent of Canadian peacekeepers in this former Yugoslav republic has been termed a diplomatic measure to prevent the war in Bosnia from spreading into Macedonia.

Sent by the United Nations at the request of the Macedonian authorities, the Canadian soldiers will patrol the country's borders with Serbia and Albania. (→ April 7)

Abortion controls tightened in Poland

Warsaw, Thursday 7
Strict limits on abortions were imposed today by the lower house of the Polish parliament. Only pregnancies resulting from rape or incest, or where the mother's life is in danger or the foetus is "severely damaged" may be terminated. The upper house has yet to debate the issue, and it is expected to impose more stringent controls demanded by the Roman Catholic Church.

U.S. raid on Somali warlord's arsenal

Marines on patrol in the capital.

Mogadishu, Thursday 7
The first major engagement of United States forces against the Somali militia led by General Mohammed Farah Aidid took place at dawn this morning. Helicopters attacked four metal warehouses which served as a weapons arsenal for Aidid's forces. Somali militiamen inside the warehouse had been engaging in sniper attacks against the U.S. patrols. (→ 15)

Serbs guilty of 20,000 rapes, says EC

Geneva, Friday 8
Serbs fighting for control of Bosnia are raping Muslim women in an "ethnic cleansing" campaign, an attempt to rid areas of the Muslim population, according to a report by a team of European Community investigators. The report, based on interviews with Muslim refugees in Croatia and Geneva, has been sent to the United Nations headquarters here and may be used as evidence in a possible war crimes trial. The report stresses that the rapes are not incidental to the fighting in Bosnia, but "a weapon of war to force the population to leave their homes." The report estimates that 20,000 women, the vast majority Muslim, have been raped. (→ 14)

The systematic rape of Muslim women by Serb fighters has shocked the world.

Israel eases stance on Arab deportees

A long wait in no man's land.

Israel, Thursday 7
Under pressure from the United Nations, Israeli authorities eased their hard-line stance toward the alleged activists of the radical Islamic fundamentalist group Hamas who have been deported to the no man's land north of Israel in southern Lebanon. A two-person Red Cross team will be allowed to go through Israeli-controlled territory to their camp. (→ Feb. 5)

U.S., Mexico to cooperate on free trade

A brief respite from trade talks.

Austin, Friday 8
After a meeting at the Texas governor's mansion, President-elect Bill Clinton and Mexican President Carlos Salinas answered questions from the press, stressing their commitment to the North American Free Trade Agreement. Although the two leaders said that the text of the agreement would not be open to renegotiation, Clinton added that he had a few reservations about the plan. Clinton wants separate agreements that would help protect American jobs and the environment. He had said during his campaign for the presidency that he would not sign the NAFTA until these issues were resolved.

Bosnian vice-premier is gunned down

Moments before the fatal shooting.

Sarajevo, Friday 8
Hakija Turajlic, the Bosnian deputy prime minister, was murdered today while under U.N. protection. He was travelling in an armored car manned by French U.N. soldiers to meet a visiting Turkish official when the vehicle was stopped at a Serbian checkpoint near the airport. Contrary to standing orders, the door was opened, and a Serb pointed a gun past two U.N. guards and opened fire, killing Turajlic. Western officials believe the killing was designed to halt the peace process. The Serbs claim their men were threatened by the French and that Turajlic cursed and insulted them. (→ 14)

Britain, Argentina seek to mend ties

Buenos Aires, Thursday 7
Foreign Secretary Douglas Hurd, making the first visit by a British cabinet minister to Argentina since the 1982 Falklands War, today held "fruitful and constructive" talks with President Carlos Menem. It is understood that they avoided the still disputed question of ownership of the Falklands, and Hurd was cool to a suggestion that President Menem should be invited to London to seal the rapprochement between the two countries. During his visit Hurd has concentrated on seeking agreement on technical matters such as oil exploration and squid fishing.

State of emergency in Tajikistan capital

Daily chores go on despite the crisis.

Tajikistan, Friday 8
A state of emergency was declared today in Dushanbe, capital of this Central Asian republic, where anarchy rules and the dangerous streets are filled with refugees from the fighting between the clans loyal to the former Communist bosses and and the Islamic-democratic alliance who are teetering on the edge of all-out war.

Moscow, worried by the threat of a complete breakdown of authority in this strategic outpost of the former Soviet empire, is trying to broker an agreement between the factions and has sent in a motorized rifle division to keep the peace. So far it has had no success with either aim. The former Communists and the Islamic fundamentalists have no common ground, and the Russian soldiers are under attack from fundamentalists operating out of Afghanistan. (→ March 30)

Saddam continues to taunt Allies

Washington, D.C., Friday 8
Saddam Hussein, despite a display of defiance, seems to be bowing to the allies' ultimatum. On Wednesday, the United States, Britain, France and Russia gave Iraq 48 hours to move surface-to-air missiles away from the air exclusion zone in southern Iraq. Iraqi Deputy Prime Minister Tariq Aziz said that Iraq would not heed the ultimatum and that "should these bases be attacked, Iraq will certainly respond in kind to the agression." But it seems that Iraq has moved the missiles today. Due to poor weather, U.S. satellites could not be sure of their exact location. (→ 17)

Jan. 5. President George Bush bids farewell at West Point.

Jan. Artist Christo unveils his project to wrap Berlin's Reichstag.

Jan. 7. Princess Margaret, 62, is in hospital with pneumonia.

January

1993

Su	Mo	Tu	We	Th	Fr	Sa
					1	2
3	4	5	6	7	8	9
10	11	12	13	14	15	16
17	18	19	20	21	22	23
24	25	26	27	28	29	30
31						

London, 10
Princess Diana, separated from her husband, wants to divorce Prince Charles, the press reports. (→16)

Italy, 10
The country's new highway code bans kissing and other amorous effusions at the wheel.

Oslo, 11
Russia and five Nordic nations agree to form a joint cooperation council.

Burma, 12
The military junta says it will hold opposition leader and Nobel Prize winner Aung San Suu Kyi indefinitely.

London, 12
Britain's first refuge for battered husbands is opened.

The Netherlands, 12
The government says it plans to cut the armed forces by up to 50% by the year 2000.

Ottawa, 13
Official statistics show that Chinese has become Canada's third most common language, after English and French.

U.K., 14
The aircraft carrier *Ark Royal* sails for the Adriatic as the spearhead of British reinforcements for operations in Bosnia. →

Colombia, 14
Nine scientists are killed when Mount Galeras volcano erupts.

Baltic Sea, 14
A Polish ferry capsizes, killing 43 people.

Somalia, 14
Five women are stoned to death for adultery.

Shetland Isles, 15
Oil from the wreck of the tanker *Braer* is dispersed by wind and waves.

Japan, 15
The strongest earthquake to hit Japan in a decade injures 193 people.

Spain, 16
Europe's biggest wind-powered energy generator is opened on Cape Tarifa.

DEATH

15. Sammy Cahn, U.S. songwriter (*1914).

Britain suffers first Bosnian casualty

Sarajevo, Thursday 14
Lance Corporal Wayne Edwards, 26, became the first British soldier to be killed in Bosnia when he was shot by a sniper today while escorting an ambulance in the town of Gonji Vkuf. He was struck in the head by one of a burst of shots fired as he drove a Warrior armored vehicle through the center of the town which has been the scene of fierce clashes between Muslims and Croats. A Royal Welch Fusilier, he was serving with the Cheshires. (→19)

U.N. peacekeepers drive cautiously through a devastated village near Vitez.

Virgin and Branson win BA lawsuit

London, Monday 11
Richard Branson won a stunning legal victory for his Virgin Atlantic airline today when British Airways, the world's biggest and most profitable airline, had to apologize unconditionally for what Branson called a "dirty tricks campaign" to rid BA of its competition. In addition to the apology, Branson is to receive damages of £500,000, and Virgin will get £110,000 in settlement of his libel action. BA also faces costs estimated at £3 million. (→Feb. 5)

Irish PM Reynolds hangs on to power

Dublin, Tuesday 12
Albert Reynolds was re-elected prime minister by the Irish parliament today after his party, Fianna Fail, which lost 10 seats in the general election seven weeks ago, entered into an unlikely right-left coalition with the Labour Party. Under the terms of the deal, the leader of the Labour Party, Dick Spring, becomes deputy prime minister and minister of foreign affairs. Spring is expected to give priority to the future of Northern Ireland.

India convulsed by religious violence

Bombay, Tuesday 12
India has been riven by religious strife since Dec. 6 of last year, when the destruction of the Babri Mosque in the northern town of Ayodhya by Hindu fanatics sparked riots and street battles between Muslims and Hindus. Over the last week there has been more violence, and an official toll of 215 dead was given by the government tonight. Many estimate a much higher figure, as much as two times the official reckoning. Activity in the commercial capital was effectively brought to a standstill by the rioting, but the chaos was not limited to Bombay. The western town of Ahmedabad was also affected, forcing the cancellation of the India-England cricket match scheduled for Saturday. Both cities are under curfew and the government has reinforced police and federal troops. (→March 12)

Video games cause youth health scare

London, Thursday 14
Reports of several cases of epileptic fits caused by prolonged exposure to video games such as Nintendo's "Game Boy" have led to calls by the government for an urgent inquiry. Apparently the seizures were prompted by repeated bursts of flickering lights.

A spokesman for the Japanese company said Nintendo was now planning to attach warnings against overindulgence to all its highly popular video games.

Branson is also a keen sportsman.

A relieved Albert Reynolds.

Is overindulgence dangerous?

Bush orders Haiti refugee blockade

Washington, D.C., Friday 15
President George Bush, in consultation with Bill Clinton, has ordered a naval blockade of Haiti to prevent boats carrying asylum seekers from leaving the island.

Clinton, in his presidential campaign, criticized the Bush policy of returning Haitians without hearings to determine their eligibility for refugee status. After his victory, many Haitians began preparing to flee. The Coast Guard has observed 200 boats being built and 1,400 ready to go, and a Coast Guard spokesman estimated that, in the worst case, up to 200,000 people could be headed for the U.S.

The Bush administration and the Clinton team responded to criticism by saying the blockade is a necessary measure to prevent drownings due to the unseaworthiness of the refugee's boats.

130 nations sign chemical weapons treaty

An entire category of weapons of mass destruction is to be eliminated.

Paris, Friday 15
The representatives of 130 countries signed a chemical disarmament treaty at a ceremony here at UNESCO headquarters today.

The agreement is a remarkable step forward; not only the use of chemical arms, but the possession and manufacture of these weapons of mass destruction, are forbidden. Signataries include Russia, the United States, China, India and Pakistan. North Korea, Iraq and Libya refused to sign.

The United Nations will supervise the elimination of the stockpiles, most of which belong to the United States and Russia.

Mafia boss Riina is caught at last

Palermo, Friday 15
The Italian police has finally arrested the most wanted man in the country. Plainclothes agents stopped the Citroën sedan in which Salvatore "Toto" Riina was riding with one unarmed bodyguard during rush hour this morning. He was jailed in a high-security prison in Palermo and then reportedly transferred to another undisclosed location.

Riina, who is said to be the "capo di tutti capi," or boss of all bosses, of the Sicilian mob, has been in hiding for nearly 24 years. He is wanted in connection with more than 100 murders and charged with responsibility for most of the political assassinations in Sicily over the last decade, including the bomb attacks last year which killed anti-Mafia Judge Giovanni Falcone and his successor Paolo Borsellino.

Somalia aid effort runs into trouble

Mogadishu, Friday 15
The situation in Somalia, despite the signing in Addis Ababa last Friday of a cease-fire agreement between 14 Somali factions, is still tense. Tuesday a U.S. Marine was killed in an ambush and yesterday a Swiss member of the International Committee of the Red Cross was shot in a confrontation over pay in Bardera. Today the Red Cross announced the suspension of all its activities in Somalia for 48 hours. (→ Feb. 24)

Ex-East German leader exiled to Chile

Berlin, Thursday 14
The attempt to bring the old communist elite of East Germany to justice is in tatters tonight following the flight of Erich Honecker to join his family in Chile. The former Communist Party leader was allowed to leave the country after his trial on manslaughter charges, arising from shootings at the Berlin Wall, was abandoned. A constitutional court ruled that Honecker, who is 80 and suffering from terminal liver cancer, should be freed because of his failing health. The decision was greeted with outrage.

Erich Honecker claims to be dying.

Royal 'love-tape' starts press storm

London, Saturday 16
The publication of six minutes of sexually intimate conversation between the Prince of Wales and Camilla Parker-Bowles, wife of courtier and horseman Brigadier Andrew Parker-Bowles, has set off a frenzy in British newspapers. Dubbed the "Camillagate" scandal, this latest exposé of royal marital problems is being examined in its minutest salacious details. Parker-Bowles is described as the woman Charles "loved and lost."

Jan. 16. England beat France 16-15 in the Five Nations championship.

Rock stars honored in Hall of Fame

Los Angeles, Tuesday 12
The Rock and Roll Hall of Fame has 11 new members, including artists from the 50s – Ruth Brown, Etta James, Frankie Lymon and the Teenagers – and the 60s – Cream, Creedence Clearwater Revival, the Doors, Van Morrison, Sly and the Family Stone – as well as Dinah Washington, a jazz singer, American bandstand host Dick Clark and producer Milt Galber.

Jan. 16. William Burroughs' new book, "The Seven Deadly Sins."

January
1993

Su	Mo	Tu	We	Th	Fr	Sa
					1	2
3	4	5	6	7	8	9
10	11	12	13	14	15	16
17	18	19	20	21	22	23
24	25	26	27	28	29	30
31						

U.K., 17
Bookmakers cut odds on the monarchy being abolished before the year 2000 from 100 to 1 to 50 to 1.

Melbourne, 18
West Indies cricketers beat Australia by four wickets to win the World Series competition.

London, 18
Prime Minister John Major expresses support for the U.S. raid on Iraq.

Cape Canaveral, 19
The shuttle *Endeavour* lands after a six-day mission.

Washington, D.C., 19
Bill Clinton pledges to bring a "spirit of innovation" into government. (→ 20)

Nairobi, 19
Kenya frees its last four political prisoners.

U.S., 19
Two weeks of heavy rain along the U.S.-Mexico border have left 35 people dead or missing.

Washington, D.C., 19
The State Department says Serbian forces in Bosnia are behaving as cruelly as the Nazis.

Los Angeles, 20
John McEnroe says he does not plan to play on the U.S. Davis Cup squad this year.

Geneva, 20
The Japanese head of the World Health Organization, Hiroshi Nakajima, is re-elected for a second five-year term.

Baghdad, 20
Iraq's official media advises President Bush to commit suicide. (→ Feb. 13)

Washington, D.C., 20
The Senate confirms Warren Christopher as Secretary of State, Lloyd Bentsen as Treasury Secretary and Les Aspin as Secretary of Defense.

London, 22
Eddie George is appointed governor of the Bank of England.

DEATHS

22. Kobo Abe, Japanese novelist (*March 7, 1924).

23. Thomas Dorsey, U.S. gospel composer (*1899).

U.S. missiles pound Iraqi targets

The sky over Baghdad is once again lit up by streaks of anti-aircraft fire.

Baghdad, Sunday 17
Two years to the day after the Gulf War began, U.S. warships in the Persian Gulf and the Red Sea fired 40 to 50 "smart" cruise missiles against what the White House termed a nuclear weapons plant outside the Iraqi capital. The attack is a response to Iraq's refusal to comply with United Nations Security Council resolutions. Bill Clinton, who becomes U.S. president in three days, said that he supported the attack ordered by President Bush.

A missile blasted a large crater outside a hotel frequented by foreign journalists, damaging the lobby and killing at least three people. It is unclear whether the explosion was caused by the U.S. bombs or anti-aircraft fire. (→ 20)

Endeavour orbits with $30-million toilet

Cape Canaveral, Sunday 17
Two astronauts from the shuttle *Endeavour* walked in space tonight for five hours. The space walk was part of tests in preparation for the construction of the space station *Freedom*, which is scheduled to begin in 1996, and for the repairs on the Hubble Space Telescope, which will be undertaken in December of this year.

One of the more controversial aspects of the *Endeavour* trip is the price tag of a special toilet designed to eliminate the problems of odor and small floating balls of escaped liquids in the ship. This marvel of hygienic technology was developed at a cost of $30 million. (→ 19)

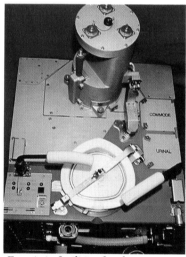

Futuristic facilities for the crew.

Elfin ambassador Hepburn dies

Switzerland, Wednesday 20
Audrey Hepburn (*May 4, 1929), model, actress and ambassador for UNICEF, the United Nations children's group, died at her Swiss home today after a long and brave battle with cancer. Her elfin looks ensured her success as a photographic model, and when she turned to acting she became one of Hollywood's most adored stars, with leading roles in *Roman Holiday* and as Holly Golightly in *Breakfast at Tiffany's*. Her later work in refugee camps around the world helped focus attention on the plight of sick and hungry children.

Jan. 17. Despite the worldwide recession and the current Motown blues, thousands flocked to the Detroit International Auto Show to admire the latest models, including this awesome Ford Mustang Mach III.

Oscar time for Rex and Audrey.

Bill Clinton is inaugurated as 42nd president

Attended by a massive crowd, today's ceremony marked the culmination of four days of festivities enjoyed by thousands of ordinary Americans.

Washington, D.C., Wednesday 20
William Jefferson Clinton swore to "preserve, protect and defend the Constitution" on his grandmother's King James Bible in today's inaugural ceremony on the steps of the Capitol. Tens of thousands of spectators turned up on the Mall on a bright, chilly day to witness the event. The ceremony included prayers led by the Reverend Billy Graham and a poem read by Maya Angelou. The new president's inaugural speech emphasized renewal, and he challenged Americans to "answer the call" to service and sacrifice in order to "reinvent America." The celebrations started Sunday with a visit to the home of Thomas Jefferson at Monticello, Virginia. His entourage then followed, by bus, the route Jefferson took to the White House. More pageantry followed, with parades and concerts, featuring such artists as Aretha Franklin, Bob Dylan and a reunited Fleetwood Mac, whose "Don't Stop Thinking about Tomorrow" had become the theme song of the Clinton campaign.

Clinton was born Billy Blythe – his father died four months after his birth – and took his stepfather's name at the age of 15. He studied at Georgetown, Yale and Oxford University. Governor of Arkansas for all but two years from 1978 until 1992, the Democrat will be the first U.S. president of the post-World War II generation. (→ 22)

The Herbie Hancock and Bill band.

Frontiersmen parade down Pennsylvania Avenue in perfect winter weather.

A solemn moment at JFK's grave.

Angola's UNITA rebels attack key oil town

Renewed fighting broke out throughout Angola about two weeks ago.

Angola, Wednesday 20

Jonas Savimbi's UNITA rebels have taken the important oil town of Sayo. The capture of the town, which accounts for about one-third of Angola's oil production, is a serious setback for the government. Petroleum production represents 90% of the country's foreign reve-

nues, and the government needs the money to finance its fight against the rebels. Many foreigners, mostly Portuguese, were evacuated, but 14 are believed to be held by rebel forces. The government now fears an attack on the enclave of Cabinda, the country's most important oil-producing area. (→ May 19)

Nuclear dispute shakes CIS unity

Minsk, Friday 22

The summit of leaders of the Commonwealth of Independent States split today over who should have control of the strategic nuclear weapons of the former Soviet Union based in Kazakhstan and Ukraine. At present, Russia has ad-

Communists take to the streets.

ministrative control of the weapons but shares political control with the states concerned. The Russian delegate demanded full control of the weapons, but this was rejected by Ukraine. After heated debate, Ukraine refused to sign a pledge for closer CIS cooperation.

Jean Plaidy dies

Athens, Wednesday 20

Jean Plaidy, one of Britain's most prolific and successful authors of romantic fiction, died today while on a cruise ship in the Mediterranean. Always guarded about her age, she was thought to be 83. Her real name was Eleanor Hibbert, but she wrote under various pseudonyms, each one a best-seller.

Knesset vote paves way for PLO talks

Tunis, Thursday 21

Peace activist Abie Nathan, by meeting here today with Yasser Arafat, has made history. He is the first Israeli to meet legally with a member of the Palestine Liberation Organization. Before Tuesday's vote in the Israeli parliament annulled a 1986 law making contacts with groups considered terrorist illegal, Nathan would have been subject to a jail term and, in fact, had previously been imprisoned for this offense. The Palestinian delegates with whom Israel has been negotiating in recent peace talks are from the West Bank and the Gaza Strip but answer to the PLO. Now the way is open to direct negotiations. (→ Feb. 24)

Clinton presidency suffers first setback

Nominee Zoë Baird under fire during her Senate confirmation hearings.

Washington, D.C., Friday 22

President Clinton is cutting his losses and dropping his nomination of Zoë Baird for attorney general. Baird had employed illegal aliens in her home and failed to make the necessary Social Security payments for them. The revelation of the story in the Senate confirmation

hearings and the resulting criticism of his choice of nominee was the administration's first setback, just two days after the inauguration. Now he faces criticism from Democrats who feel that he is letting his nominee down, but he obviously feels that fighting for Senate approval would be worse. (→ Feb. 11)

Privatization for British Rail announced

London, Friday 22

The government published today the bill designed to turn Britain's railway system back to private ownership. Under the provisions of the bill, all British Rail's passenger services will be franchised to private-sector operators. It is expected that there will be as many as 40 of these operators, who will hold their fran-

chises for five years or more. The bill will not have an easy passage. There is complete disapproval on the Labour benches, and a number of Tories are unhappy over some of its provisions, especially the uncertainty surrounding the fate of cut-price saver fares and travel cards. Investors are also wary of BR's daunting losses.

Massive march against racism in Vienna

Vienna, Saturday 23

In the biggest demonstration in Austria since World War II, about 200,000 people marched in Vienna to protest racism and xenophobia. The march was supported by all of Austria's political parties with the

exception of the far-right Freedom Party. Indeed, the march was conceived in opposition to a petition which will be circulated by the Freedom Party and which calls for the addition of an anti-immigration article to the Constitution.

An estimated 200,000 Austrians march peacefully through central Vienna.

January
1993

Su	Mo	Tu	We	Th	Fr	Sa
					1	2
3	4	5	6	7	8	9
10	11	12	13	14	15	16
17	18	19	20	21	22	23
24	25	26	27	28	29	30
31						

Washington, D.C., 24
Treasury Secretary Lloyd Bentsen outlines plan based on an energy tax to reduce the deficit.

London, 24
John Habgood, archbishop of York, warns that the public's tolerance of the behaviour of the royal family "has its limits."

Vatican, 24
The Vatican criticizes the Clinton administration's abortion policies.

U.S., 25
Sears Roebuck & Co. says it will eliminate 50,000 jobs and cease publication of its legendary catalogue.

Cairo, 25
President Mubarak vows to end Islamic fundamentalist violence. (→ Feb. 28)

New Delhi, 25
John Major expresses full support for India's economic reforms. (→ 28)

U.K., 26
Britain's interest rates are lowered to 6%, the lowest level in 15 years.

Germany, 27
A Jewish cemetery is desecrated in the former GDR.

United Arab Emirates, 27
The use of children as jockeys in camel races is banned.

Seattle, 27
Boeing confirms it plans to study the feasibility of building a 550-to-800-seat "super-jumbo" with the Airbus consortium. (→ Feb. 22)

U.S., 29
The Census Bureau reports that the number of women in managerial jobs climbed 95% to 6.2 million between 1980 and 1990.

Kenya, 30
At least 133 people are killed when a train falls into a river.

New York, 31
The pound is quoted at $1.76.

DEATHS

26. Jeanne Sauve, Canada's first woman governor general (*April 26, 1922).

30. Queen Alexandra of Yugoslavia (*1922).

Thurgood Marshall dies at 84

Bethesda, Maryland, Sunday 24
Two years after retiring from the Supreme Court because of health problems, Thurgood Marshall died today of heart failure. He was born July 2, 1908, in Baltimore.

Marshall became the first black Supreme Court justice in 1967. As the court moved rightward in his latter years of service, the staunch liberal and ardent defender of civil rights often found himself in the minority, expressing his beliefs through his dissenting opinions. He headed the NAACP Legal Defense and Educational Fund from 1940 to 1961. His greatest victory as a lawyer came in the Brown v. Board of Education case of 1954, when the court banned segregation in "separate but equal" public schools.

He served 24 years on the Court.

First Lady to head Health Task Force

Washington, D.C., Monday 25
Less than a week after arriving at the White House, Hillary Clinton has been named by her husband to head a Task Force on National Health Reform. The president said the plan would be ready to present to Congress in 100 days. The main problems to attack are coverage and cost. Some 20 million Americans are badly covered by the $840-billion system, the world's most expensive, and 35 million have no health insurance at all.

Sumo glory for 446-pound Hawaiian

The new champion, aged just 23, was a high-school basketball player.

Tokyo, Sunday 24
American wrestler Chad Rowan is poised to make sumo history. After winning his second consecutive tournament, it is very likely he will be named the first foreigner to become a *yokozuna*, or grand champion. Akebono, Rowan's Sumo name, has only been wrestling for five years, a record time for an ascension to the top. He must be promoted by Japan's Sumo Association, but few are chosen – only about 60 in the last 300 years.

Turkish reporter killed by bomb

Ankara, Sunday 24
Ugur Mumcu, editorial writer and investigative reporter for the leftist daily newspaper *Cumhuriyet*, was killed today when a bomb placed under his car exploded. The journalist was known for taking strong positions on controversial subjects in his country, especially on the rise of Islamic fundamentalism.

Mystery killings at CIA headquarters

Maclean, Virginia, Monday 25
Today in front of the CIA headquarters, a man walked past a line of cars waiting to enter the compound and shot five people. Two were killed and three wounded. The CIA confirmed that some of the people were CIA employees but could not say how many. The man's motives remain a mystery.

Jan. 26. "Britannia" may well be the last of the royal yachts, as Parliament considers the future of the ship, which costs £11 million to run annually.

Havel is first president of Czech Republic

The first president of the young Czech Republic thanks his supporters.

Prague, Tuesday 26
After an argumentative three-hour session of parliament, Vaclav Havel was elected by 109 votes out of 200 to the presidency of the Czech Republic. Havel was supported by the governing center-right coalition. Opposing him were candidates from the Communist Party and the extreme-right Republican Party. The new Czech presidency is a less powerful one than the old federal post he had occupied until last July. Havel himself admits he will serve more as a symbol of the new era than as chief executive.

Row over Hoover plant move to Scotland

Dijon, France, Wednesday 27
A furious demonstration blocked the center of the town here today as workers from the Hoover factory protested against the American company's decision to close it down and switch its operations to Cambuslang in Scotland. Amid accusations that the British government had made an under-cover deal with Hoover, Pierre Beregovoy, the French prime minister, attacked the abrupt closure of the plant after 30 years and threatened to take Britain to the European Court for misuse of EC funds. The French also claim the Scots will be used as "slave labor."

Jan. 30. Japanese tycoon Takeo Mori (*1905), said to be the world's richest man, dies.

IRA bombs Harrods and injures four

London, Thursday 28
The IRA bombed Harrods for the third time in 20 years today. A device thought to contain one pound of Semtex exploded in a litter bin near one of the store's front doors, injuring four people. The bin was one of a number which had been removed on the advice of police but replaced by the Kensington and Chelsea council because of the mess caused by shoppers at a Harrods sale. The IRA sees the store as a legitimate target because of its establishment links. Six people were killed by an IRA attack on Harrods nine years ago. (→ Feb. 27)

Queen's envoy goes overseas underwater

Sanglatte, Calais, Friday 29
Sir Christopher Mallaby, Britain's new ambassador to France, today became the first representative of Her Majesty's Government to travel to an overseas post entirely by land. He arrived here after riding for 3 hours and 40 minutes on a grimy works train through the Channel Tunnel to claim his place in the history books. He also broke tradition by wearing a boiler suit, reflective jacket, rubber boots and a hard hat instead of normal diplomatic attire. He remained, however, the epitome of unruffled Foreign Office tact, telling the welcoming committee waiting at the tunnel entrance: "It's marvellous."

Sir Christopher arrives in France.

Albanian dictator's widow sent to prison

The dictator's widow is aged 72.

Tirana, Wednesday 27
Nexhmije Hoxha was sentenced today to a prison term of nine years for misusing $75,000 worth of public money during the five years between the death of her husband Enver Hoxha, who had run Albania with an iron hand for 40 years, and the fall of the Stalinist regime in 1990. Prosecutors said the Hoxhas had used their office to enrich themselves while the country grew poorer and more isolated. Hoxha's co-defendant, Kino Buxheli, former head of a government agency that provided money to the Communist leaders, was sentenced to four years for abuse of power.

Foreigners flee Zaire as soldiers rampage

Kinshasa, Thursday 28
Rioting erupted today after soldiers were paid with new five million zaire notes. The transitional government has declared them worthless, and shopkeepers reject them. The government declared sovereignty last April, but President Mobutu Sese Seko refuses to hand over power. The violence has affected the foreign community. France's ambassador was killed in an attack on the embassy, and at least seven other foreigners have been killed.

Angry soldiers say the government is paying them with worthless money.

Dallas Cowboys corral Buffalo Bills, 52-17

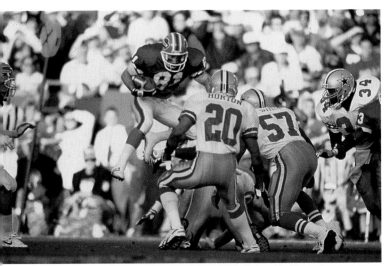

Cowboys seem more than ready to tackle a high-flying Buffalo player.

Pasadena, California, Sunday 31
Troy Aikman, Dallas quarterback and most valuable player of Super Bowl XXVII, led his team to victory over Buffalo tonight at the Rose Bowl. An estimated 100 million people in the United States and an additional 650 million in the rest of the world watched the game, and so advertisers happily coughed up $850,000 for 30-second spots. The entertainment went far beyond the game itself – the half-time show featured Michael Jackson and the NFL set up a football theme park next to the stadium.

John Major sues over infidelity rumors

London, Thursday 28
John Major issued writs for libel today against the left-wing magazine *New Statesman and Society* and a satirical magazine, *Scallywag*, after they had printed rumors about the prime minister and Clare Latimer, a Whitehall caterer. Latimer also instructed solicitors to sue the two magazines. Officials travelling with Major on his tour of India and the Gulf said that he was in a "cold fury" over the allegations which were "completely untrue." Major thus becomes the first prime minister for 25 years to sue for libel. Both magazines will defend the actions. (→ Feb. 18)

Clinton seeks compromise on gay soldiers

Washington, D.C., Friday 29
President Clinton today moved toward ending the ban on gays in the military, saying that applicants would not be asked if they were homosexual and that gays would not be thrown out of the armed forces solely because of their sexual preference. Defense Secretary Les Aspin was given six months to draft an executive order ending the ban, and a study of the problems posed by the change will be conducted during this period. Clinton called his decision a compromise, short of ending the ban outright as he promised he would in his campaign. The Joint Chiefs of Staff of the armed forces object to the change.

Anti-gay sign by a Florida road.

Massive bomb kills 20 in Bogota

Bogota, Saturday 30
A car loaded with 220 pounds of explosives was detonated today not far from the presidential palace. Twenty people, including schoolchildren buying textbooks for the new term, were killed and 30 were injured by flying glass and falling debris. The whole of the center of the city was rocked by the blast. This is the third explosion since Pablo Escobar, the drug baron who made a spectacular escape from prison last July, threatened to renew his campaign of terrorism. Officials fear there is worse to come.

'Three Little Pigs' offensive to Islam?

London, Sunday 31
The three little pigs, whose adventures with the wolf remain firm bedtime favorites, have run into a new danger: Publishers are huffing and puffing at authors to keep all mention of pigs out of children's books for fear of offending Islamic fundamentalists. According to PEN, the international writers' society, this is only one of the examples of "political correctness" being imposed on authors. Middle-class pursuits like ballet and pony-riding are out and so are symbols of wealth such as grassy lawns.

Jan. 31. For his spring-summer 1993 Paris collection (left) Chanel designer Karl Lagerfeld chose airy lightness and refined femininity, while Gianfranco Ferre of Dior opted for pleats and sunset-to-sunrise colors.

Jan. 31. Jim Courier makes like Crocodile Dundee after beating Stefan Edberg, 6-2, 6-1, 2-6, 7-5, to win the Australian Open. Earlier, Monica Seles defeated Steffi Graf, 4-6, 6-3, 6-2, to win the Women's Final.

February

1993

Su	Mo	Tu	We	Th	Fr	Sa
	1	2	3	4	5	6
7	8	9	10	11	12	13
14	15	16	17	18	19	20
21	22	23	24	25	26	27
28						

Brussels, 1
The EC begins formal talks on admitting Austria, Finland and Sweden by 1995.

London, 1
Prince Charles quips "this is rather like unveiling a mummy" as he unveils a bust of the Queen.

Perth, Australia, 1
West Indies cricketers defeat Australia by an innings and 25 runs to win the Test series.

Los Angeles, 3
The new trial of the four LAPD officers involved in the beating of Rodney King opens. (→ April 17)

France, 3
French women have the highest life expectancy in Europe, 81.1 years, eight years more than French men, official statistics show.

The Netherlands, 3
Parliament backs plans to allow euthanasia under controlled conditions.

London, 3
The pound falls to a record low of 2.35 against the Deutsche mark. (→ 4)

Hong Kong, 3
Governor Chris Patten undergoes a successful heart operation.

New York, 3
Chrysler Corp. says its stock sale raised $1.78 billion.

Chicago, 3
Marge Schott, owner of the Cincinnati Reds, is suspended from baseball for one year and fined $250,000 for racial slurs.

Germany, 4
Police launch a crackdown against far-right rock groups.

Washington, D.C., 5
President Clinton signs into law a bill, his first, that guarantees workers up to 12 weeks of unpaid leave a year to deal with family medical emergencies.

DEATHS

5. Lord Bernstein, British business executive (*Jan. 30, 1899).

6. Sheikh Saad a-Din el-Alami, Great Mufti of Jerusalem (*1911).

Mafia millions pour into Monte Carlo

Paris, Wednesday 3
A French parliamentary investigative commision has issued a report saying that France and Monaco are targets for money-laundering activities of the Italian mafia. The lax banking regulation that has made Monaco a tax haven serves to hide the source of money. Once profits from illegal activities are laundered, they are invested in legitimate businesses. The favorite targets for investment seem to be real estate and, unsurprisingly, casinos.

Monaco property, a Mafia favorite.

Cambodia offensive

Cambodia, Monday 1
The government acknowleged today an offensive against Khmer Rouge rebels in western and north-central Cambodia. United Nations officials condemn the offensive, the largest since the UN sent in peace-keeping forces after the government and three rebel groups signed a peace treaty in 1991. (→ May 28)

Bundesbank steps in to help save ERM

Currency speculators once again cause havoc on European money markets.

Frankfurt, Thursday 4
The Bundesbank, much against its own wishes, cut the German interest rates today and a great sigh of relief went round the financial markets. The cut is not large – 0.5 points in the Lombard rate and 0.25 points in the much more important discount rate – but it had an immediate effect on the exchange rate mechanism where pressure on the weaker currencies had become unsustainable. The pound, which has taken a terrible battering this week, closed three pfennigs up against the mark, and Chancellor Norman Lamont has been given some respite. Lamont was not overly grateful. He said the cut "should have taken place somewhat earlier."

Mirror in space

Moscow, Thursday 4
Russia used a giant mirror to reflect sunlight onto the earth, casting a dim beam of light across Europe tonight. The thin mirror, 20 meters in diameter, is made of Kevlar, a tough plastic. The hope is that eventually it may be used to light northern cities or to provide emergency lighting in disaster areas.

Ex-FBI boss gay?

Washington, D.C., Friday 5
According to a new book, *Official and Confidential: The Secret Life of J. Edgar Hoover*, by Anthony Summers, mafia bosses used pictures of the FBI chief engaging in homosexual acts to blackmail him. The book also claims mafiosi influenced Hoover by fixing horse races he had bet on.

Feb. 4. Bugatti, which has not produced a new model for 40 years, unveils its stunning EB 110 supercar. The 212-mph two-seater sells for £265,676.

Feb. 2. A multi-million-dollar golf course opens in arid Dubai.

Palestinians reject Israeli return offer

Lebanon, Friday 5

Israel has offered to allow 101 of the 415 Palestinians deported for allegedly being supporters of Hamas and Islamic Jihad to return and given the Red Cross a list of names. But the deportees insist that all must be allowed to come back, or none of them will. "We'll even refuse to receive the list of names," said a spokesman for the deportees. U.S.-brokered Mideast peace talks stalled after the deportations last December, and there is little chance of getting them restarted if the issue is not resolved. (→ 24)

A few of the exiled Palestinians brave the icy cold to say their prayers.

Tennis great Ashe dies

Arthur Ashe and his wife are honored by New York Mayor David Dinkins.

New York, Saturday 6

Arthur Ashe, one of America's most loved and respected athletes, has died of pneumonia brought on by AIDS. Ashe, born in Richmond, Virginia, on July 10, 1943, was not only a great tennis player, but a human-rights and AIDS activist, Washington Post columnist, television sports commentator and author of a three-volume history of America's black athletes. He was the first black athlete to win a Grand Slam event, in the first U.S. Open in 1968, and the first to win at Wimbledon, in 1975. (→ 10)

BA chief Lord King steps down early

London, Friday 5

Lord King, the dynamic businessman who has spent "twelve memorable years" as chairman of British Airways, announced today that he was retiring, six months early. At an emotional press conference, he angrily denied that his decision to step down had anything to do with the settlement by BA of the libel action brought by Richard Branson of Virgin Atlantic Airways.

Heart failure claims Joseph Mankiewicz

Bedford Hills, New York, Sunday 7

Joseph Mankiewicz (*Feb. 11, 1909) died at his home here today. An urbane and witty writer and director, his work is best summed up by All About Eve, a story of backstage rivalry played with acid brilliance by Bette Davis and George Sanders. A string of successes followed but the hugely expensive Cleopatra, with its off-screen love-affair between Elizabeth Taylor and Richard Burton, slipped from his control and nearly ended his career.

He was one of Hollywood's giants.

Belgian kingdom to be federal state

Brussels, Saturday 6

The Kingdom of Belgium, created in 1830, has just survived a test of its unity. Parliament has adopted Article 1 of the Constitution, which makes the country a federal state. This change gives the regions of Wallonia, Flanders and Brussels their own governments.

Diplomacy, defense and overall economic policy will remain under central authority.

True love conquers deep Ulster hatreds

Belfast, Friday 5

A Roman Catholic woman, Anna Moore, 46, and a Protestant man, Bobby Corry, 43, both serving life sentences for terrorist murders are to marry in Maghaberry top security jail. This unlikely romance between sworn enemies blossomed in letters passed between the jail's male and female sections. They made contact on relatives' visiting days. There will be no honeymoon.

Muscovites buy guns as crime spreads

Black-market guns are cheapest.

Moscow, Saturday 6

President Yeltsin's decree published yesterday allowing Russian citizens to buy arms to defend themselves will not make much difference. People are already armed to the hilt, mostly with guns sold by hungry soldiers, in face of a soaring crime rate with the murder rate up by 40% and robbery up by 60% last year. Shoot-outs in expensive restaurants, casual murder and corruption reaching high into the government are part of everyday life.

Feb. 5. British stuntman Tip Tipping is killed while skydiving.

February

1993

Su	Mo	Tu	We	Th	Fr	Sa
	1	2	3	4	5	6
7	8	9	10	11	12	13
14	15	16	17	18	19	20
21	22	23	24	25	26	27
28						

Algeria, 7
The state of emergency imposed a year ago in the face of growing Islamic fundamentalist violence is extended indefinitely.

Singapore, 7
Britain's Nick Faldo wins the $825,000 Johnnie Walker Classic golf tournament.

Iran, 7
A mid-air collision between an airliner and a jet fighter kills 132 people.

Prague, 8
At the same time as Slovakia, the Czech Republic introduces its new currency.

Washington, D.C., 10
President Clinton orders 100,000 federal jobs to be cut over the next four years.

Taiwan, 10
Lien Chan, a U.S.-educated politician, is named prime minister.

Richmond, Virginia 10
Thousands of people, including New York Mayor David Dinkins, attend the funeral of Arthur Ashe.

Kuala Lumpur, 11
Malaysia's nine hereditary rulers agree to limit their vast privileges.

New York, 11
The hijacker of a Lufthansa jetliner with 104 people aboard surrenders to police.

U.K., 11
University lecturers are ordered by their union to declare all sexual and romantic relationships with their students.

Cambodia, 12
French President François Mitterrand says France's war in Indochina in the 50s was "a mistake."

Mali, 12
Former dictator Moussa Traore is sentenced to death for the killing by police of 200 demontrators in 1991.

U.K., 12
Inflation falls to 1.725-year low.

Baghdad, 13
Saddam Hussein says he favors dialogue with the Clinton administration.

Michael Jackson reveals secrets on TV

Santa Ynez, Calif., Wednesday 10
In Michael Jackson's first interview in 14 years, live on television, the reclusive, self-proclaimed "King of Pop" refuted rumors about himself that have circulated in the press. At his ranch in southern California, he told talk-show host Oprah Winfrey that his complexion is light because of a skin disease, not because he bleaches his skin, he didn't fake the moonwalk, and he doesn't sleep in a oxygen tent. But yes, he is in love with actress Brooke Shields.

The eccentric star speaks out.

U.S. auto giants post record losses

Detroit, Thursday 11
Ford Motor Co. posted a $7.4-billion loss for 1992 yesterday, the largest in American corporate history. The record did not stand for long. General Motors Corp. broke it today with their announcement of a $23.5-billion loss for last year. The red ink in both cases was primarily due to new accounting rules which make for bookkeeping losses from the write-off of estimates of future costs of health benefits for retired workers. The benefits had been negotiated in lieu of pay rises. Ford's losses were also attributable to its losses in Europe – $1.1 billion last year. A GM spokesman called their losses a "paper hit" and said that their cost-cutting drive should allow the company to at least break even next year.

Feb. 8. Rodin's famous sculpture, "The Thinker," arrives in China.

Taxman has a date at Buckingham Palace

London, Thursday 11
The Queen is to join her subjects in paying income tax and capital gains tax on her private income. She is expected to pay £2 million in taxes on the annual income from her personal fortune, which is estimated at some £50 million. She will also take over Civil List payments to junior members of the royal family.

Prime Minister John Major told the Commons today that the arrangement had been initiated by the Queen a year ago. There is little doubt, however, that her advisers were forced to make the move to stem growing public unease at the monarch's tax-exempt wealth at a time when Britain is groaning under the impact of the recession.

The only significant concession she has won is an exemption from inheritance tax on what she hands on to her successor. Major said

We are definitely not amused.

there could be no question of taxing assets such as royal palaces, crown jewels and art treasures which the Queen owns as sovereign and not in a private capacity.

Feb. 9. New Yorkers can now go to a "sumo bar" to practice.

U.S. plan for Bosnia

Washington, D.C., Wednesday 10
Secretary of State Warren Christopher said tonight that America is willing to send troops to Bosnia to enforce a peace agreement. In a six point initiative to end the Balkan war, he called for tougher economic sanctions against Serbia, a tightening of the no-fly regulations, the creation of a war crimes tribunal and the appointment of a U.S. envoy to oversee the crisis. But, he said the only solution is negotiation between the warring parties. (→ 25(→ 25

Ex-Italian Premier quits in scandal

Rome, Thursday 11
Former Prime Minister Bettino Craxi resigned as leader of the scandal-plagued Italian Socialist Party today claiming that he was the victim of "unjust aggression." Craxi has received six separate notifications from Milan magistrate alleging corruption, extortion and violating the law on the financing of political parties. He is one of many leading politicians to be disgraced in the drive against Italy's endemic corruption. He claims the anti corruption drive has destabilized the country. (→ April 19)

Clinton picks woman as attorney general

President Clinton hopes Janet Reno will be confirmed as attorney general.

Washington, D.C., Thursday 11
President Clinton has named Janet Reno, a 54-year-old prosecutor from Miami, to be attorney general. If confirmed by the Senate, she will be the first woman to head the Justice Department. Clinton called her an example of the "best of America's statehouses and courthouses" and an outsider to Washington. "No agency needs an injection of innovative spirit more than the Department of Justice," he said.

Reno is Clinton's third choice. His first two picks, women as well, were dropped after revelations that they had hired illegal aliens as household help.

Zafy elected president in Madagascar

Madagascar, Thursday 11
The official results, though partial, from the second round yesterday of the presidential elections show opposition leader Albert Zafy winning in a landslide over President Didier Ratsiraka. The surgeon was health minister in the regime prior to that of Ratsiraka, who has ruled since 1975. Zaf, as he is known by his young supporters, was at the head of anti-government demonstrations in 1991 and was subsequently named premier of a short-lived transitional government. He came in well ahead of Ratsiraka in the first round last November and two days ago told a crowd of supporters, "After February 10, our history will be a happy one!"

Feb. 13. Ukrainian champion Sergei Bubka soars 6.14 meters at Lievin, France, to smash his own world indoor pole-vault record for the 17th time.

Feb. 13. Watch your step: a young French bride sets her sights on a world record with her 277.60-meter-long train.

Pope criticizes Islamic leaders in Sudan

Khartoum, Wednesday 10
Pope John Paul II, speaking today in the Sudanese capital, called for an end to persecution of the Christian and animist minorities in the Muslim-dominated country, saying that the strife was causing "a terrible harvest of suffering." The Pope addressed General Bashir, the country's leader, stressing the importance of minorities' rights to exist and to keep their traditions and the state's moral obligation "to leave room for their identity and self-expression." Later, speaking to priests and nuns, he compared the Christians' situation to the crucifixion of Jesus.

Thousands are dying of hunger.

King David was gay, says Israeli MP

David slays the giant Goliath.

Jerusalem, Wednesday 10
King David was a homosexual, opined Yael Dyan, Labor member of parliament and daughter of former Defense Minister Yoshe Dyan, in a session of the Knesset. In a debate on discrimination against homosexuals in the armed forces, she called for Israel and the Knesset to "come out of the closet." She supported her assertion by quoting from the Second Book of Samuel, where David speaks of his friend Jonathon, saying, "Wonderful was thy love to me, passing the love of women," and suggested that religious members of the Knesset might want to censor the Bible. She asserted other great Jewish leaders from the past had been gay as well.

Clinton set to tax wealthy Americans

Washington, D.C., Thursday 11
Speaking to a group of business leaders, President Clinton said that he would ask Congress to raise taxes on the wealthy and on corporations. The business community, he asserted, had "known for years that something had to be done about our deficit." He asked for their support, saying that higher taxes were necessary to reduce the national debt. The tax increases would be offset by "changes in the tax code that will plainly reward investment, as opposed to consumption, in the business sector." (→17)

Royal heir slams 'PC elitism' in U.S.

Williamsburg, Va., Saturday 13
The Prince of Wales let fly at "misguided" trendy teachers in a speech here tonight, condemning as "real elitism" the view that children from poorer backgrounds should not be made to study the classic works of literature. "It amounts to telling these children that because they live in ghettos or slums ... because they are poor or parentless, they must be deprived of the greatest of human thought and the beauty of human expression. This is a sad perversion of the genuine egalitarian nature of literature."

Su	Mo	Tu	We	Th	Fr	Sa
	1	2	3	4	5	6
7	8	9	10	11	12	13
14	15	16	17	18	19	20
21	22	23	24	25	26	27
28						

Tehran, 14
Iran again demands Britain hand over British author Salman Rushdie, sentenced to death by Ayatollah Khomeini four years ago today.

Slovakia, 15
Michal Kovac, a banker, is elected as the new nation's first president.

U.S., 15
Scientists announce the discovery of a huge range of volcanos, many of them active, deep under the South Pacific.

Germany, 16
U.S. folk singer Joan Baez is refused admission to a discotheque because she is foreign.

China, 17
Two student leaders arrested after the 1989 pro-democracy uprising are freed.

Lebanon, 17
Heavy fighting breaks out between pro-Iranian guerrillas and Israeli forces.

Oxford, 17
Students of Somerville College protest a decision to admit men into their all-women establishment.

Washington, D.C., 18
The Senate blocks a White House bid to end the ban on immigration of people infected with the AIDS virus.

Seattle, 18
Boeing Co. announces plans to cut 28,000 jobs by mid-1994. (→ 22)

Kuwait, 19
Kuwait City's zoo reopens, two years after most of its animals starved to death or were eaten by Iraqi troops during the Gulf war.

Moscow, 19
President Yeltsin calls for the replacement of the parliament's speaker, Ruslan Khasbulatov. (→ March 13)

Tripoli, 20
Libya denies reports that it is building an underground chemical weapons plant.

DEATH

18. Leslie Norman, British film producer (*Feb. 23, 1911).

Blueprint for recovery unveiled by Clinton

The new president delivers his first State of the Union speech to Congress.

Washington, D.C., Wednesday 17
President Clinton, in tonight's State of the Union address to Congress, presented his economic plan for the country, as well as his intentions to reform the health and welfare systems and to establish a national service corps for young people.

The plan has two seemingly contrasting objectives: jump-starting the economy and reducing the monstrous deficit. So tax increases – an increase of the top rate on income and a new energy tax – and selective spending cuts – a freeze on federal employees' pay and cutbacks on big science projects – are coupled with increased government spending on construction, education and other projects intended to stimulate the economy. Republicans charge that the plan is simply "tax and spend," while Clinton replies that the plan must be judged over the long term, not on the immediate tactics.

Emirates, France sign big arms deal

Abu Dhabi, Sunday 14
France has won a bitterly fought battle to supply the United Arab Emirates with a fleet of 436 main battle tanks. After desert trials, the UAE chose the Leclerc, despite power problems with the engine, over to America's M1A2 Abrams and Britain's Challenger 2.

Former communist Lithuania leader

Vilnius, Sunday 14
First results from the polls indicate that the former Communist Party leader Algirdas Brazauskas has been elected president of Lithuania by a huge majority in today's election, easily defeating Stasys Lozoraitis, an emigré for 50 years. Despite his communist background, which he has now disavowed, he is regarded as the best man to deal with the economic crisis. He insists that neither he nor his close colleagues were communist by conviction and that they are now dedicated to pragmatic social democracy.

Brazauskas seeks foreign investment

Cyprus election won by rightist leader

Nicosia, Sunday 14
Veteran right-wing politician Glafcos Clerides was elected president of Greek Cyprus today, defeating incumbent George Vassiliou by less than 1%. His election bodes ill for U.N. plans to reunite the island with Greeks and Turks running a two-zone republic.

Hundreds drown as ferry sinks off Haiti

Haiti, Thursday 18
The Haitian Navy and the U.S. Coast Guard have begun a search for survivors of a ferry that sank in a storm Tuesday night. It is estimated the ferry was carrying up to 2,000 people, mostly Haitian farmers taking their produce to market in the capital.

Feb. 14. Latest in a crop of royal dramas, Sky Television's elaborate mini-series, "Diana: Her True Story," covers 27 years of Princess Di's life.

Feb. 14. London's gay community celebrates St. Valentine's Day.

Antarctic triumph for two British trekkers

Two boys charged with toddler's murder

John Major welcomes home polar heroes Sir Ranulph and Dr. Michael Stroud.

Blurred video pictures record the moment when baby James is led away.

London, Friday 19

Sir Ranulph Fiennes and Dr. Michael Stroud spoke today of the dangers and hardships of their record-breaking 95-day trek across 1,345 miles of Antarctica. They estimated that when they were lifted off the ice a week ago they were within seven days of death from frostbite, hunger and exhaustion. "It was certainly the nastiest expedition I have been on in 29 years," said Sir Ranulph. Dr. Stroud agreed, "I hope I remember how bad it was and never do it again." They walked for ten, sometimes 13 hours a day, at temperatures of -25° C, pulling sledges loaded with nearly 500 pounds of equipment and had rested for only one day when a 100-mph blizzard forced them to halt. They completed the longest unsupported polar crossing and the first crossing of Antarctica on foot. "We were either lucky or God was good to us," said Sir Ranulph.

More than three million jobless in U.K.

London, Thursday 18

The government faced a wave of anger in the House of Commons today following the publication of figures showing that unemployment rose to 3,062,065 last month, the highest level since April 1987. The passing of the politically sensitive three million mark provoked rowdy and bitter exchanges in the Commons, while thousands demonstrated outside Parliament and Job Centres. In an attempt to calm the anger, the government announced that measures to help industry and provide training for the jobless would be a key part of next month's budget. Prime Minister Major said, "We are determined to bring unemployment down." (→ March 16)

ANC girds for post-apartheid election race

Johannesburg, Sunday 21

The African National Congress held an international convention here this weekend, the first in South Africa since the group was made legal three years ago. The ANC, beginning its transformation from liberation movement to political party, is trying to raise campaign funds for elections expected to be held by spring 1994. The ANC also set a timetable for the lifting of the remaining sanctions against South Africa. Yesterday, also looking forward to the elections, President de Klerk appointed two mixed-race "coloreds" and an Indian to his cabinet, also a first. (→ April 10)

Liverpool, Saturday 20

Two boys aged ten were charged tonight with the abduction and murder of two-year-old James Bulger, who wandered away from his mother in a Bootle shopping centre nine days ago. His body was found by children two days later on a railway embankment two-and-a-half miles away. The two boys, from Walton, have also been charged with attempting to abduct a second two-year-old boy. The second youngest defendants ever to face a murder charge in Britain, they cannot be named for legal reasons. Their arrest followed intensive inquiries by 200 police officers who were helped by computer enhanced video pictures taken by security cameras which showed two boys leading James from the shopping center. James's death has led to an outpouring of grief and anger. Hundreds of bouquets and toys have been left where he died. (→ March 1)

Feb. 16. Harvard's drama club honors Whoopi Goldberg.

Feb. 18. A $30,000 White House jogging track for Bill Clinton.

Feb. 20. Italian automobile pioneer Feruccio Lamborghini (*1917), designer of the legendary Countach and Miura SV, dies in Perugia, Italy.

February

1993

Su	Mo	Tu	We	Th	Fr	Sa
	1	2	3	4	5	6
7	8	9	10	11	12	13
14	15	16	17	18	19	20
21	22	23	24	25	26	27
28						

U.K., 21
A poll shows that nearly 50% of Britons would emigrate if they could, highest since 1948.

London, 22
A Turner landscape is sold for a record £11 million to the Getty Museum in California.

Paris, 23
Fishermen protesting against U.K. fish imports cause $6 million worth of damage.

Bombay, 23
Cricket: India beat England by an innings and 15 runs to win the Test series 3-0.

Germany, 24
Munich's 945-foot-high Olympic Tower, which has been visited by 27.2 million people, is 25 years old.

London, 24
A painting bought for $3 by an American tourist at a junk sale is found to be worth $40,000.

Washington, D.C., 24
CIA director James Woolsey warns that Russia appears unable to control the illegal export of nuclear technology.

California, 24
Governor Pete Wilson declares an end to the state's six-year drought.

U.S., 25
28were to unmarried women, an all-time high.

Moscow, 25
The Kremlin claims to have cut its troop levels in the Far East by half, to 120,000, in the past five years.

Brussels, 26
France and other NATO allies refuse to assist the U.S. airdrop in Bosnia. (→ March 1)

U.S., 28
Public and private installations are placed on a level of alert not seen since the Gulf War. (→ March 5)

DEATHS

21. Harvey Kurtzman, U.S. cartoonist and a founder of *Mad* magazine (*1925).

27. Eddie Constantine, U.S. actor (*Oct. 29, 1917).

28. Ruby Keller, Canadian-born dancer (*Aug. 1909).

Clinton gets tough on Europe's Airbus

Clinton tells Boeing workers he intends to protect U.S. aerospace jobs.

Seattle, Monday 22
Speaking to Boeing Co. employees today, President Clinton blamed European subsidies of the Airbus jetliner for job losses in the U.S. aircraft industry. He said the U.S. would closely monitor European compliance with a 1992 agreement limiting subsidies. "You know, I've seen these agreements made for years. I've seen people promise us they'd do this, that and the other thing, and then nothing happens," he added. Clinton said European governments had plowed $26 million into the industry.

U.S. envoy hopeful about Mideast peace

Jewish settlers are afraid they will have to leave the Occupied Territories.

Jerusalem, Wednesday 24
Warren Christopher, the U.S. secretary of state, expressed optimism on prospects for restarting the Mideast peace-talks after meeting with Israeli Premier Yitzhak Rabin and with a group of Palestinian negotiators. His first tour of the region has finished, and although no date has been set for resumption of the talks and the dispute over the 401 Palestinian deportees which led to the break-off of the talks has not been settled, he said "all parties want the negotiations to succeed, they want them to resume and succeed at an early date." (→ March 16)

Mulroney to resign

Toronto, Wednesday 24
Prime Minister Brian Mulroney resigned today as leader of the Progressive Conservative Party after ten years in office and two election victories. It is thought that the prospect of defeat in the upcoming elections prompted his decision. His premiership was soured by his failure to appease French-speaking Quebec by making it distinct while remaining part of Canada. His likely successor is the Minister of Defense Kim Campbell. (→ June 13)

Major supports U.S Bosnia airdrop plan

Washington, D.C., Thursday 25
President Clinton announced toda that the U.S. Air Force is to beg airdrops of food and medicine Muslims besieged in Bosnia. He i sisted the operation was for "stric ly humanitarian purposes" and tha aid would also be available for Serb and Croats. Prime Minister Joh Major, who flew home today afte talks with the president, praised th plan as an imaginative way to hel communities cut off by the fightin but made it clear that he regarde escorted road convoys as the mos reliable way of delivering aid an

Major briefs White House reporters.

that Britain would not become in volved with the air drops.

In another development, the Un ited Nations, shocked by the hor rors of "ethnic cleansing" and mass rape in Bosnia, has voted to estab lish the first war crimes tribuna since World War II. (→ 26)

Feb. 23. 60,000 soldiers join in an anti-Yeltsin demonstration.

World Trade Center rocked by massive bomb

New York, Friday 26

An explosion shook the 110-floor twin towers of the World Trade Center today at 12:15 p.m. The explosion was apparently caused by a bomb in a parking garage below the towers. Five people were killed and hundreds suffered from smoke inhalation. A crater 100 feet in diameter was formed, and a fire raged through a commuter-train station, sending a pillar of smoke up through the stairways. Near the site of the blast, concrete walls were split open and steel beams bent.

More than 40 telephone calls claiming responsibility were received after the explosion. The extent of the damage and the number of casualties make the blast the worst terrorist attack in U.S. history. The U.S., which has enjoyed relative freedom from terrorist attacks, has many major buildings with vast parking garages located directly underneath.

Rescuers scramble to help evacuate a few of the hundreds of blast victims.

The World Trade Center, second in height only to the Sears Tower in Chicago, accommodates 55,000 workers and 80,000 visitors a day. The center, located in lower Manhattan, is one of the world's largest financial and market hubs, housing New York's commodity and mercantile exchanges, many banks and brokerage firms. (→ 28)

Bobby Moore dies

A farewell to his millions of fans.

London, Wednesday 24

Bobby Moore (*April 12, 1941), the captain of the England football team which won the World Cup at Wembley in 1966, died today from cancer of the liver. Typically, he kept his illness private until last week when he issued a dignified statement in answer to the increasing number of inquiries about his health. He was regarded not only as a great footballer but as a great ambassador for the sport. Tributes to him are pouring in from all over the world. He was, said Pele, the Brazilian genius, "the perfect English gentleman."

Mt. Everest cleanup operation planned

Chamonix, France, Wednesday 24

Lightweight carbon-fiber sleds are being built here for a unique expedition to Mount Everest. A French-Nepalese team will climb to the pass where 400 climbers from 147 expeditions have camped over the last 40 years since Edmund Hillary and Tenzing Norgay conquered the Himalayan peak. They will clean up the nearly 17 tons of junk – oxygen bottles, tents, ropes and so on – left by the alpinists.

Feb. 24. Eric Clapton walks away with six Grammy Awards.

Mogadishu mobs attack U.S., U.N. forces

A tense face-off as a crowd of angry Somalis surrounds a U.S. Marine.

IRA blast injures 18 in north London

London, Saturday 27

An IRA litter-bin bomb exploded in crowded Camden High Street today, injuring 18 people. Commander Bernard Luckhurst of Scotland Yard later accused the bombers of herding people towards the bomb by telephoning a warning indicating the bomb was 400 yards away from the real scene. He said this "was clearly designed to injure as many people as possible."

Mogadishu, Wednesday 24

Rampaging mobs attacked U.S. and U.N. troops here in the Somali capital last night and today, taking the Egyptian embassy until it was recaptured by U.S. troops. The worst of the disturbances was at a traffic circle where roads to the airport, the seaport and the Marine's headquarters meet. The attacks were incited by Mohammed Farah Aidid, who used radio broadcasts to accuse the U.S. and U.N. of allowing his rival, Mohammed Said Hersi Morgan, to take territory near the southern port city of Kismayu. (→ April 26)

Bloody shootout at cult's compound in Texas

Federal agents surround Ranch Apocalypse, HQ of the Branch Davidians sect.

Waco, Texas, Sunday 28

A deadly gun battle erupted this afternoon when federal agents attempted a raid on the compound of a heavily armed religious cult. Four federal agents and two cult members were killed. At least 12 agents were wounded.

Agents from the Bureau of Alcohol, Tobacco and Firearms had been practicing for the raid for days. They had planned to arrest the leader of the Branch Davidians, David Koresh, on federal firearms charges and confiscate the cult's arsenal of guns and explosives.

More than 200 police had en circled the compound when the fe eral agents began their approach hiding in livestock trailers. Cu members fired at them, and at lea one agent was hit by fire from .50-caliber machine gun, a gu used to shoot down planes. A ceas fire was agreed 45 minutes late but there was a subsequent shoo out when three cult members cam out of the compound and fired.

Koresh, born Vernon Howel told CNN tonight that he had bee "shot through the guts" during th attack. (→ March 8)

Armed agents storm the heavily fortified compound outside Waco but are soon forced to withdraw as cultists direct a hail of gunfire through walls.

Muslim militants target Cairo café

Cairo, Sunday 28

A bomb planted by Muslim militants exploded in a café in the city center Friday, killing four people and injuring 16. The Wadi Nil café in Tahrir Square is frequented by foreigners, and Americans, Germans and Swedes were among the wounded.

The Egyptian minister of the Interior told the parliament today that the man who had planted the bomb was killed in the explosion. Several people were arrested Friday night in connection with the attack, one of the worst acts of terrorism in Cairo for many years, and the government said that they planned to arrest other members of the extremist group.

Hollywood star Lillian Gish dies at 96

New York, Saturday 27

Lillian Gish (*Oct. 14, 1896), acclaimed as the finest actress to emerge from the silent cinema, died today at her Manhattan home. She had important parts in D.W. Grif-fith's celebrated epics, *The Birth of a Nation* and *Intolerance*, and despite a break from her career with the arrival of the talkies, this frail-looking woman of delicate beauty was still acting in her nineties.

Miss Gish (right) plays her final role in the 1987 film "Whales in August."

Doubt cast on value of breast X-rays

Bethesda, Maryland, Saturday 27

At a conference on mammography sponsored by the American Cancer Society, it was reported that mammographs, X-rays of breast tissue intended to find cancers in the early stages, are not much use to women under 50.

The findings of several independent studies from Canada, Sweden and Britain showed that mammographs were useful for women over 50, but no difference could be found in death rates of younger women who had had mammograms and those who had not. The finding contradicts usual medical advice given to women, that mammograms are very useful in detecting potentially deadly breast cancer.

March

1993

Su	Mo	Tu	We	Th	Fr	Sa
	1	2	3	4	5	6
7	8	9	10	11	12	13
14	15	16	17	18	19	20
21	22	23	24	25	26	27
28	29	30	31			

Germany, 1
The government announces it will push for a seat on the U.N. Security Council despite British and French opposition.

U.S., 1
The government reports that the number of food-stamp recipients reached a record 26.6 million on January 1.

Bogota, 1
Jose Posada, the Medellin drug cartel's financial adviser, surrenders to police.

Fort Lauderdale, Florida, 1
George Steinbrenner, owner of the New York Yankees, returns to baseball after a 30-month suspension for corruption.

U.K., 3
Tony Bland, the last victim of the April 15, 1989, Hillsborough soccer disaster, is allowed to die by his doctors.

Mozambique, 3
The first U.N. peacekeepers arrive to enforce peace accords between RENAMO guerrillas and government forces.

London, 3
Rolls Royce announces plans to open a showroom in China.

London, 4
Barclays Bank announces a £242-million loss, the first in its 97-year history.

U.S., 4
Authorities admit that more than 40% of U.S. military rations parachuted into Muslim enclaves in Bosnia contain pork.

Havana, 5
President Fidel Castro says Hillary Clinton is "a beautiful woman."

Nepal, 6
Princess Diana ends a visit to Kathmandu, her first solo visit abroad since the break-up of her marriage.

DEATHS

2. Carlos Marcello, reputed head of the oldest organized crime family in the U.S. (*1910).

3. Albert Sabin, U.S. virologist (*Aug. 26, 1906).

4. Lord Ridley, British politician (*Feb. 17, 1929).

NY bomber caught

New York, Thursday 4
The FBI has arrested a suspect in connection with the bombing of the World Trade Center in lower Manhattan. FBI agents found that the van they believe transported the bomb had been rented by Mohammed Salameh, a 26-year-old Palestinian with a Jordanian passport. He reported it stolen on February 26, the day of the blast. Today, when he came to get back the deposit on the van, he was arrested by FBI agents. The identification papers he presented had traces of nitrates similar to those found at the site of the explosion. (→ 8)

Mohammed Salameh is aged 26.

U.S. food airdrops to Bosnia begin

Bosnia, Monday 1
American Hercules aircraft dropped food and medical supplies last night to the embattled Muslims of Cerska, who have had no aid since the war broke out ten months ago. Flying over the mountains from their bases in Germany, the aircrews pushed out 30 crates which floated down on parachutes over their target.

Nine of the crates have been spotted by American satellites and their positions passed on to the Bosnian government. Washington officials say that some were within "easy walking distance" of Cerska, but it is feared that tons of the supplies have been lost in the rugged countryside or fallen into the hands of the advancing Serbs. Some officials regard the airdrop plan as an ineffectual gesture, but the Hercules will be flying again tonight.

Ben Johnson banned for life for doping

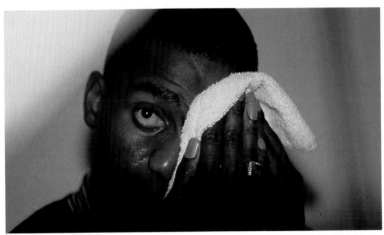

The world's fastest man ponders the sad end of a brilliant track career.

Paris, Friday 5
Canadian sprinter Ben Johnson was suspended for life from racing by the International Amateur Athletic Association today. A drug test the 31-year-old athlete took in January showed that he had used testosterone; this is the second time he has been caught using proscribed performance-enhancing substances. Johnson had been stripped of a gold medal won in the 1988 Olympics when post-race testing showed he had used an anabolic steroid.

Few surprises in vast French sex survey

France, Wednesday 3
A report on a major survey of the French on the subject of sex has been released. The survey shows that little has changed since the last survey of this kind was done in 1973. The age of the first sexual experience dropped and the number of partners went up, but there has certainly not been a sexual revolution. Nor has the advent of AIDS made a big difference: Only 16% said they had changed their behavior because of the disease.

State of emergency declared in Zambia

Lusaka, Thursday 4
The Zambian government imposed a state of emergency today following reports that opposition parties were planning a coup. Justifying the move, President Frederick Chiluba said: "Our young democracy is at stake. The danger is real and the consequences could be grave." Reports speak of leading members of the opposition being rounded up, but ex-President Kenneth Kaunda said the state of emergency had been imposed for no reason.

March 1. Hundreds of mourners attend the funeral of James Bulger, aged two. Two 10-year-old Liverpool boys have been charged with his murder.

Su	Mo	Tu	We	Th	Fr	Sa
	1	2	3	4	5	6
7	8	9	10	11	12	13
14	15	16	17	18	19	20
21	22	23	24	25	26	27
28	29	30	31			

South Korea, 7
President Kim Young Sam grants amnesty to 41,000 criminals and dissidents.

U.K., 8
A 1,400-year-old yew, the oldest tree in Britain, dies.

New York, 8
The Dow Jones industrial average hits a record high of 3,469.42 points.

Cairo, 8
The extremist Islamic Group threatens to hit U.S. targets if action is taken against its leader, Sheikh Omar Abdul Rahman, over the bombing of the World Trade Center (→ 25).

Frankfurt, 8
Two rightist Germans are indicted for a racist firebombing that killed two Turks last November.

U.K., 9
Leading film stars, including Anthony Hopkins and Michael Caine, call for an end to movie violence.

Indonesia, 10
President Suharto, in power since 1965, is re-elected for a fifth term.

Montreal, 10
The international aviation organization reports that the number of airline accident deaths rose to 1,097 in 1992, up from 653 in 1991.

Switzerland, 10
Ruth Dreifuss, 53, becomes the first woman to be elected to the Swiss cabinet.

Pyongyang, 11
North Korea pulls out from the nuclear Non-Proliferation Treaty.

Washington, D.C., 12
The Pentagon calls for the closure of 31 major military bases in the U.S.

U.K., 12
Eldorado, the much-criticized £10-million television soap opera set in Spain, is scrapped.

DEATHS

8. Billy Eckstine, U.S. jazz singer (*July 8, 1914).

10. Cyril Northcote Parkinson, British historian and author of Parkinson's Law (*July 30, 1909).

Waco cult leader David Koresh tells FBI he's 'ready for war'

The self-proclaimed messiah of Waco vows to fight to the death if necessary.

Waco, Texas, Monday 8
Cult leader David Koresh has told the FBI that he is "ready for war." Previously Koresh had said that he was willing to come out of the compound, which has been surrounded by federal agents for more than a week following their failed raid, but that he was awaiting instruction from God. Koresh has released 2 children and two elderly women but says that 17 children and 9 adults, some of whom are British and Australian, remain. According to an Australian man who left the Branch Davidians in 1989, Koresh was obsessed with keeping a year's stockpile of food in anticipation of a coming war. (→ 22)

Tory rebels humiliate Major in Parliament

London, Monday 8
Tory Euro-rebels dealt Prime Minister John Major a bruising defeat over the Maastricht treaty in the House of Commons today.

Despite fierce pressure by the Whips, 26 Conservatives voted for a Labour amendment and 18 others deliberately abstained. Amid uproar and cries for the government to resign, the crowded house carried the amendment by 314 votes to 292.

This humiliation means that it is unlikely that Britain will be able to ratify the treaty until the autumn and that the government's standing in the European Community will be severely damaged. In domestic terms it highlights the Tories' bitter divisions over Europe. (→ May 7)

Immigration fears boost German rightists

Bonn, Sunday 7
The far-right Republican Party, led by former Waffen-SS officer Franz Schonhuber, has scored massive gains in today's provincial elections in Hesse. The result will send shivers down the government's spine for it reflects not only nationwide discontent with the mainstream parties but the continuing growth of support for the right-wingers' anti-immigration policies. The rightists are striking a violent chord with many recession-hit Germans who see the immigrants as the source of their troubles. (→ 8)

March. Russian authorities are trying to put a stop to illegal pit-bull fights in Moscow.

March 9. Demi Moore wins the People's Choice Award for her role in "A Few Good Men."

Afghan warlords sign peace accord

Islamabad, Pakistan, Sunday 7
The leaders of rival factions signed a peace agreement here today after months of fighting which has left thousands dead. The factions overthrew the Communists last April after 14 years of insurrection and then began fighting amongst themselves for control of the country. Burhanuddin Rabbani will remain president, and his enemy Gulbuddin

Hardliner Gulbuddin Hekmatyar.

Hekmatyar will become prime minister. A point of contention not solved by the agreement is the naming of the defense minister. Hekmatyar insists that it is his "duty" to name the defense chief, a post currently held by a member of Rabbani's party.

Hundreds are killed in Bombay bombings

The car bomb exploded as the bus drove by, killing all 65 people aboard.

Bombay, Friday 12
A devastating wave of car-bomb explosions killed up to 300 people and injured hundreds more today. The first blast ripped through the city's stock exchange, and minutes later, a dozen slightly less powerful explosions rocked the city. The bombing assault appears to have been a carefully planned operation, although no one has yet claimed responsibility. The devices were clearly meant to cause maximum loss of life and damage to property.

Smarten up chaps, cricketers are told

London, Wednesday 10
England's cricketers, soundly defeated in India, have been told by the game's authorities that their personal appearance has caused "disquiet." Captain Graham Gooch's "designer stubble" is not specifically mentioned but is likely to disappear under the "smarten-up" orders.

Labour hangs on to power in Australia

Australia, Saturday 13
Prime Minister Paul Keating and the Labour Party have won the general elections, despite the worst economic crisis here since the 1930s. The defeat of the more conservative Liberal Party is largely due to Keating's attacks on their proposal to introduce a 15% value added tax.

Sarajevo holds first Bosnia atrocities trial

The accused face the death penalty.

Sarajevo, Friday 12
Two Serb militiamen, Borislav Herak, 21, and Sretko Damjanovic, 30, were accused of murder and rape here today in Bosnia's first war crimes trial. Ljubo Lukic, the prosecutor, said the crimes were part of the "ethnic cleansing" of villages around Sarajevo. Nada Tomic, girlfriend of Damjanovic who was arrested with the two men when they drove through a Muslim checkpoint by mistake, was accused of looting Muslim homes.

Both men were said to have confessed to multiple murders, and Herak is said to have raped and killed 12 Muslim women. (→ 30)

Abortion foe guns down Florida doctor

Pensacola, Florida, Thursday 11
David Gunn, a 47-year-old doctor has been gunned down by an anti-abortion activist. At today's court hearing, Michael Griffin, who admitted killing Gunn outside an abortion clinic here, told the judge he wished to represent himself in court and asked to be permitted to keep his Bible with him in jail as a "legal document." Last Sunday, Griffin attended a church service in which he led a prayer for his future victim and expressed a wish that Gunn give his life to Jesus. Abortion-rights activists say the increasingly militant tactics of pro-lifers has created a climate of intolerance that led to the killing.

Griffin admits killing Dr. Gunn.

Yeltsin reels after clash with Parliament

Boris Yeltsin needs loyal supporters.

Moscow, Saturday 13
The Congress of People's Deputies dispersed today after four tumultuous days in which they flouted President Yeltsin's authority and approved a resolution cutting his powers while strengthening those of the hardline congress. Yeltsin, reeling under this assault, gathered his papers together and stormed out of the parliament when a deputy called for his dismissal yesterday. He made it plain that he intends to go ahead with his referendum on who rules Russia whatever the congress decides. One bright spot for him is President Clinton's insistence that he is the "duly-elected president of Russia." (→ 20)

March. Thanks to a new art book, "Caressing Picasso," blind Britons can now "see" the artist's famous Goat by feeling the raised lines.

March

1993

Su	Mo	Tu	We	Th	Fr	Sa
	1	2	3	4	5	6
7	8	9	10	11	12	13
14	15	16	17	18	19	20
21	22	23	24	25	26	27
28	29	30	31			

Andorra, 14
The tiny Pyrenean principality becomes independent.

Detroit, 15
General Motors announces its head of purchasing, Ignacio Lopez de Arriortua, has quit to join Volkswagen.

New York, 15
The U.S. formally approves a link in routes and ownership between British Airways and USAir.

Brussels, 15
Unemployment in the EC reaches 10% for the first time since 1988.

France, 16
Ostrich meat is officially declared fit for human consumption.

U.S., 16
The final death toll of the East Coast blizzard reaches 184.

France, 17
The government announces plans to disband the army's century-old carrier-pigeon unit.

Washington, D.C., 17
Jean Kennedy Smith, sister of the late President John Kennedy, is appointed U.S. ambassador to Ireland.

Nome, Alaska, 17
Alaskan Jeff King wins the 1,160-mile Iditarod Trail Sled Dog Race in a record 10 days, 15 hours and 38 minutes.

U.S., 18
Pioneer sex researchers William Masters and Virginia Johnson divorce.

Atlanta, 19
After the withdrawal of Milan's candidacy, Olympic officials say that Sydney is the front-runner to host the 2000 Olympic Games. (→ Sept. 23)

Sri Lanka, 20
Cricket: England end a disastrous tour by losing to Sri Lanka by eight wickets in the final one-day Test.

Sydney, 20
Brazil beats Ghana, 2-1, to win the World Youth Soccer Championship.

DEATH

17. Charlotte Hughes, Britain's oldest inhabitant (*1878).

U.S. hit by 'storm of the century'

New York and other East Coast cities are virtually shut down by the storm.

U.S., Sunday 14
The eastern United States was hit this weekend by what meteorologists are calling a "snow-a-cane" because the giant storm combined characteristics of a hurricane and a blizzard. Cities from Atlanta to Boston were brought to a standstill as roads and airports were closed. The winter storm affected more Americans over a greater area than any other in history. Emergency conditions were in effect in 12 states, and more than 127 people died. Although more snow fell in the north, the storm had its greatest effect in the south. Florida had 50 tornadoes and records were set in Birmingham, Alabama, and Chattanooga, Tennessee, as 21 inches of snow fell in both towns. (→ 16)

Death sentence for rapist policeman

Rabat, Monday 15
Mohammed Mustapha Tabet, chief police commissioner of Morocco, was found guilty of more than 1,500 sex crimes, including rape, and was sentenced to death today. Evidence presented to the court included 118 videos Tabet had made with hidden cameras in his flat over a period of three years of he and his friends having sex with 518 women and girls. He sometimes demanded sex in return for passports and other official documents.

Budget for recovery unveiled by Lamont

London, Tuesday 16
Chancellor Norman Lamont performed an economic juggling act with his budget today, seeking to balance the nation's books and curb borrowing without harming the prospects of recovery. It involves three years of rising taxes including the controversial imposition of VAT on domestic fuel, electricity and gas. MPs were startled by its toughness. One said Lamont "was taxing the future to pay the debts of the past." (→ April 26)

China gets tough in talks on Hong Kong

Beijing, Wednesday 17
China threatened today to set up a shadow government in Hong Kong if Chris Patten, the colony's governor, continues with his democratic reforms. The threat, from Lu Ping, head of the Hong Kong Affairs Office, was couched in the Chinese idiom: "We need to set up a second kitchen," which is what happens when a squabbling family splits up. "If Governor Patten insists on confrontation," said Lu Ping, "we will take corresponding measures."

March 14. In Prague, 16-year-old Oksana Baiul from Odessa, in Ukraine, delivers a nearly flawless routine before being crowned figure-skating champion of the world for 1993.

March 15. Author V.S. Naipaul wins the £30,000 David Cohen British Literature Prize.

March 16. Prince Charles discusses strategy with officers of the British peacekeeping force in Croatia while convoys carrying food and medicine are blocked by Serb militiamen in Bosnia.

28

IRA targets Mother's Day shoppers

Warrington, Saturday 20

Children shopping for Mother's Day presents were mown down by two IRA bombs in the center of this Cheshire town today. The bombs, timed to explode a minute apart, were planted in metal litter bins which were turned into shrapnel by the explosions. As people ran to help those injured in the first explosion they were caught by the full blast of the second. Jonathan Ball, aged three, was killed as he walked out of a sports shop with his mother, and Tim Parry, 12, is so badly hurt he is not expected to live. Fifty five people were wounded. A warning was given, but it named a site in Liverpool, 16 miles away. Police believe this was done deliberately to confuse the security services. (→ 25)

Police and explosives experts sift through the bomb debris looking for clues.

Legendary actress Helen Hayes dies

Nyack, New York, Wednesday 17

Helen Hayes Brown, born October 10, 1900, died today of congestive heart failure. Although she won two Oscars – best actress in *The Sin of Madelon Claudet* in 1931 and best supporting actress in *Airport* in 1970 – she was best known as America's leading theatrical actress. Having seen her play the title role in *Victoria Regina*, which opened in 1935, Noel Coward called her "the greatest living actress." She began acting at the age of five and continued until she was 72, playing more than 70 major roles in the theater, as well as dozens in films and on television. After retiring from the stage she wrote an autobiography, *My Life in Three Acts*.

West Bank violence cuts short PM's trip

Washington, D.C., Tuesday 16

After outbreaks of violence in the Occupied Territories, Prime Minister Yitzhak Rabin has decided to cut short his U.S. visit; he will return Friday. Yesterday in the West Bank, Jewish settlers killed an Arab in a drive-by shooting after two Israelis had been run over by an Arab truck driver. Today in Gaza, rioting Palestinians threw stones and a homemade bomb at Israeli soldiers. Troops opened fire, killing two and wounding at least 45 people. (→ 30)

U.K. decides to ban porno TV channel

London, Friday 19

The pornographic TV channel, Red Hot Television, beamed from Holland, is to be banned in Britain. Announcing this move today, Heritage Secretary Peter Brooke said: "The sexually explicit content of Red Hot Television is unacceptable and has the potential to cause great harm to children who may see it. It repeatedly offends against good taste and decency." If the transmissions are not stopped, the supply of decoders will be made illegal.

Boris Yeltsin set to rule by decree

Moscow, Saturday 20

Fears of an armed confrontation rose tonight when President Yeltsin declared he was taking "special powers" to stop his hardline opponents reviving communism while they accused him of mounting a coup. In a television address to the nation, Yeltsin virtually declared war on the Congress of People's Deputies. Russia faces ruin at their hands, he said, and "the president is forced to assume responsibility for the country." (→ 29)

The doyenne of American theater.

March 20. Welsh defenders Neil Jenkins (right) and Paul Arnold fail to stop a 26-10 French victory in the Five Nations rugby tournament.

March. Japanese engineers unveil their Techno Super-Liner, or TSL, project. The TSL-F vessel shown here, due to begin operational testing next year, has been designed to carry 1,000 tonnes of cargo over a distance of 550 miles at speeds of up to 45 mph, even during rough weather. The futuristic ship's 280-foot hull can slice through 18-foot waves.

March

1993

Su	Mo	Tu	We	Th	Fr	Sa
	1	2	3	4	5	6
7	8	9	10	11	12	13
14	15	16	17	18	19	20
21	22	23	24	25	26	27
28	29	30	31			

France, 21
Pierre Bérégovoy's Socialist government is routed by rightists in the first round of parliamentary elections. (→ 29)

Florida, 22
Steve Olin and Tim Crews, both Cleveland Indians pitchers, are killed when their power boat crashes.

Geneva, 23
U.N. experts say that record ozone lows have been registered over a large area of the Western Hemisphere.

London, 23
Organizers of the 1994 Tour de France announce that the famous cycle race will pass through the Channel Tunnel, due to be opened next year.

Jerusalem, 24
Ezer Weizman, an advocate of peace with Israel's Arab neighbors, is elected president.

Berlin, 24
A 38-year-old Briton is beaten up after speaking to a gang of youths in English.

Warrington, 25
Tim Parry, the boy injured in the recent IRA bombing, dies. (→ 28)

New York, 25
The BBC and ABC television networks agree to coordinate their news-gathering operations worldwide.

U.S., 26
Scientists announce the discovery of the gene that causes Huntington's disease.

Bonn, 26
Nearly 100,000 steelworkers demonstrate against planned job cuts.

South America, 26
Frenchman Bruno Peyron, who is attempting to sail round the world in 80 days aboard the *Commodore Explorer,* rounds Cape Horn. (→ April 20)

Belgium, 27
Some 300,000 people join in festivities to celebrate the designation of Antwerp as the 1993 Cultural Capital of Europe.

DEATH

24. John Hershey, U.S. author (*June 17, 1914).

Nigel Mansell wins his first IndyCar race

Surfers Paradise, Sunday 21
Briton Nigel Mansell, world champion Formula One racing driver, won his first IndyCar Grand Prix race today, 65 gruelling laps round the streets of this Queensland, Australia, resort. He won just over five seconds ahead of Emerson Fittipaldi, another former Formula One champion, and then ran out of fuel immediately after crossing the finishing line.

Mansell made a poor start but quickly carved his way through the field. "It was a fantastic race," he said afterwards. "These cars are hard to drive but I really enjoyed it. I can't remember the last time I enjoyed a race so much."

"Still a lot to learn," says Mansell.

Tibetan chants are new Waco weapon

Waco, Texas, Monday 22
After considering Billy Ray Cyrus's hit country song, "Achy Breaky Heart," the FBI has decided that broadcasting Tibetan chants over loudspeakers would be more annoying to David Koresh and his 90 followers still holding out in the cult's compound. Messages are being broadcast to inform the "Davidians" about their legal status and opportunites to leave without being harmed. The FBI has also cut the electricity in a bid to make them give themselves up. (→ April 19)

South Africa admits to A-bomb program

Johannesburg, Thursday 25
President de Klerk admitted today that South Africa had built six nuclear devices but he insisted that, contrary to many reports, it had "never conducted a clandestine test." All six bombs, he said, had now been dismantled and he had decided to disclose the facts to the world, "South Africa's hands are clean. We are concealing nothing." Foreign Minister "Pik" Botha said later that a special auditor had ensured every gram of uranium used had been accounted for.

Bosnia reluctantly accepts UN plan

New York, Thursday 25
President Izetbegovic, head of th Muslim-led government of Bosnia signed the Vance-Owen peace pla at the United Nations today. It wa done reluctantly, because the pla cedes territory to the Serbs and th Serbs themselves are not happy

Bosnia's president accepts new map.

about the plan. "We will decide fo ourselves," said Radovan Karad zic, the Bosnian Serb leader, whe he arrived at the U.N. The plan puts the onus for making peace on the Bosnian Serbs. Muslims hope U.S. pressure will prevail. (→ 31)

International chess body disqualifies two rebel grandmasters

World champion Garri Kasparov.

Switzerland, Tuesday 23
Chess grandmasters Nigel Short and Garri Kasparov were banned by Fide, the World Chess Federation, today. Fide also said that the Professional Chess Organization set up by Kasparov, the world champion, and Short, his challenger, had no legal basis. The row stems from the anger of the two men at the way in which they felt they were being railroaded into playing their challenge match in Manchester without being properly consulted. They then set up their own breakaway organization and asked for bids to stage their match. Short's reaction to his banning is that it is "completely irrelevant" and that Fide's statement is "mendacious."

Challenger Nigel Short of Britain.

Blind cleric is focus of World Trade Center blast investigation

New York, Thursday 25
Five men charged with bombing the World Trade Center pleaded not guilty at a U.S. courthouse here today. Since the first arrest in the case three weeks ago, federal investigators have been focusing on connections between the accused and an Egyptian cleric who preaches at a Jersey City mosque.

After the cleric, Sheikh Omar Abdul Rahman, was acquitted in Egypt of charges linking him to the 1981 assassination of President Anwar Sadat, he left for a self–imposed exile. He entered the U.S. from the Sudan on a tourist visa in 1990, despite the fact that he was regarded in Egypt as the leader of that country's branch of the fundamentalist Islamic Jihad and was on the U.S. terrorist list.

The sheikh is known for his fiery speeches, which rail against the

Sheikh Abdul Rahman, aged 55, has been based in New Jersey since 1990.

Egyptian government and call for an Islamic state in his country. Cassettes of his speeches made in the U.S. are bought by his followers in Egypt. One such speech, threaten-

ing the assassination of Egyptian President Hosni Mubarak, was recently broadcast by a radio station owned by the Hezbollah, or Party of God, in Lebanon. (→ June 24)

Boat Race victory for Cambridge crew

London, Saturday 27
The Cambridge eight beat Oxford by 4 lengths in the 139th University boat race along the Thames from Putney Bridge to Mortlake today. It was only the second victory for Cambridge since 1975. They started as underdogs but, using their big new "cleaver" oars to telling effect, soon drew away to win in 17 minutes, the fourth fastest time ever. Cambridge president, James Behrens said: "This is the beginning of a new era for us. I expect to see us dominating this event for the next few years."

The race, a favorite in Britain's sporting calender, has taken on an international aspect recently. This year three Americans, two Germans, a Yugoslav, a Canadian and an Australian took part.

Briton is first woman to be Concorde pilot

London, Thursday 25
Barbara Harmer, 39, became civil aviation's first woman supersonic pilot today when she flew as first officer on the Concorde. It was, she said, "the achievement of a long–held ambition." She began as an air traffic controller, learning to fly privately. She became a flying instructor to get a commercial licence then joined British Caledonian to pilot BAC 1-11s before converting to long-haul DC-10s. She is one of 40 women pilots currently employed by British Airways.

She will fly the London-NYC route.

Kim Basinger to pay for reneging on film

Los Angeles, Thursday 25
Kim Basinger is to pay $8.9 million for backing out of the film *Boxing Helena*. Carl Mazzocone of Main Line Pictures argued that she had promised to play the woman whose limbs are cut off by an admirer in order to keep the beauty to himself. Basinger countered that she had not signed a contract. The court found that she must pay the estimated difference in what the film would have made with Basinger in the role and what it will make with the lesser-known Sherilyn Fenn.

A costly ruling for Kim's no-show.

March 22. Bill and Hillary Clinton leave the Little Rock hospital where the First Lady's 81-year-old father, Hugh Rodham, is critically ill.

March 27. Chinese Communist Party leader Jiang Zemin is elected president.

March 27. "Marcus" celebrates his appointment as the official mascot of the Channel Tunnel.

March

1993

Su	Mo	Tu	We	Th	Fr	Sa
	1	2	3	4	5	6
7	8	9	10	11	12	13
14	15	16	17	18	19	20
21	22	23	24	25	26	27
28	29	30	31			

Washington, D.C., 28
General Colin Powell, chairman of the Joint Chiefs of Staff, announces he will leave his post on September 30.

Hollywood, 28
Sylvester Stallone and Melanie Griffith are among the "winners" of this year's Razzie Awards for worst films. (→ 29)

London, 29
A two-year-old stallion and a carpet, given by the president of Turkmenistan, are among the presents received by Prime Minister John Major on his 50th birthday.

South Korea, 29
The government agrees to pay financial support to women who were forced into having sex with Japanese troops during World War II.

Jamaica, 30
The People's National Party, led by Prime Minister Percival Patterson, wins general elections.

Thailand, 30
The last camp for Cambodian refugees is closed; in one year, the U.N. has repatriated 350,000 such refugees.

Sarajevo, 30
The two Serb militiamen on trial for war crimes are sentenced to death.

Dushanbe, 30
Sangak Safarov, leader of Tajikistan's Popular Front, the country's main fighting force, is assassinated.

Germany, 31
The government approves plans to compensate Nazi victims in the former East Germany.

Bosnia, 31
U.N. food convoys to the besieged town of Srebrenica are halted after six Muslims are killed in a stampede to board trucks for evacuation. (→ April 6)

New York, 31
The pound is quoted at $1.52.

DEATHS

27. Roy "Wrong Way" Riegels, former U.S. football player (*1909).

30. Richard Diebenkorn, U.S. artist (*April 22, 1922).

Anti-IRA demonstrators march in Dublin

Demonstrators at the General Post Office, center of the 1916 Easter Rising.

Dublin, Sunday 28
Some 10,000 people, appalled by the IRA bombing in Warrington a week ago which killed two young boys, braved pouring rain here today to call for an end to terrorist violence. The rally was inspired by Susan McHugh, the Dublin housewife who decided to make a stand for peace after the bombing. She urged the rally to bring about an end to the violence. "All I can see is a trail of misery and devastation," she said. "I am the voice of a child saying please, please, make it stop." The rally was addressed by churchmen and community workers from the north and south of the Irish border and from Britain. The Irish pop singer Sinead O'Connor sang a new anthem for peace. Many observers doubt, however, that this upsurge of feeling will prove strong enough or last long enough to have any effect on the political situation. (→ April 7)

China frees trade

Beijing, Monday 29
China has made official the opening of its economy advocated by top leader Deng Xiaoping. A constitutional amendment replaces the "planned economy on the basis of socialist public ownership" with a "socialist market economy." The legislature also re-elected Prime Minister Li Peng and chose Jiang Zemin as president.

Channel fish war

Guernsey, Monday 29
Thirty French fishing boats sailed into Saint Peter Port here today to protest the enforcement of fishing regulations by the Royal Navy. This is the latest in a series of incidents in a fishing war which has seen a French trawler sail away with three officers from a British boarding party and the burning of a Royal Navy white ensign.

Impeachment bid fails to oust Yeltsin

Moscow, Monday 29
Hardliners in the Congress of People's Deputies failed tonight by only 72 votes out of nearly 900 cast to get the two-thirds majority they needed to impeach President Yeltsin. The vote came at the end of a dramatic day which saw Yeltsin turning to the people for support, climbing onto a bus outside the Kremlin and telling a huge crowd: "The time for compromise is over." With his position secure, at least for the time being, he can now hold the plebiscite he plans for April 25 which he is confident will confirm his position as Russia's first democratically elected leader. (→ April 25)

No easy ride for Russia's president.

Vote first in Canada

Charlottetown, Tuesday 30
Catherine Callbeck has become the first woman to be elected premier of a Canadian province. The incumbent Liberal Party won 31 out of 32 seats in the Prince Edward Island legislature; the Conservative Party won the remaining seat. This first was virtually inevitable, as the Conservatives are also led by a woman, Patricia Mella.

March 28. Driving a McLaren, Ayrton Senna wins the Brazilian Grand Prix, his 37th victory, just 16 seconds ahead of Britain's Damon Hill.

March 28. Kevin Schwantz of Texas wins the Australian GP.

Right wins historic landslide in France

President Mitterrand (right) tries to put a brave face on the Socialists' rout.

Paris, Monday 29
Edouard Balladur was appointed prime minister by President François Mitterrand tonight following the stunning victory of the right wing alliance in the French general election. The announcement came as no surprise. Balladur, a moderate right-wing technocrat, is backed by all sections of the right and the isolated president had no option but to name him. The defeat of the Socialists is so great that their representation in the National Assembly has slumped from 282 to 70 while the right-wingers can muster 484 seats, the largest majority yet of the Fifth Republic. (→ May 1)

Tropical diseases spreading, WHO reports

Washington, D.C., Wednesday 31
The World Health Organization reports that tropical diseases are spreading at an alarming rate. By the year 2010, four million people may die each year, more than twice the present rate. One in ten people in the world is infected by the most common tropical diseases, with malaria affecting 270 million.

Violence leads Israel to close West Bank

Jerusalem, Tuesday 30
Prime Minister Yitzhak Rabin has ordered the West Bank closed after weeks of violence that has left 15 Israelis and 26 Palestinians dead. Palestinians in the Occupied Territories will not be allowed to cross over the pre-1967 Israeli borders.

There has been an increase in shooting and stabbings of Israelis, and today in Hadera two policemen were killed by assailants with Uzi submachine guns. The Islamic Resistance Movement, the armed wing of Hamas, claimed responsibility. Rightist politicians criticized Rabin, calling for stronger measures to protect Israelis, such as declaring a national emergency and introducing the death penalty.

Intifada gets bloodier every day.

Hoover chief fired in free flight row

London, Monday 29
William Foust, president of Hoover Europe, and two other senior officers were fired today after the company's American parent, Maytag, said that sales promotions involving free air travel had caused "tremendous difficulties" and had cost the company more than £20 million. The promotions, which offered two £400 air tickets with each sale worth over £100 were vastly oversubscribed.

Murdoch back again at New York Post

Feisty Murdoch takes control.

New York, Monday 29
Rupert Murdoch has been granted control of *The New York Post* pending approval of his purchase of the tabloid by the Federal Communications Commission. Murdoch, who owns WNYW-TV in New York, hopes the FCC will grant a waiver on a rule barring ownership of a newspaper and broadcast outlet in the same market. Murdoch had to sell the *Post* in 1988 because of the rule. The paper has been in financial trouble since last year. When multimillionaire Abe Hirschfeld bought the paper and fired editor Pete Hamill and other employees earlier this month, the remaining staff rebelled, publishing an edition that attacked Hirschfeld, calling him "evil," a "nut" and a "liar." Hamill has turned down an offer by Murdoch to write a column and be "editor at large."

Clint Eastwood, Emma Thomson reap Oscars in Los Angeles

A well-deserved award for Emma.

Hollywood, Monday 29
Clint Eastwood, who had never won an Oscar before the Academy Awards ceremony tonight, took best film and best director Oscars for *Unforgiven*. Gene Hackman was named best supporting actor for his performance in the western. Al Pacino, another first-time winner, won the best actor award for *Scent of a Woman*.

Britain was well represented. Emma Thompson was named best actress for *Howard's End*, Neil Jordan's *The Crying Game* won the best original screenplay award, and Vanessa Redgrave, Joan Plowright and Miranda Richardson were nominated for best supporting actress. But American Marisa Tomisei won that award for *My Cousin Vinnie*.

You've made my day, beams Clint.

April

1993

Su	Mo	Tu	We	Th	Fr	Sa
				1	2	3
4	5	6	7	8	9	10
11	12	13	14	15	16	17
18	19	20	21	22	23	24
25	26	27	28	29	30	

London, 1
Britain agrees to send a squadron of warplanes to help enforce the no-fly zone over Bosnia.

Tokyo, 1
Japan agrees to cut its auto exports to the EC by 8.1%.

Australia, 1
A record 69% of Australians want their country to become a republic, a poll shows.

U.S., 1
More than 20% of Americans are infected with a sexually transmitted viral disease, a study claims.

U.S., 2
Unemployment figures show 7% to be out of jobs.

Moscow, 2
The Kremlin admits that the Soviet Union systematically dumped nuclear waste in Arctic and Eastern seas.

London, 4
Food critic Egon Ronay insures his taste buds for £250,000.

Baltimore, 5
On major league baseball's opening day, President Clinton throws the first ball; the Texas Rangers then trounce the Baltimore Orioles 7-4.

New Orleans, 5
The North Carolina Tar Heels beat Michigan, 77-71, to win the NCAA championship.

New York, 7
The former Yugoslav republic of Macedonia becomes a member of the U.N.

Tehran, 10
Iran says its tourist income rose by 50% over the past year.

DEATHS

1. Don Juan de Borbon, father of King Juan Carlos of Spain (*June 20, 1913).

1. Lord Zuckerman, British scientist (*May 30, 1904).

4. Alfred Butts, U.S. inventor of the board game "Scrabble" (*1900).

7. Hugh Rodham, father of Hillary Clinton (*1911).

8. Marian Anderson, U.S. opera singer (*Feb. 27, 1902).

Britain's RAF celebrates its 75th birthday

Indoor ceremony on a rainy day.

Norfolk, Thursday 1
The Royal Air Force, the oldest air force in the world, celebrated its 75th birthday today, but the fly-past of 149 planes at RAF Marham had to be cancelled because of torrential rain. The presentation of new sovereign's colours to mark the occasion was moved to a hangar normally housing Tornados where the Queen praised the service for its gallantry, determination and devotion to duty throughout its 75 years: "We should remember today those members who have given their lives for their country, and think also of your colleagues who are serving the cause of peace in the world."

Scientists challenge AIDS drug AZT

London, Thursday 1
The largest study yet carried out to evaluate the effectiveness of AZT in treatment of people with HIV indicates that the anti-viral drug does little to prevent the onset of AIDS. The three-year study, carried out in England, Ireland and France, showed that 92% of HIV-positive patients who received AZT survived, and 93% who received a placebo survived. The rate at which patients developed AIDS was the same in both groups, 18%. The drug is commonly prescribed to prevent development of the disease.

April 1. Brandon Lee, son of the late martial arts film star Bruce Lee, is killed during the filming of "The Crow," an action movie.

The Grand National ends in disarray

Liverpool, Saturday 3
Aintree Racecourse officials have declared this year's chaotic Grand National void. John White, whose mount, Esha Ness, came in first, was in tears. The trouble began when animal-rights demonstrators ran onto the course just before the off. When calm was restored, the jittery horses broke through the tape in a false start. On the second attempt there was a second false start, but the front runners carried on, believing that the shouts of officials trying to stop the race were those of protesters.

U.S.-Russia summit held in Vancouver

Bill and Boris get away from it all.

Vancouver, Sunday 4
In the first meeting between Bill Clinton and Boris Yeltsin, the accent was on butter, not guns.

Clinton emphasized his support for Yeltsin's reforms and a $1.6-billion aid package was announced. The largest part of the package was $700 million in agricultural credits for purchase of grain. It also included a fund to help Russia's privatization program, shipments of medical supplies, aid for developing business and help for repairing an oil-pipeline system and dismantling nuclear weapons.

But they insisted the summit was about more than just money: "I don't view this as a talk about aid. This is a talk about a long-term partnership," said Clinton. (→ 15)

Armenians broaden Karabakh offensive

Terrified Azerbaijani civilians are airlifted out of the combat zones.

Azerbaijan, Sunday 4
Azerbaijani authorities say that Armenian forces have taken a tenth of Azerbaijani territory, including the town of Kelbadzhar, and have begun an attack using tanks and artillery on the town of Fizuli, south of Nagorno-Karabakh. Both countries lay claim to the enclave which lies within Azerbaijian. Armenia denies that its armed forces are involved, saying that the fighting is being conducted by Karabakh "self-defense forces." (→ June 30)

Brutal war in Bosnia is now one year old

Sarajevo's Serb snipers turn even life's simplest tasks into a nightmare.

Sarajevo, Tuesday 6
The first anniversary of this terrible internecine war which has seen men murder families who had once been their neighbors and whole villages wiped out by "ethnic cleansing" was marked in this besieged city today by the usual barrage of shells and crack of snipers' bullets. It was just another day in the war.

Western leaders, meanwhile, appeared to be edging closer to military intervention. David Howell, chairman of the House of Commons foreign affairs committee, joined U.S. Secretary of State Warren Christopher in suggesting the arms embargo on the Muslims be lifted: "The mood of the world is beginning to say that the democracies must intervene." (→ 12)

Vatican fuels clash over women priests

The Vatican, Wednesday 7
The Roman Catholic Church intervened directly today in the Church of England's crisis over the ordination of women priests. The Vatican issued a statement saying that it "has responded positively" to requests from Anglicans opposed to women's ordination and also that the Church must respect the conscience of those who "find themselves in difficulty within the Anglican communion." Vatican sources say that more than 1,000 Anglican clergy, including some bishops, may very well defect.

Emotional farewell for Warrington victims

Warrington, Wednesday 7
Prince Philip, representing the Queen, and Mary Robinson, president of Ireland, sat side by side in the parish church of Saint Elphin today, attending an emotional remembrance service for Jonathan Ball, 3, and Timothy Parry, 12, killed by IRA bombs on Mother's Day eve. John Major flew to the service from Belfast, where he had announced plans for the resumption of peace talks.

President Clinton sent a letter in support of the peace efforts to coincide with the service. "Violence," he wrote, "from whatever quarter can never be justified." (→ 24)

Young and old mourn dead boys.

U.S. abortion foe under fire in U.K.

London, Friday 9
An American anti-abortion activist has been ordered to leave the country. The deportation order calls the presence of Don Treshman, head of Rescue America, as "not conducive to the public good."

A group of abortion-rights activists demonstrated outside his headquarters here today. Treshman had wanted to spread his message in Europe, but plans to go to France, Scotland and Ireland had to be canceled because he must remain in Britain to appear at an appeals hearing.

April 7. Would you betray your husband for $1 million? That's the question posed by "Indecent Proposal," out in the U.S. today.

Sampras ends Courier's reign as No. 1

A quarterfinal victory for top spot.

Tokyo, Friday 9
Pete Sampras has displaced fellow American Jim Courier as the highest ranked tennis player in the world. The 21-year-old defeated David Wheaton, 6-3, 3-6, 6-4, in the quarterfinals of the Japan Open. "I heard that if I won the match I would be number one," he said. "I was thinking about it a couple times during the match."

The Association of Tennis Professionals' ranking is generated by computer. The ranking is based on the player's 14 best scores over the previous 52 weeks. Sampras has a ATP score of 3,591 points, and Courier, who was upset by Jonathan Stark 4-6, 2-6, is second with 3,563 points.

Communist leader killed in South Africa

Hani was a hero to black militants.

Boksburg, Saturday 10
Chris Hani, hardline leader of South Africa's militant youth, was shot to death outside his home here today by a white gunman. Hani, 50, was also head of the South African Communist Party and a powerful member of the national executive of the African National Congress. He was seen by many as the successor to the ailing Nelson Mandela. His death seems certain to cause more bloodshed; young men in the black townships have sworn vengeance and are performing the "toyi-toyi" war dance. The police said tonight that Januzu Wallus, a South African of Polish origin, has been arrested in connection with the murder. Other arrests may follow.

April
1993

Su	Mo	Tu	We	Th	Fr	Sa
				1	2	3
4	5	6	7	8	9	10
11	12	13	14	15	16	17
18	19	20	21	22	23	24
25	26	27	28	29	30	

London, 11
Professor Stephen Hawkin, author of the best-selling *A Brief History of Time*, is named "Brain of the Year."

Manila, 11
Clashes betwwen Philippine troops and Communist guerrillas leave 42 dead.

Dublin, 11
Ebony Jane, ridden by Charlie Swan, wins the Irish Grand National steeplechase.

France, 12
The Euro Disney theme park, near Paris, celebrates its first anniversary.

London, 13
Former Prime Minister Margaret Thatcher launches a savage attack on British policy on Bosnia.

New York, 13
The *Washington Post* wins three Pulitzer Prizes.

Washington, D.C., 13
The State Department announces that new U.S. passports will have green covers instead of blue ones.

Prague, 13
The Czech Republic bans abortions for foreign visitors.

Paris, 13
France announces that the outspoken commander of U.N. forces in Bosnia, General Philippe Morillon, is to be replaced.

Tokyo, 13
Japan unveils a $116-billion plan to rescue its economy.

Kuwait, 14
Former President George Bush gets a hero's welcome as he visits the emirate. (→ 26)

Moscow, 14
Twelve leaders of the August 1991 bid to topple President Mikhail Gorbachev go on trial for treason.

Birmingham, 15
Gymnast Vitali Scherbo of Belarus wins the all-round title at the Worlu Championships.

London, 16
Ruben Palacio of Colombia becomes the first world champion to be stripped of his WBO featherweight title after testing positive for the AIDS virus.

NATO planes enforce 'no-fly' over Bosnia

German airmen set off for a surveillance mission aboard an AWACS plane.

Bosnia, Monday 12
Operation Deny Flight was launched today, with American, Dutch and French fighter pilots enforcing the U.N. air-exclusion zone over Bosnia. Six RAF Tornados are also on call, and after a decision by the constitutional court only four days ago, German AWACS crews will man the surveillance planes in the first deployment of German troops abroad since 1945. (→ 13)

Tourists in fear of U.S. mean streets

New Orleans, Monday 12
The murder of Scottish tourist Adrian Strasser, 36, here this weekend following the killing of a German visitor, Barbara Meller, in Miami 10 days ago highlights the dangers facing foreign tourists who wander away from the bright lights in America. Seven foreigners have been killed in Miami since October. British travel officials today urged tourists to "get streetwise."

April 13. Bill Clinton honors Thomas Jefferson on the 250th anniversary of his birth.

A miracle shot nets $1 million bonanza

Bloomington, Ill., Wednesday 14
NBA pros make a lot of money, but they don't come close to getting a million dollars for one shot. That is what 23-year-old Don Calhoun, a Chicago office-supplies salesman, won here tonight at half-time of the Chicago Bulls-Miami Heat game. He sank a basket from the foul line at the other end of the court – 75 feet away. Eighteen others had tried and failed in previous games.

Hillary out-earns President Clinton

Washington, D.C., Thursday 15
Hillary is the one who brings home the bacon in the Clinton household. According to tax data from the White House released today, the First Lady earned $203,172 last year working for the Rose law firm in Little Rock. Her husband took home $34,527 from his job as governor of Arkansas. The couple's combined gross adjusted income was $290,697, and they had a tax bill of $70,228. President Clinton called it "a pretty good lick," but they would have paid $6,120 more under his proposed tax rise.

Augusta Masters' title for German

Augusta, Georgia, Sunday 11
German Bernhard Langer has won the 57th Masters here at Augusta National, his second time to don the winner's green jacket. He shot a 2-under-par fourth round to finish with a total of 277, 11 under. The victory is especially sweet for Langer because it is the first major

Nicklaus faces the new generation.

tournament he has won since 1985, the last time he took the Master's title. Runner-up Chip Beck finished with a 7-under 281. Last year's winner Fred Couples, the only American to win in the last six years, was well down the list at 288. Grand old man Jack Nicklaus, who had led the field for a while in the first round, shot a one-over 289.

April 14. The Pope tells Roman Catholic nuns to leave their controversial convent at the Auschwitz concentration camp.

'The Saint's' father was not an angel

Windsor, Thursday 15
Leslie Charteris (*May 12, 1907), creator of the debonair rogue Simon Templar, alias *The Saint*, died in hospital here today. The success of his books with their stickman trademark enabled him to indulge his love of "eating, drinking, horse-racing, loafing." He loafed so well that his later books were written not by saints but by ghosts. Born in Singapore, he was the son of an Englishwoman and a prosperous Chinese surgeon who claimed descent from the Shang emperors. He married four times.

Richest states offer Russia massive aid

Tokyo, Thursday 15
Ministers of the Group of Seven leading industrialised countries meeting here today promised Russia $21 billion in "pragmatic, visible, tangible and effective" aid. Kabun Muto, Japan's foreign minister, explained: "We want to see a democratic, stable and economically strong Russia, firmly integrated into the community of democratic states and into the world economy." Douglas Hurd, the British foreign minister, was optimistic that the aid would give a "very substantial" political advantage to Yeltsin who faces a referendum on his reforms in 10 days time.

Rodney King verdict eases tensions in LA

Wall art illustrates the black community's anger over the orginal verdict.

Los Angeles, Saturday 17
Los Angeles has been a tense city for the last week. The jury in the civil-rights trial of four policeman accused in the beating of Rodney King went into deliberations last weekend. Gun sales were up in anticipation of a repeat of last year's riots. Since Friday night 6,500 police have been on the streets and the National Guard has been standing by. That tension was lifted today when the jury came in with its verdict. Sgt. Stacey Koon, the ranking officer present at the beating, was found guilty of allowing excessive force to restrain King. Officer Laurence Powell, who was seen to strike most of the blows against King in the video of the beating made by a bystander, was convicted of using excessive force. The other officers, Theodore Briseno and Timothy Wind, were acquitted.

Dinosaur mystery puzzles paleontologists

New York, Saturday 17
Paleontologists from the American Museum of Natural History say they have found a 75-million-year-old fossil that is an evolutionary link between dinosaurs and birds. *Mononychus olecranus*, as they have named it, was found in Mongolia's Gobi Desert. It has a dinosaur's long neck and tail and sharp teeth and a bird's keeled breastbone. But many ornithologists disagree, insisting that birds evolved from reptiles only distantly related to dinosaurs.

Gloves come off as Japan, U.S. clash

Washington, D.C., Friday 16
President Clinton and Japanese Prime Minister Kiichi Miyazawa made it clear in a joint press conference here today that there were serious differences in their views on the current trading situation between the two economic giants. Clinton criticized Japan as being

A lighter moment after tough talks.

closed to American imports. Miyazawa responded that Japan would increase access to its markets, but added that the U.S. must do more to increase the quality of its products in order for them to sell well in Japan. The total U.S. trade deficit stands at $7.2 billion, more than half of which, $4.13 billion, is the deficit with Japan.

Heart attack claims Turkey's president

Ankara, Saturday 17
President Turgut Ozal died today, hours after suffering a massive heart attack and six years after undergoing heart surgery for a triple bypass. Ozal, aged 66, was a man of vision, determined to make Turkey a modern regional power. He introduced radical economic changes, applied for full membership of the EC, and spread Turkey's influence into the Moslem states of the former Soviet Union. He also earned the goodwill of the U.S. by putting Turkey and its airfields on the side of the allies in the Gulf War. His likely successor is Prime Minister Suleyman Demirel. (→ June 13)

The pugnacious leader was aged 66.

Pakistan's premier is deposed in coup

Islamabad, Saturday 17
Pakistan's Prime Minister, Nawaz Sharif, accused President Ghulam Ishaq Khan of conspiring against his government in nationally televised speech today.

The bitter power struggle began early in the year, when Ishaq Khan appointed the commander of the military without consulting Sharif. At the end of February, Sharif said the president's office should be weakened by repealing a constitutional amendment that allows the president to dismiss the government and dissolve parliament. (→ 18)

April. A U.S.-built Amac .50-caliber supergun, similar to rifles used by the IRA in Ulster. It can blow a man's head off from a distance of 1.5 miles.

Su	Mo	Tu	We	Th	Fr	Sa
				1	2	3
4	5	6	7	8	9	10
11	12	13	14	15	16	17
18	19	20	21	22	23	24
25	26	27	28	29	30	

Bosnia, 18
The Muslim town of Srebrenica falls to Serb forces.

Wembley, 18
Arsenal beats Sheffield Wednesday, 2-1, in the final of soccer's League Cup.

Pakistan, 18
President Ishaq Khan ousts premier Sharif.

Tokyo, 20
The dollar drops to 110.25 yen, its lowest level since 1945.

Stockholm, 20
Swedish television rejects a British sex education program, saying it is "much too tame."

U.S., 21
A poll shows that 93% of Americans blame David Koresh for the Waco tragedy.

Egypt, 21
Information Minister Mohammed Sherif escapes an assassination attempt.

Rome, 22
Prime Minister Giuliano Amato resigns. (→ 26)

China, 22
The government says its birth control policies led to a big drop in the 1992 birthrate.

Isle of Man, 23
A public outcry forces the Manx government to abandon plans to remove punishment by birching from the statute book.

Geneva, 23
The World Health Organization declares tuberculosis a global emergency, saying TB could kill 30 million by 2003.

DEATHS

18. Elizabeth Frink, British sculptor (*Nov. 14, 1930).

20. Henry Brandon, former *Sunday Times* correspondent in Washington, D.C., (*March 9, 1916).

20. Mario Moreno, "Cantinflas", Mexican comic actor (*Aug. 12, 1911).

22. Andreis Truernicht, founder of South Africa's Conservative Party (*Feb. 19, 1921).

24. Oliver Tambo, South African anti-apartheid leader (*Oct. 27, 1917).

Waco siege ends in fiery tragedy

Waco, Texas, Monday 19
At 5:55 this morning an FBI negotiator telephoned the beseiged compound holding David Koresh and the Branch Davidians. He warned Steve Schneider, Koresh's right-hand man: "There's going to be tear gas injected into the compound. This is not an assault. Do not fire. The idea is to get you out of the compound." The FBI negotiator heard Schneider order the cultists to put on gas masks, and then the telephone was thrown out of the window. Agents backed by armored vehicles advanced on Ranch Apocalypse and loudspeakers repeated the warning: "Come out now and you will not be harmed." Tanks punched holes through the walls of the fortified compound. As the world's media looked on, the tanks pumped CS gas into the build-

Long-range cameras record the final moments of the 51-day stand-off.

ings in the hope that the cult members would surrender. FBI snipers say they saw two people setting fires about noon. The blaze spread rapidly, engulfing the buildings as police and reporters watched helplessly. Nine cult members, including two Britons, escaped from the self-inflicted inferno. Among the dead are at least 17 children. (→ 21)

Warsaw ghetto's Nazi victims honored

Eternal flame burns at Birkenau, where more than one million Jews died.

Warsaw, Monday 19
The 50th anniversary of the gallant but doomed defense of Warsaw's ghetto by poorly armed Jewish youths against the might of the German army was commemorated here today. Prime Minister Yitzhak Rabin of Israel, U.S. Vice President Al Gore, President Lech Walesa of Poland and German parliamentarians laid wreaths in tribute to the fighters whose sacrifice first drew the world's attention to the Holocaust. Thousands of Jewish visitors wept as Rabin praised the dead: "They had no chance, but they do now because in the history of mankind they will remain as defenders of the fire of honor."

'Too old' racer wins London's marathon

London, Sunday 18
Eamonn Martin, the 34-year-old runner who was written off as too old by sponsors, stormed home to win the London Marathon today in his first attempt at racing the distance.

Shrugging off his years, he outsprinted Mexican Isidro Rico over Westminster Bridge to collect the winner's prize of £58,000. He said that he had enjoyed the race and added, "There are always people who break the rules on age."

EBRD chief Attali is called to account

London, Sunday 18
Jacques Attali, the head of the European Bank for Reconstruction and Development, is under fire for lavish spending on the bank's new headquarters. According to press reports, tons of Carrara marble and flashy sculptures have been brought in to outfit the offices of bank officials. The cost of equipping the plush headquarters is said to have been about £200 million, about double the amount disbursed by the EBRD. (→ June 25)

Italian voters reject old political system

Rome, Monday 19
Italians, weary of political scandal and corruption, voted overwhelmingly today to reform the political system. No less than 82% voted in favor of replacing proportional representation with a simple first-past-the-post system. Even more, 90% voted to end the public financing of political parties. President Scalfaro is expected to form a new government immediately to push through the reforms and emergency economic measures. (→ 22)

Phileas Fogg's record falls to Frenchman

Brest, Tuesday 20

Phileas Fogg's fictional record of 80 days around the world was broken today when the French yachtsman Bruno Peyron and his five-man crew brought their 85-foot catamaran *Commodore Explorer* into harbor here with less than a day to spare. His time was 79 days, 6 hours, 20 minutes. Peyron's voyage was hardly less adventurous than Fogg's. Two other competitors in the challenge race were forced to retire, and Peyron's boat split its starboard hull, fought a storm off Cape Horn and collided with a whale. Nobody expected him home so soon. A trophy, designed by the American artist Tom Shannon, is still on the drawing board. He and his crew will share a prize of £120,000.

Land ahoy: Peyron's journey ends.

Massive IRA bomb rips heart out of City

London, Saturday 24

The IRA devastated the heart of the City of London today with one of the biggest bombs ever detonated on the mainland. The bomb, hidden in a truck close to the Nat-West Tower, left a crater of some 14 square yards. Edward Henty, a photographer, was killed and 44 others were injured. The medieval church of Saint Ethelburga the Virgin was destroyed and over a million square feet of office space was made uninhabitable. First estimates suggest insurance claims will total £1 billion. Security experts say that the IRA's resumption of prestige attacks is a sign the terrorists believe they have recovered from the bad publicity following the Warrington bombing.

The cost of devastation: £1 billion.

Chilling Holocaust Memorial Museum opens in Washington

Washington, D.C., Thursday 22

The Holocaust Museum, a federal museum built with private donations, was dedicated today. It documents the history of the Nazi attempt to wipe out European Jews. The museum shows various artifacts such as Zyklon B canisters used in death camp gas chambers, a Polish railcar used to take victims to the camps, a Danish boat that ferried Jews to safety as well as photographs, drawings, films and documents.

The five-level domed building, whose architecture recalls the death camps, was designed by James I. Freed, a Jew who escaped Nazi Germany at the age of nine.

A $90-million museum to bring home the full horror of the Holocaust.

Brazilian royalists suffer vote setback

Rio de Janeiro, Wednesday 21

The various pretenders to the throne of Brazil – about a dozen in all – will be deeply disappointed by the first results of today's referendum in which 90 million Brazilians were supposed to vote on what form of government they want. They could have voted for the restoration of the Braganza monarchy, which was deposed 103 years ago, but the electorate was so confused by the terms of the referendum that half of them stayed away from the polls or spoilt their papers. Of those that did vote, only 10% want a king – whoever he might be.

April 21. Drop dead chic: Anti-fur activists use a dead fox for their new campaign in Britain.

Cesar Chavez, farm union hero, dies

Yuma, Arizona, Friday 23

Farm labor organizer Cesar Estrada Chavez was found dead today in the town where he was born on March 31, 1927. From 1952 to 1962 he worked for the Community Service Organization, founded by Saul Alinsky. In 1962, he founded the labor organization that became the United Farm Workers. Called a "heroic figure" by Robert Kennedy, Chavez led boycotts of grapes and other produce in the 1960s in order to gain leverage with growers.

April 20. The Rock Ridge Saloon, in Greenwich Village, offers a bizarre new sport each Tuesday: human 'bowlees' versus six 5-foot-high pins.

April

1993

Su	Mo	Tu	We	Th	Fr	Sa
				1	2	3
4	5	6	7	8	9	10
11	12	13	14	15	16	17
18	19	20	21	22	23	24
25	26	27	28	29	30	

Tirana, 25
Pope John Paul II begins his first visit to Albania, until recently the world's only officially atheist state.

Boston, 25
Responding to criticism about the first 100 days of his presidency, Bill Clinton says: "You can't expect instant results."

Nottingham, 26
Brian Clough, manager of Nottingham Forest for 18 years, says he is to retire from the club.

London, 26
Norman Willis, general secretary of the TUC, announces his early retirement.

Kuwait, 26
The government says Iraqi agents have been arrested for trying to assassinate former President Bush during his recent visit. (→ June 26)

Colombia, 26
Flash floods kill an estimated 100 people.

Rome, 26
Carlo Ciampi, 72, is named prime minister. (→ June 20)

Washington, D.C., 27
A CIA report accuses French spies of targeting U.S. defense and aerospace firms.

Yemen, 27
The governing General People's Congress defeats an Islamic fundamentalist party in parliamentary elections.

Asmara, 27
The Ethiopian province of Eritrea votes overwhelmingly in favor of independence.

U.K., 28
A record 5.6 million crimes were recorded in England and Wales last year.

London, 28
The Smith and Wesson .44 used by Bob Ford to kill outlaw Jesse James is sold to a U.S. collector for £115,000.

London, 29
Lloyds of London, facing losses of £6 billion, announces the most drastic reorganization in its 305-year history.

South Africa, 29
President de Klerk apologizes for apartheid for the first time.

President Yeltsin wins crucial vote of confidence in Russia

Moment of truth as the presidential couple prepare to cast their ballots.

Moscow, Sunday 25
President Yeltsin has won a clear victory in the referendum held today to pass judgement on his leadership and his reforms. Some 60% of the voters backed his leadership, and 53% supported his economic reforms. In Moscow he has won more than 70% of the votes. President Clinton was delighted. He said it was "a very good day" not only for Russians but for Americans. However, Yeltsin's hardline opponents scoffed at the results. Ruslan Khasbulatov, the parliament's speaker, said that the vote "would have neither winners nor losers." Aleksander Rutskoi, the vice president, said: "So what happened? We had a sociological opinion poll, that's all." (→ May 6)

U.K. recession is over, chancellor claims

London, Monday 26
A jubilant Norman Lamont, the chancellor of the exchequer, announced today that Britain's worst recession since the dark days of the 1930s is officially over. The chancellor based his upbeat comments on figures just released which show that ouput grew by 0.6% in the first quarter, after more than 30 months of stagnation.

Economists, who are warning against complacency, say this spurt is due to increased exports resulting from lower interest rates and the reduction of the pound's value after Britain's pull-out from the European exchange-rate mechanism last September. (→ May 7)

New optimism for Norman Lamont.

U.S. Marines leave Mogadishu to U.N.

Mogadishu, Monday 26
Control of the Somali capital was handed over from U.S. Marines to Pakistani peacekeepers. The 2,500 Marines, who had been charged with policing the city, will fly home Wednesday. They were part of the 24,000 U.S. troops sent to assure delivery of food and medical aid and halt clan fighting in the country. About 2,200 Marines will be deployed on a ship off the Somali coast in case they are needed as reinforcement. The Pakistani regiment is part of a U.N. force of 30,800 troops who will officially take control of Somalia. (→ May 4)

April 26. Prince Andrew, aged 33, assumes his first command.

Princess Di tells of despair over bulimia

London, Tuesday 27
The Princess of Wales, who has suffered from bulimia, spoke passionately today about the "secret spiral of despair" of the victims of eating disorders. She told a conference of health workers that the problem starts in childhood with "feelings of guilt, of self revulsion and low personal esteem." The illness that develops, she said, becomes a "shameful friend." By focusing their energies on controlling their bodies, they had found a refuge from having to face more painful issues at the center of their lives.

Di reveals traumatic experiences.

Bosnia's Serbs reject peace plan and defy U.N. sanctions

Belgrade, Monday 26
After a grim and often passionate all-night sitting, the Bosnian Serb parliament voted unanimously this morning to reject the Vance-Owen peace plan and to defy the harsh new sanctions threatened by the U.N. The mood was summed up by one member who emerged after the 6 am deadline set by the U.N. to say: "If the Vietnamese survived a war against the Americans, so can we." The sanctions which will now come into force are meant to cut off the Serbs from the outside world. They will stop shipments along the Danube, stop Yugoslav ships passing through U.N. countries, freeze funds in foreign banks and stop all goods except humanitarian aid edtering by land. (→ May 6)

Peace efforts by Lord Owen (center) and Cyrus Vance (right) suffer new blow.

Wartime roles for U.S. women pilots

Washington, D.C., Wednesday 28
Secretary of Defense Les Aspin today ordered an end to the ban on women pilots in combat. He also asked Congress to repeal a law that barred women from navy combat ships. The law against women combat pilots had been repealed in 1991. But Aspin stopped short of allowing women combat roles on the ground. Heads of the various military branches indicated they would cooperate fully with the order. At present there are 999 women pilots and flight officers in the American armed forces, about 2% of the total. Women account for 11.6% of the nearly two million members of the military.

China, Taiwan end 40 years of enmity

Singapore, Tuesday 27
Ending four decades of rivalry and bitter hatred between Communist China and Taiwan, senior officials from both countries met here today at the start of historic bilateral talks.

Although this initial meeting is not expected to lead to major concrete results, it is seen as an important first step towards the reunification of the Nationalist island with the Chinese mainland. Both sides readily agree that Taiwan is part of China, but both also regard themselves as the sole legitimate government of China.

Monica Seles stabbed in back by pro-Graf fanatic during match

Hamburg, Friday 30
The guard working the Hamburg Open noticed a bald man walking along the bottom row of seats just behind a thin, three-foot-high wall that separates the court area from the stands, but thought little about him. But the man suddenly reached into a bag he was carrying, pulled out a knife and stabbed Monica Seles in the neck. The man was wrestled to the ground by two spectators and the guard, and his arm was broken. When questioned later by police after his arrest, he explained he had wanted to wound Seles because she was the top-ranked tennis player in the world, ahead of his favorite, Steffi Graf.

As guards struggle with the assailant, friends rush to help stricken Seles.

April 25. Gay Americans march: hundreds of thousands of gay-rights activists gather in Washington to call for an end to discrimination.

April 29. The Queen announces that Buckingham Palace is to open for visitors. Money will finance repairs to fire-damaged Windsor Castle.

May

1993

Su	Mo	Tu	We	Th	Fr	Sa
						1
2	3	4	5	6	7	8
9	10	11	12	13	14	15
16	17	18	19	20	21	22
23	24	25	26	27	28	29
30	31					

Newmarket, 1
Zafonic, ridden by Pat Eddery, wins 2,000 Guineas race.

South Africa, 1
Six whites and one black are killed in an attack on a hotel; authorities blame the Pan-Africanist Congress. (→ 25)

Moscow, 1
Pro-Communist demonstrators clash with police after May Day celebrations. (→ 6)

Louisville, Kentucky, 1
Sea Hero, ridden by Jerry Bailey, wins Kentucky Derby.

Kuwait, 2
Government announces plans to build a 120-mile ditch, ten feet deep and 16 feet wide, along the border with Iraq.

U.K., 2
Manchester United win Football League trophy for the first time in 26 years.

U.S., 3
Levi Strauss & Co. announces it will not do business in China.

Cambodia, 4
The Khmer Rouge ambush a convoy of U.N. peacekeepers and attack a U.N. camp. (→ 21)

Northern Cyprus, 4
Polly Peck founder Asil Nadir jumps £3.5-million bail and flies to Northern Cyprus. (→ June 24)

London, 5
British Safety Council calls Buckingham Palace a "potential death trap" and urges safety measures be put in place before opening the palace for public visits.

Las Vegas, 8
Lennox Lewis is first British world heavyweight champion in 20th century, beating Tony Tucker in WBC title fight.

DEATHS

2. Julio Gallo, American vintner (*March 21, 1910).

5. Irving Howe, American political and literary critic (*June 11, 1920).

6. Ian Mikardo, British politician (*July 9, 1908).

8. Alwin Nikolai, American designer, choreographer and composer (*Nov. 25, 1912).

France's ex-premier commits suicide

Paris, Saturday 1
Pierre Bérégovoy (*Dec. 23, 1925), France's former prime minister, has committed suicide. He had been driven to a canal near Nevers where he often went on solitary walks. He took his bodyguard's gun without

A close ally of François Mitterrand.

his knowledge and shot himself. He was found near the canal and died four hours later en route to a hospital in Paris.

Bérégovoy had been traumatized by the Socialists' humiliating defeat in the March general elections and was extremely upset over allegations of financial impropriety stemming from an interest-free loan from a businessman friend who has been indicted for insider trading.

U.N. forces take over Somalia operation

Coming home: Marines get a White House welcome from Bill Clinton.

Mogadishu, Tuesday 4
The colors of the United Nations have replaced the Stars and Stripes here in the Somali capital. Most of the Americans have gone home. The remaining 3,625 soldiers will serve under U.N. command, the first time U.S. troops have done so. Another 1,381 infantrymen will be part of a quick reaction force under U.S. command. Officials say the objective of the mission, keeping the peace and assuring aid routes, has not changed. (→ June 5)

Sri Lanka president is killed by a bomb

Colombo, Saturday 1
A suicide bomber wiped out President Ranasinghe Premadasa of Sri Lanka and his entire staff today as he led a May Day parade through the capital. The assassin, who was blown to pieces, had a bomb strapped to his chest, mirroring the killing of India's Rajiv Gandhi. It is thought he was a follower of opposition leader Lalith Athulathmudali, who was murdered last week.

Trial of top spy opens in Germany

Dusseldorf, Tuesday 4
Markus Wolf, East Germany's brilliant spymaster, went on trial here today charged with treason and bribery. Wolf, much admired by his opponents in the spy game, was novelist John Le Carre's model for George Smiley's opponent, Karla. Joking with reporters at the court, he said Le Carre should have consulted him in order to draw his characters "more realistically."

May 1. Thorvald Stoltenberg of Norway replaces former U.S. Secretary of State Cyrus Vance as U.N. mediator for Bosnia.

May 4. Laura Ashley's famous frocks are 40 years old today.

May 5. British daredevil Jim Greenshields makes aviation history by being first to land a microlight on a moving truck.

osnian Serbs reject U.N. peace proposal

Pale, Bosnia, Thursday 6
After a tempestuous all-night sitting, the self-styled parliament of the Bosnian Serbs has refused to ratify the Vance-Owen peace plan and has mockingly used a charade of democracy to ensure its failure. The deputies insisted on putting the issue to a referendum, a process impossible to carry out in this war-torn country. President Milosevic of Serbia, fearful of the threat of western military action, had tried to persuade them to accept the peace plan and has responded to their refusal by imposing sanctions. Lord Owen says that the sanctions might help them accept reality, but today's frustrating developments bode ill for the peace plan. (→ 22)

Defiant as ever, Radovan Karadzic (right), leader of Bosnia's Serbs.

Yeltsin denounces enemies in parliament

Anti-Yeltsin militants clash with police during a May 1 demonstration.

Moscow, Thursday 6
President Yeltsin went on television tonight to tongue-lash his conservative opponents, accusing them of planning the May Day riot in which a policeman was killed and more than 500 people were injured. He threw down the gauntlet to the conservative-dominated parliament by announcing that he will put forward a bill ordering fresh elections before the end of the year. He also threatened to purge officials opposed to his drastic reforms of the economy but, in what is seen as a bid to gain support from the bureaucrats, ordered pay rises of up to 40% for state officials. (→ July 12)

FBI files show Disney was special agent

U.S., Thursday 6
The creator of Mickey Mouse was a rat, according to a new book. Marc Eliot, author of *Walt Disney – Hollywood's Dark Prince*, made FBI files he used in researching the unauthorized biography available to the *New York Times*, which judged them authentic. The files show that Disney began working as a Tinseltown spy in 1940, providing reports to the FBI on colleagues he suspected of being Communists. In 1954 he was named a Full Special Agent in Charge, Contact. The book also portrays Disney as a heavy drinker and a neurotic, obsessed with washing his hands.

Revelations that are no Mickey Mouse affair for Walt Disney's image.

NFL and players' union reach labor pact

New York, Thursday 6
The National Football League's management council has approved a collective bargaining agreement with the Players Association. The last such contract between the NFL and the players' union expired in 1987, and the two camps have been battling it out in the courts since then. The contract must now be ratified by a majority vote of the players. The seven-year pact liberalizes the terms of free agency and increases benefits for players. Life insurance and pension benefits will double, and protection for players injured in the line of duty will triple over the life of the agreement.

Tories in trouble after local poll setback

London, Friday 7
The Tories were reeling today after a stunning series of setbacks in the Newbury by-election and local elections. At Newbury, the Liberal Democrats demolished a Tory majority of 12,357 and took the seat by 22,055 votes. In the shire elections, Tories lost control of 15 councils and now hold only one of the 47 county councils in England and Wales. The scale of the disaster has led some Tories to question John Major's future as Tory leader. His reaction is to concede that his government has been given "a bloody nose," but "we'll be back." (→ 27)

It's downhill for John Major.

May

1993

Su	Mo	Tu	We	Th	Fr	Sa
						1
2	3	4	5	6	7	8
9	10	11	12	13	14	15
16	17	18	19	20	21	22
23	24	25	26	27	28	29
30	31					

Iran, 9
Swiss national is sentenced to three years in prison for disclosing state secrets.

China, 10
Foreign investment is welcome in oil industry but prohibited in telecommunications, the government announces.

New York, 11
Paul Cézanne's *Les Grosses Pommes* sells for $28.6 million, a record for the artist.

London, 11
John Major meets Salman Rushdie, his first meeting with a British premier since Iran issued the *fatwa* against the author. (→Aug. 11)

Paris, 12
Two wood slivers said to be from Jesus's cross are sold at auction for $18,500.

Italy, 12
Franco Nobili, head of Italy's largest public corporation, is arrested on corruption charges.

Europe, 13
Spanish peseta is devalued 8%; Portuguese escudo is devalued 6.5%.

Cleveland, 13
George Brett becomes one of only six baseball players with 3,000 hits and 300 home runs; his Kansas City Royals beat the Cleveland Indians 7-3.

Italy, 13
Senate removes parliamentary immunity of Guilio Andreotti, accused of Mafia collusion.

London, 14
Tottenham Hotspur's chief executive, Terry Venables, is fired by owner Alan Sugar then reinstated by a High Court judge.

Baltimore, 15
Prairie Bayou wins Preakness Stakes.

DEATHS

9. Penelope Gilliat, British author and film critic (*March 25, 1932).

10. Dame Freya Stark, British explorer and writer (*Jan. 31, 1893).

13. Wolfgang Lotz, the Israeli "Champagne spy" (*1921).

14. Edouard Pignon, French cubist painter (*Feb. 12, 1905).

Pope John Paul II warns Mafia bosses on their home turf

An unprecedented condemnation of organized crime by the Catholic Church.

Agrigento, Sicily, Sunday 9
The pope, clearly angry, denounce the Mafia at the end of mass her today. "The Sicilian people canno always live under the pressure o a civilization of death," he sai "God once said, 'Do not kill.' N human group, Mafia or whatever can trample on this most sacred law of God." He also paid tribute to magistrates murdered while seeking to bring the Mafia to justice.

But this visit, Pope John Paul' third to Sicily, was not enough to silence the critics who accuse the church of doing too little, too late to counter the spread of organize crime worldwide.

Joyrider who took the A train is arrested

New York, Monday 10
If he hadn't broken the speed limit, perhaps Keron Thomas wouldn't have been arrested for impersonating a subway motorman. Last Saturday, this 16-year-old who loved trains arrived at the terminus wearing a motorman's shirt and carrying a motorman's tools and took control of the A train. He drove it for three-and-a-half hours before he broke the speed limit and the train stopped automatically. He was taken to headquarters to undergo a drug test but fled the scene. The police caught up with him today.

Blaze kills 220 in Bangkok toy factory

Bangkok, Monday 10
A fire that destroyed a four-story toy factory here today and killed at least 220 people, including many children, was the most deadly of its kind in history. The fire apparently started when a spark from faulty electrical works ignited synthetic material used in making dolls. The blaze brought down the steel frame and reduced the building to a heap of smoking rubble. As many as 1,600 workers were at the plant, which was poorly equipped for fire safety. Most of the victims were young women who worked at low-wage jobs and often brought their children to work with them.

Landmark elections held in Paraguay

Asuncion, Sunday 9
Paraguayans flocked to the polling booths today to elect their first civilian president in the first fully democratic election since the country achieved independence 182 years ago. The polls were supervised by teams of international observers, including former U.S. President Jimmy Carter. Early results indicate victory for Juan Carlos Wasmosy, leader of the ruling Colorado Party. Wasmosy's success surprises many who thought him tainted by the wealth he acquired under the dictatorship of General Stroessner, but he says: "Nothing can cloud the clarity of this legitimate electoral victory."

May 9. The world's first test-tube baby, Louise Brown, born in Manchester on July 26, 1978, launches National Fertility Week in Britain today.

May 10. Dire Straits star Mark Knopfler receives an honorary degree at Newcastle University.

May 11. Garth Brooks (left), pictured with the veteran crooner George Jones, is named entertainer of the year at the Academy of Country Music Awards.

Whaling summit harpoons Japan's hopes

Canned whale meat is popular, although many Japanese prefer it fresh.

Kyoto, Friday 14
A Japanese request for a one-time allocation to catch 50 minke whales was rejected by the International Whaling Commission, whose five-day meeting has come to an end. Norway wanted approval to resume whaling, too, and says it will recommence this summer, despite the ruling. Japan and Norway based their request on the commission's scientific committee's report that a limited number of minkes could be killed without endangering the species. But anti-whaling nations argued that this step would lead to resumption of large-scale whaling. The commission also endorsed the creation of a whale sanctuary in the oceans around Antarctica.

Paris school drama over

After killing "Human Bomb," police commandos rush the children to safety.

Neuilly-sur-Seine, Saturday 15
Masked police commandos burst into a booby-trapped classroom here in this Paris suburb today, ending a hostage drama with a hail of gunfire. They shot dead the "Human Bomb," as Eric Schmitt, an unemployed, divorced loner called himself. For 46 hours, police had waited for Schmitt, who had demanded 100 million francs ($18 million) in ransom, to fall asleep. His six remaining captives, girls aged three and four, were rushed outside to their parents. The two young women, Laurence Dreyfus, a teacher, and Evelyne Lambert, a pediatrician, who cared for the children during their ordeal have been awarded the Legion of Honor for their bravery.

Income-related fines abandoned in U.K.

London, Thursday 13
Home Secretary Kenneth Clarke abolished the discredited unit-fine system today. The system was meant to impose a fairer system of punishment, with the rich paying more than the poor for the same offense, but it led to a series of ludicrous anomalies because of the complexity of the system. The case that finally led to the downfall of the system was that of Vaughan Watkins, an unemployed man fined £1,200 for littering. In another case, a man was fined £500 for refusing to pay a £36 parking ticket after his car broke down in a no-parking zone. Such absurdities led to the resignation of 30 magistrates and caused much indignation.

Star Wars program is officially dropped

Washington, Thursday 13
President Reagan's futuristic Star Wars plan to defend the United States from ballistic missiles died today when Defense Secretary Les Aspin announced that the project, which has cost $32 billion, is being downgraded to counter the more likely threat from short-range missiles such as Scuds. Often scorned as a waste of time, the Star Wars project has made much progress with systems like "Brilliant Pebbles" to smash incoming missiles, but more importantly, it is credited with helping to bring about the end of communism by forcing Mikhail Gorbachev to acknowledge that the Soviet Union could no longer compete economically with the U.S.

May. New Yorkers are flocking to arcades offering virtual reality games, at $5 for three minutes.

May. A new street version of the prize-winning Lotus racing bike.

Press great Hearst dies of heart attack

New York, Friday 14
William Randolph Hearst, Jr., born January 27, 1908, son of the legendary publishing tycoon and editor in chief of the Hearst empire, died today after suffering a cardiac arrest. Hearst made his mark when he and two colleagues interviewed Soviet leaders after the death of Stalin. The resulting articles won him the Pulitzer Prize in 1956. He used his Editor's Report column, which appeared in Hearst papers for 40 years, to espouse anti-communism and a strong U.S. defense policy.

May 15. Niamh Kavanagh, a 25-year-old Dubliner, wins the Eurovision Song Contest with the song "In Your Eyes."

May

1993

Su	Mo	Tu	We	Th	Fr	Sa
						1
2	3	4	5	6	7	8
9	10	11	12	13	14	15
16	17	18	19	20	21	22
23	24	25	26	27	28	29
30	31					

Turkey, 16
Premier Suleyman Demirel is named president. (→ June 13)

London, 16
Edward Teller and other scientists warn that Earth is in danger of being hit by a comet – in 100 years' time.

Rome, 16
Jim Courier wins Italian Open, beating Goran Ivanisevic 6-1, 6-2, 6-2.

Mount Everest, 17
Rebecca Stephens is the first British woman to reach the summit.

Paris, 17
OECD predicts unemployment will reach 11.6% in Europe in 1993.

Egypt, 17
President Mubarak says direct-dial phone links with Pakistan, Afghanistan, Iraq, Sudan and Iran will be cut as part of fight against Islamic extremists.

London, 17
Governor-elect of the Bank of England, "Steady" Eddie George, takes a five-year pay freeze.

Moscow, 18
Russia's central bank puts its first treasury bills to auction.

Italy, 20
Giorgio Benvenuto resigns as head of Socialist Party.

Kabul, 21
The Red Cross says 4,500 have been wounded in nine days of shelling of the Afghan capital.

Cambodia, 21
Khmer Rouge says it will not accept results of next week's election. (→ 29)

South Africa, 22
30 are killed in fighting between ANC and Inkatha.

London, 22
Inflation falls to 1.3%, lowest since 1964.

DEATHS

18. Walter Wood, American explorer (*1908).

21. Major General John D. Frost, British paratroop leader (*Dec. 31, 1912).

22. Mieczyslaw Horszowski, Austrian pianist (*1893).

Danes finally vote for Maastricht treaty

Anti-EC youths and anarchists riot in Copenhagen as results are announced.

Copenhagen, Tuesday 18
The Danes said "Yes" to Maastricht today, reversing last year's "No" decision by 56.8% to 43.2% in a massive 85.6% turnout of voters. Their decision came as a great relief to the EC and especially to John Major, giving him the impetus to complete Britain's ratification of the treaty. The voting took place calmly, but late tonight rioting broke out. Police opened fire on stone-throwing demonstrators to save an injured officer. (→ 20)

British nurse found guilty of murders

Nottingham, Monday 17
Nurse Beverly Allitt, 24, was found guilty at Crown court here today of murdering four children and attacking 13 others in her care at Grantham hospital. Over a 59-day period, she injected her victims with insulin or suffocated them. An inquiry will examine why she was employed when it was known she had a dangerous personality disorder and why action was not taken sooner.

Deal paves way for media of the future

New York, Monday 17
The telephone company U.S. West Inc. is buying a 25% stake in entertainment purveyor Time Warner Inc. Their collaboration will let their customers order the movie, sporting event or other program they want, when they want it. Time Warner can provide the goods and U.S. West can provide the telecommunications and switching capacity necessary to make the system work.

Clinton's costly trim causes political row

Los Angeles, Tuesday 18
Two runways at Los Angeles International Airport were shut down for nearly an hour today as the take-off of the presidential plane, Air Force One, was delayed. The delay was not due to weather or technical

A $10 short back and sides it isn't.

problems, just an Arkansas good ol' boy getting his ears lowered. President Bill Clinton kept the plane on the ground so Beverly Hills hair stylist, Christofe, could cut his hair. The presidential 'do raised a ruckus in Washington, where foes said that he was wasting taxpayers' money and interfering needlessly with air transport. Christofe's average fee is $200, but it is not known how much the president paid. (→ 29)

May 16. Mexico's Raul Alcala wins the gruelling 1,085-mile, 11-day Tour DuPont race, just 2 minutes and 26 seconds ahead of U.S. rider Lance Armstrong.

May 17. Central London ground to a standstill as thousands came to see the star-studded £1.6-million opening bash of the Planet Hollywood eatery.

Clinton gets tough with Angolan rebels

Washinton, D.C., Wednesday 19

The United States has recognized formerly Communist Angola. President Clinton said the strides toward democracy made by President José Eduardo dos Santos's government led to his decision. The government has agreed to sign a peace accord with the UNITA rebels, led by Jonas Savimbi. UNITA, which had been backed by the U.S. in the past, refuses to sign the agreement. In 1991 the two groups signed a peace agreement, but after dos Santos won the first round of the nation's first multiparty elections, Savimbi relaunched his guerrilla war.

Assisted suicide ban is struck down

Detroit, Thursday 20

A law passed by the Michigan state legislature to stop Jack Kevorkian, known as "Dr. Death," from assisting terminally ill people in committing suicide has been struck down on a technicality by a Detroit judge. Kevorkian, a pathologist, has aided 16 people in ending their lives. The most recent instance was on Sunday – the first after the assisted suicide ban was passed in February. The judge, Cynthia Stevens, said that even if the technical fault in the law was corrected, she would block its enforcement. "This court cannot envisage a more fundamental right than self-determination," she wrote in her decision.

May 19. Prince Charles, guarded by secret service agent Katia Ignatowicz, ends a week-long official visit to Poland.

Serbs claim final victory in Bosnia war

Serb militamen say they are now in control of 70% of Bosnian territory.

Bosnia, Saturday 22

Exultant Serbs claimed victory today after the United States reluctantly accepted a "peacekeeping" formula which, in effect, will allow the Serbs to keep the land they have occupied and "ethnically cleansed." They now have the land they want, and as far as they are concerned, the war is over. President Milosevic, who under the threat of western military intervention was urging the Bosnian Serbs to accept the Vance-Owen peace plan only two weeks ago, now no longer mentions it.

These developments follow intense diplomatic activity, including a visit to the White House by Andrei Kozyrev, the Russian foreign minister, and leave President Clinton disillusioned by his failure to coax his allies into tougher action. (→ June 1)

Constitutional crisis flares up in Ukraine

Kiev, Friday 21

The government of the Ukraine is in chaos tonight, with a president who wants power but cannot get it and a prime minister who wants to resign but is not allowed to. President Kravchuk's attempt to seize power was blocked when parliament refused to give him the constitutional authority he needs to carry out economic reforms and at the same time refused to accept Prime Minister Kuchma's resignation.

There is a serious aspect to this situation: It could prevent the implementation of the START-1 nuclear arms treaty, which Ukraine must ratify. (→ June 17)

No more laughs on tap at 'Cheers' bar

Boston, Thursday 20

The cast of the hit TV show *Cheers* gathered here at the Bull & Finch, the bar that served as a model for Sam's watering hole, to watch the final episode. Advertisers are betting that huge numbers of Americans will join them: They're paying $650,000 for each 30-second spot aired during the special 98-minute show. *Cheers*, which debuted on Sept. 30, 1982, was a critical as well as a popular success. The show won 26 Emmies and was nominated for 111, and it was seen in 38 countries, with six million viewers in Britain.

A grand total of 275 episodes.

House of Commons approves EC treaty

London, Thursday 20

The House of Commons finally gave the Maastricht treaty bill its third reading tonight, despite the biggest revolt by Tory MPs during its tortuous year-long passage through the House. It now goes to the House of Lords. Ministers, much relieved to see the end of the bill after marathon debates lasting 200 hours, celebrated the result with champagne in the smoking room. Although 41 Tories voted against government, the Labour Party's decision to abstain on the third reading gave the bill an easier passage than expected, by 292 votes to 112. (→ July 23)

Venezuela's leader faces trial for graft

Caracas, Friday 21

President Carlos Andrès Pérez, who survived two attempted military coups last year, was today ordered to stand trial on corruption charges by Venezuela's congress. He is accused of using a discretionary fund to make a $10-million profit by changing bolivars to dollars and back to take advantage of a devaluation of the bolivar. The president declared his innocence in a bitter speech but agreed to step down while he is tried, and he seems to be resigned to the end of a political career spanning 50 years. The news was greeted by Venezuelans as a long overdue blow against a corrupt political elite.

May 19. A rare 19th-century mechanical calculator is sold at Christie's in London for £7.7 million, far more than expected.

Su	Mo	Tu	We	Th	Fr	Sa
						1
2	3	4	5	6	7	8
9	10	11	12	13	14	15
16	17	18	19	20	21	22
23	24	25	26	27	28	29
30	31					

Germany, 23
Eastern Germany's largest strike in 60 years ends.

Tibet, 24
Violence breaks out during anti-China demonstration.

Europe, 24
EC poll shows 55% favor military intervention in the former Yugoslavia.

London, 24
The Treasury announces plans to sell nearly all its 22% stake in British Telecom.

U.S., 24
Sega announces that its video games sold in U.S. will carry violence ratings.

U.S., 24
Charles Barkley, forward for the Phoenix Suns, is voted the NBA's most valuable player.

Iraq, 25
Iranian jets strike rebel base 60 miles into Iraqi territory.

South Africa, 25
73 officials of the Pan-Africanist Congress, the group linked to recent attacks on whites, are arrested.

Guatemala, 25
President Jorge Serrano Elias dissolves Congress and Supreme Court and suspends constitutional rights. (→ June 5)

Pakistan, 26
Supreme Court reinstates Prime Minister Nawaz Sharif and parliament.

Germany, 26
Constitutional guarantee of asylum to any politically oppressed person is revoked.

New York, 28
Monaco and Eritrea join U.N.

New York, 28
The pound is quoted at $1.56.

Poland, 29
A man is killed and many injured in violence following Poland-England soccer game, which ended in a 1-1 tie.

DEATHS

26. Joseph Pulitzer, Jr., American newspaper publisher (*May 13, 1913).

27. Lord (Joe) Gormley, British trade unionist (*July 5, 1917).

30. Sun Ra, American jazz musician (*ca. 1914).

Chancellor Lamont dismissed by Major

Kenneth Clarke takes over.

London, Thursday 27
Rumors of a shakeup in Prime Minister John Major's cabinet were confirmed today as he dismissed his chancellor of the exchequer. Kenneth Clarke, the home secretary, is to take over from Norman Lamont. The prime minister's move is seen as an attempt to restore public confidence in his government, following Major's continuing slide in opinion polls, increasing criticism on economic policy and the setback in local elections earlier this month. The news broke this morning when Lamont's mother, Irene, revealed to reporters that her son had called to tell her he had quit. (→ June 3)

British, Irish heads of state meet

London, Thursday 27
The Queen welcomed Mary Robinson, the Irish president, to Buckingham Palace today in an historic meeting, the first between an Irish head of state and the British sovereign since Ireland gained independence 71 troubled years ago. After 40 minutes of talk over tea and biscuits, Robinson said: "It was very significant that we could meet as two heads of state with so many bonds in common – so much in the past and more particularly in the present and future." The meeting was carefully choreographed in order not to give offense to either side in the always delicate relationship between Britain and Ireland. There is now speculation that a member of the royal family could make a reciprocal visit to Dublin.

Florence's Uffizi Gallery wrecked by bomb

Florence, Thursday 27
A car bomb severely damaged the Uffizi Gallery today, killing the caretaker and his family and destroying or damaging a number of paintings and sculptures. Among the works of art destroyed was *The Birth of Christ* by the Dutch artist Gerrit van Honthurst, but the collection's most important paintings, in a corridor unaffected by the blast, were not harmed. This is the second car bomb in less than two weeks, and they are being blamed on Mafia terrorism. Six people died, 30 were injured and the gallery will be closed for a long time.

The blast shocked the world of art.

Double first for the Cannes Film Festival

Best actress prize for Holly Hunter.

Cannes, Monday 24
The Golden Palm, the top honor of the Cannes film festival, was awarded jointly to *The Piano*, by Australian Jane Campion, and *Farewell to My Concubine*, by Chinese Chen Kaige. It was the first time the award went to a film directed by a woman or a Chinese. Briton Mike Leigh was named best director for *Naked*, and the star of the film fellow Briton David Thewlis, won the best actor award. The award for best actress went to American Holly Hunter, of *The Piano*.

Killer of Japanese student is acquitted

Japan, Monday 24
The top news story in Japan is the acquittal yesterday of Rodney Pears, the Louisiana man who shot and killed a Japanese exchange student he had mistaken for a robber last October. Pears shot the boy when he did not respond to his shouted command, "Freeze!" The Japanese increasingly see the U.S. as a barbarically violent society and worry that the U.S. government is more interested in promoting tourism than making the streets safe.

May 26. AC Milan fail to stop Basile Boli of Olympique Marseille from scoring a goal to give OM their first European Champions' Cup, by 1-0.

ormer Reagan hand chosen by Clinton

ashington, D.C., Saturday 29
resident Clinton has replaced his
oung communications director,
eorge Stephanopoulos, with a for-
er advisor to presidents Nixon,
ord and Reagan. David Gergen,
, will be charged with, as he puts
"the intersection of policy and
olitics and communication."

Clinton counts on Gergen, who
rchestrated President Reagan's
ublic relations in his first term, to
ead off gaffes like the haircut fias-
o that have haunted the Clinton
dministration. The move is also an
ttempt to emphasize Clinton's com-
itment to bipartisanship. (→ 31)

Gergen, known as a wily operator.

Five Turks die in fire set by neo-Nazis

Solingen, Germany, Sunday 30
Two thousand people took part in
an anti-Nazi march here today, in
protest of the arson attack on the
home of a Turkish family. Three
women and two young girls were
killed in the attack. Outrage at this
incident of racist thuggery swept
across Germany, with protests in a
number of cities. Foreign Minister
Klaus Kinkel sent a telegram of
regret to his Turkish counterpart,
while Interior Minister Rudolf Sei-
ters visited the scene of the fire.
The federal prosecutor is handling
the case, and a hunt is on for right-
wing extremists seen near the blaze.

Angry Turks protest at Solingen.

ttacks fail to deter ambodian voters

hnom Penh, Saturday 29
ambodian voters flocked to the
olls this week, defying threats by
e Khmer Rouge to disrupt voting
y attacking the polling stations.
he attacks did not deter voters,
nd there was an astonishing 90%
urnout. Final results will not be
nown for some days, but first re-
urns indicate support for the Cam-
odian People's Party and Funcin-
ec, Prince Norodom Sihanouk's
oyalist party. (→ June 16)

Walesa faces new political problems

Warsaw, Sunday 30
Poland will likely have its fifth
prime minister since the fall of communism in 1989. The government
of Hanna Suchocka lost a no-
confidence vote yesterday after the
premier refused to increase wages
and pensions for public employees.
President Walesa did not accept
Suchocka's resignation, choosing
instead to dissolve parliament and
call for new elections, to be held in
three or four months.

Mystery illness killing Navajos in West

Navajo Nation chief Peterson Zah.

Navajo Reservation, Monday 31
A mysterious illness researchers are
calling "unexplained adult respiratory distress syndrome" has killed
12 people here on the Navajo reservation that is at the borders of
Arizona, New Mexico, Colorado
and Utah. The victims, not exclu-
sively Navajo, first notice mild flu-
like symptoms, then hours or days
later suddenly die from respiratory
failure. Navajo nation President
Peterson Zah is encouraging reservation residents to collaborate with
the medical authorities.

Winston Churchill speech unleashes storm

ondon, Sunday 30
Vinston Churchill, grandson of the
vartime leader, has enraged his col-
eagues with a speech calling for
halt to the "relentless flow" of
immigrants, to preserve "the British
way of life." His comments were
condemned by Prime Minister John
Major and by leaders of the ethnic
communities, but he is unrepentant.

Bill Clinton booed at Vietnam Memorial

Washington, D.C., Monday 31
President Clinton was booed today
at the Vietnam Veterans Memorial.
Although most of the crowd obser-
ving Memorial Day here applauded
the president's speech, others called
him a coward and a traitor because
of his avoidance of military service
and his protests against the Vietnam War as a student. (→ June 5)

**May 30. Brazil's Emerson Fittipaldi, driving a Penske-Chevrolet, wins
his second Indianapolis 500, ahead of Arie Luyendyk of Holland. Nigel
Mansell of Britain finished third despite sideswiping a wall.**

**May 29. Despite the suffering all around, life goes on in Bosnia: Imela
Nogic is elected Miss Sarajevo and calls for the world to help her city.**

June

1993

Su	Mo	Tu	We	Th	Fr	Sa
		1	2	3	4	5
6	7	8	9	10	11	12
13	14	15	16	17	18	19
20	21	22	23	24	25	26
27	28	29	30			

Sarajevo, 1
At least 11 people are killed when mortar fire hits a crowd at a soccer match. (→ 4)

Mexico, 1
Two men are arrested on suspicion of involvement in the drug-related killing of the archbishop of Guadalajara last week.

New York, 2
The Irish rock band U2 signs a $195-million recording deal with Polygram's Island Records.

London, 2
British Telecom announces it will pay $4.3 billion for a 20% share in MCI, America's second-largest long-distance phone company.

Bujumbura, 2
Melchior Ndadaye wins Burundi's first free presidential elections. (→ Oct 21)

U.K., 2
Queen Elizabeth marks the 40th anniversary of her cororation.

Belgrade, 2
U.N. peacekeepers have suffered 500 casualties, including 42 deaths, since they arrived in the former Yugoslavia 450 days ago.

U.K., 3
Latest opinion polls show John Major's popularity rating at 21%, the lowest for any premier since polling began in Britain in the 1930s.

Zurich, 3
FIFA partially lifts Iraq's nearly three-year ban from world soccer.

Moscow, 4
The famous GUM department store near Red Square celebrates its 100th anniversary.

New York, 4
The U.S. signs the "biodiversity treaty," aimed at protecting plants and animals, which was agreed at last year's U.N. environment conference in Rio.

Belmont, New York, 5
Colonial Affair, ridden by Julie Krone, the first woman to ride a winner in a Triple Crown race, wins the Belmont Stakes.

U.N. to protect six Bosnia safe havens

New York, Friday 4
The resolution, supported by Russia, passed the Security Council to send a further 5,000 troops to Bosnia to protect six safe havens for a million Muslims. Third World countries were reluctant to pass the resolution, arguing that it would pen the Muslims into refugee camps, turning them into the Palestinians of Europe. Meanwhile, in Belgrade, opposition leader Vuk Draskovic is still being held after violent protests against the regime earlier this week. (→ 13)

Opposition leader Vuk Draskovic.

Somali gunmen kill 24 U.N. peacekeepers

Pakistani troops were caught in a series of simultaneous attacks.

Mogadishu, Saturday 5
A bloody series of ambushes mounted by troops loyal to the Somali clan leader General Aidid has left 24 Pakistani "blue berets" dead. Fighting broke out when the peacekeeping troops tried to inspect an armory belonging to Aidid. The city was filled with the sound of battle as the U.N. troops fought their way to safety. Tonight, both sides are poised for further confrontation with U.N. helicopter gunships preparing for action. (→ 17)

Guatemalan leader is human rights aide

Guatemala City, Saturday 5
Ramiro de Leon Carpio, human rights prosecutor of this strife-torn country, was elected president today in a restoration of democratic rule following the army's overthrow of Jorge Serrano, who seized near dictatorial powers ten days ago. The new president pledged to unite the country.

President Clinton suffers double setback

Controversial pick Lani Guinier.

Washington, D.C., Saturday 5
President Clinton has suffered two political blows at a crucial time for him: His deficit-reduction bill goes to the Senate for discussion next week. Today in Texas, Republican Kay Bailey Hutchison was elected to the Senate by a 2-1 majority over the Democratic candidate. Thursday, he dropped the nomination of his old friend Lani Guinier to the post of assistant attorney general for civil rights after Republican opposition to Guinier's leftist views.

Conway Twitty dies

Springfield, Ill., Saturday 5
Conway Twitty, the teen rock idol who crossed the musical divide to win the title of "high priest of country music," died today. He recorded dozens of hit singles, of which the best known was "It's Only Make Believe." He was born in Friars Point, Mississippi on Sept. 1, 1933.

June 3. Seven die as the "British Trent" burns off Belgium.

England stunned by soccer defeat in Oslo

London, Wednesday 2
England's soccer team, and especially their manager, Graham Taylor, are under fierce attack today following their 2-0 defeat at the hands of Norway's part-timers. The defeat leaves England teetering on the brink of exclusion from the World Cup. David Pleat, manager of Luton, summed up the debacle: "A shabby performance of inadequate ideas, tired minds and poor spirit." To add insult to injury, English fans ran amok after the game, fighting the Oslo police and wrecking a bar.

June
1993

Su	Mo	Tu	We	Th	Fr	Sa
		1	2	3	4	5
6	7	8	9	10	11	12
13	14	15	16	17	18	19
20	21	22	23	24	25	26
27	28	29	30			

Liberia, 6
More than 270 civilians are massacred when rebel forces of the National Patriotic Front attack a rubber plantation near Monrovia.

Switzerland, 6
Voters approve government plans to buy 34 U.S.-built F-18 fighters at a cost of $2.4 billion.

London, 6
The government says that, from October, women soldiers will serve in Northern Ireland for the first time.

U.K., 6
Lady Chatterley's Lover, the D.H. Lawrence novel that scandalized many Britons and was the subject of an obscenity trial in 1960, is sceened by the BBC; viewers find it rather tame.

Germany, 7
Drazen Petrovic, the Croatian shooting guard who led the NBA's New Jersey Nets in scoring last season, is killed in a car crash.

Paris, 8
René Bousquet, a leading official of France's pro-Nazi Vichy regime, is shot dead.

The Vatican, 9
The Pope warns that sex scandals involving clerics in the U.S. could undermine public trust in Roman Catholic priests.

Montreal, 9
The Montreal Canadiens win hockey's Stanley Cup after beating the Los Angeles Kings 4-1; after the game, rampaging youths cause $10 million worth of damage.

Jerusalem, 11
The Israeli Army bans discrimination against gay men and women.

London, 12
The Queen's Birthday Honours List includes life peerages for film director Sir Richard Attenborough and violinist Sir Yehudi Menuhin.

DEATHS

10. Les Dawson, British comedian (*Feb. 12, 1933).

10. Arleen Auger, American soprano (*Sept. 13, 1939).

Spain's Gonzalez wins vital election

Socialist supporters celebrate.

Madrid, Sunday 6
First results indicate that the Socialists will retain power in Spain following today's election, but they will no longer enjoy an absolute majority. Analysts say they will probably turn to the Catalan nationalists and possibly even the Basques for support. The result is seen as a triumph for Felipe Gonzalez, the charismatic premier who has led his party to victory despite Spain's economic woes. (→ July 13)

Woody Allen loses a bitter court battle

New York, Monday 7
Dylan, Moses and Satchel will remain with their mother. After Mia Farrow and Woody Allen broke up last year after 13 years together, they began a fight for custody of their three children. The judge in the case found that Allen was an unfit father and questioned a psychological report that said that he had not sexually abused his adopted daughter Dylan, as Farrow alleges. The couple, who had never married, split after Farrow discovered nude photos taken by Allen of her adopted daughter Soon-Yi, 21 at the time, with whom he was having an affair.

Woody and Mia in happier days.

U.S. refugee drama

New York, Sunday 6
More than 200 illegal Chinese immigrants fled the 150-foot freighter *Golden Venture* after it ran aground at 2:00 this morning, and 100 more were brought ashore by the police. Police suspect the ship was beached intentionally to offload the immigrants. Four people drowned and two others died later.

Tonys for 'Tommy'

New York, Sunday 6
Who guitarist Pete Townshend's rock opera *Tommy*, a sleek mix of music, dancing and technology which tells the story of a deaf, dumb and blind pinball wizard, won five Tony awards tonight. It shared the award for the best original score and won the prizes for best director, design, lighting and choreography.

Gorbunovs, a former Communist, is elected president of Latvia

Riga, Sunday 6
The Latvian Way, a right-of-center coalition led by former Communist Anatolijs Gorbunovs, is emerging as the winner of Latvia's first free election since it won independence from the Soviet Union. Gorbunovs, former ideology secretary of the Communist Party, is now firmly committed to a market economy. He also supports the law which says that only those who were Latvian citizens before the war and their descendants have the right to vote, thus disenfranchising most of the 700,000 "non-citizens," nearly 25% of the population, who arrived during the Soviet occupation.

Tennis stars Courier, Fernandez bite the dust at French Open

A Grand Slam win for Steffi Graf.

Paris, Sunday 6
German ace Steffi Graf and Spaniard underdog Sergi Bruguera are the singles champions of the 1993 French Open.

Graf, not at her best, made heavy work of her game but defeated American Mary Joe Fernandez 4-6, 6-2, 6-4. The win brings her total of Grand Slam titles to 12.

Sergi Bruguera, against all the odds, beat another American, the defending champion Jim Courier. Bruguera, who had not even reached the quarter-final of a previous Grand Slam tournament, produced some dazzling shots to win 6-4, 2-6, 6-2, 3-6, 6-3 in an exhausting game which lasted four hours.

Barcelona-born Sergi Bruguera.

Jurassic dinos set to conquer world

Dinosaur man Steven Spielberg.

U.S., Thursday 10

Steven Spielberg's heavily hyped dinosaur megamovie *Jurassic Park* roared into movie theaters across the country today. The stars are, of course, the dinos, and their development began more than two years ago. New computer graphics software – more than 200 programs – and robotic technologies, including a life-size T-rex robot using flight simulator machinery, were designed to bring them to life. The movie is accompanied by a brontosaurus-sized marketing campaign, including T-shirts and toys and a new *Jurassic* ride to be built at Universal Studios' theme park. (→17)

A $56-million thrill for dinobuffs.

American rookies beat England squad

Boston, Wednesday 9

England's soccer team was humiliated again today, this time by the United States, where the game is still in its infancy. The Americans' 2-0 victory is being treated by the U.S. press as "another in a series of shots heard around the world" and by the British press as the ultimate national disgrace. When Graham Taylor, the England manager, was asked about the defeat at the Foxboro Stadium, he was downcast: "What can you do? All I can do is look for the starting point. ... When people get knocked in life, it saps your confidence."

A mystery ailment hits Gulf War vets

Washington, D.C., Wednesday 9

Today a House subcommittee on Veterans Affairs heard testimony from federal officials and veterans groups on mysterious ailments suffered by thousands of veterans who served in Kuwait, Saudi Arabia and Iraq during the Gulf War. The veterans claim the illnesses are caused by their exposure to contaminents during Operation Desert Storm. Army and Veterans Affairs Department officials acknowledged the complaints but denied that there is any evidence of an outbreak of a specific disease among veterans who served in the Persian Gulf region.

'Forbes' says royal fortune has shrunk

New York, Thursday 10

The Queen's fortune shrank by a third last year to $7.9 billion, according to *Forbes* magazine's annual list of the world's richest people. She is now only the eighth wealthiest person in the world in a list headed by the oil-rich Sultan of Brunei, who is said to be worth $37 billion. The Duke of Westminster, whose fortune is based on property in Mayfair, also suffered last year. His wealth shrivelled to $2.3 billion, some 40% less than he was worth in 1987. He has dropped 60 places to be merely 88th in the list of the truly seriously rich.

President Rafsanjani is re-elected in Iran

Tehran, Friday 11

President Ali Akhbar Rafsanjani has been returned to office as Iran's leader. The turnout for the vote was only 57.6%, and many more people voted for the runner-up, newspaper editor Ahmad Tavakkoli, than had been expected. Campaigning on the slogan "Less luxury and more austerity for leaders," he received 25% of the votes cast. This support reflects the widespread discontent in the country and the increasing anger with the high living, fast cars and luxurious villas enjoyed by the mullahs. Some graffiti has even compared Rafsanjani with the late Shah. Tavakkoli said the result showed "the population is unhappy."

The result of the Islamic republic's election was a foregone conclusion.

June 9. A Shinto ceremony at the Imperial Palace for the wedding of Crown Prince Naruhito of Japan, 33, and his bride, Masako Owada, 29.

June 12. More than 60,000 easy riders, including 100 Britons, gather in Milwaukee, Wisc., for the 90th anniversary of Harley-Davidson "hogs."

June
1993

Su	Mo	Tu	We	Th	Fr	Sa
		1	2	3	4	5
6	7	8	9	10	11	12
13	14	15	16	17	18	19
20	21	22	23	24	25	26
27	28	29	30			

Bosnia, 13
Serbian shells hit a hospital in the Muslim town of Gorazde, killing 50 people. (→ 17)

Italy, 14
At the 45th Venice Biennale, Briton Richard Hamilton wins a Golden Lion for painting; U.S. artist Robert Wilson takes the sculpture award.

U.S., 15
A national health survey indicates that cholesterol levels in Americans have dropped rapidly since 1980.

Iran, 15
First-class air travel, banned after Khomeini came to power in 1973, is to resume.

Washington, D.C., 15
The Pentagon says a USAF general who called Clinton a "dope-smoking, draft-dodging" commander in chief is to be disciplined.

Belgrade, 16
The black market exchange rate for the Yugoslav dinar reaches a million to $1.

Germany, 16
The government announces plans to impose a special purchase tax on cars that get less than 31 miles to the gallon.

U.S., 17
Jurassic Park breaks box office records: it has the best first week ever, with $81.7 million in ticket sales. (→ July 15)

Paris, 17
President Mitterrand warns that the U.N. could become "an instrument of U.S. imperialism."

Belfast, 18
Irish President Mary Robinson causes a storm of protest when she shakes hands with Sinn Fein leader Gerry Adams at the start of a visit to Ulster.

London, 18
Researchers say five women athletes at the 1992 Barcelona Olympics had male genes.

DEATHS

13. Donald "Deke" Slayton, U.S. astronaut (*March 1, 1924).

15. John Connally, former Texas governor (*Feb. 27, 1917).

Canadian and Turkish voters decide to put women at the helm

Kim Campbell, Canada's premier.

Sunday 13
In Canada and Turkey, countries thousands of miles apart in geography and light-years apart in tradition, two women have just been elected head of their parties and designated premier.

In Canada, Kim Campbell, an extrovert lawyer with a sharp wit and sharper tongue, was narrowly chosen as head of the Progressive Conservative Party, in succession to long-serving Brian Mulroney.

In Turkey, Tansu Ciller, a Yale-educated economist who admires Maggie Thatcher, defied Islam to become head of the ruling True Path party. "We have changed Turkish history," she said. (→ 25)

Tansu Ciller wins in Turkey.

London's gay world terrified by a killer

London, Wednesday 16
A serial killer who has strangled five homosexual men in London, four of them in the past 17 days, has telephoned the police, taunting them and threatening to kill one man a week. The murders, all involving sado-masochistic practices, have spread fear through the capital's gay community. The victims were aged from 33 to 45. All were killed in their own homes, indicating they picked up their murderer in a gay bar and took him home for sex. A friend of one of the murdered men said, "I don't know when the gay scene will recover."

Racing legend Hunt dies of heart attack

Formula One champion in 1976.

London, Tuesday 15
Flamboyant motor racing champion James Hunt (*Aug. 29, 1947) was found dead at his Wimbledon home this morning. It is believed he suffered a heart attack in his sleep. Hunt, who won the Formula One championship in 1976 and later became an articulate and professional BBC commentator, was a man who lived life to the fullest, and he had the scars and the heartaches to prove it. He had two failed marriages, and his first wife later wed Richard Burton. Lord Hesketh, his former Grand Prix team boss, said of him: "He was truly outstanding and represented the archetypal British sportsman."

June 14. Women's rights pioneer Ruth Ginsburg is nominated to be America's second woman to serve on the Supreme Court.

June 15. Royal Ascot gateman Eric Petheridge fails to recognize Princess Anne and bars her from entering the course.

June. An Arkansas firm jumps onto presidential bandwagon.

Cambodian factions agree to share power

Prince Sihanouk (third from left) is likely to head the new government.

Phnom Penh, Wednesday 16
The communist and royalist parties agreed today to form an unlikely alliance which will rule the country until a new constitution comes into effect in September. The deal, arranged by Prince Norodom Siha-nouk, establishes Cambodia's fifth government in two weeks, a record even for this turbulent country. One of Sihanouk's sons, Prince Rannaridh, and Hun Sen, the communist prime minister, will serve as co-chairmen.

U.S. gunships fail to get Somali warlord

General Aidid's supporters are increasingly hostile to U.S. troops.

Mogadishu, Thursday 17
U.N. ground troops, backed up by U.S. attack helicopters and gunships, launched a dawn raid on the headquarters of General Mohammed Farrah Aidid. The operation, which left scores of Somali fighters and civilians dead, was a retaliator strike at Aidid following the attac 12 days ago in which 24 Pakista peacekeepers were killed. Today raid inflicted heavy damage on A did's headquarters but failed to cap ture the warlord. (→ July 12)

Bosnia plan 'dead'

Geneva, Thursday 17
Lord Owen conceded today that his Bosnia peace plan, based on the division of the country into 10 semi-autonomous provinces under a unified state, is dead. He could only urge President Izetbegovic of Bosnia to accept the plan proposed by his victorious enemies, the Serb and Croat presidents Slobodan Milosevic and Franco Tudjman. The plan calls for partitioning Bosnia into three ethnically homogenous states, with the Muslims getting only 10% of the total territory. (→ July 22)

Black Sea accord

Moscow, Thursday 17
President Yeltsin of Russia and President Kravchuk of Ukraine today agreed to divide the old Soviet Black Sea Fleet and so end a dangerous quarrel which has bedevilled relations between the two states since the collapse of the USSR. The fleet, with 380 ships and more than 70,000 men, is the largest naval force in Europe. Its division will start in September. The agreement also clears the way for Ukraine to ratify the START-1 and nuclear non-proliferation treaties.

Literature Nobel Sir William Golding dies

Truro, Cornwall, Saturday 19
Sir William Golding (*Sept. 19, 1911), the Nobel prize-winning author of *Lord of the Flies* and *Rites of Passage*, died suddenly at his home near here today. Among the many colleagues paying tribute to him is the author A.S. Byatt, who says: "He was a visionary who came from the same line as Coleridge and Blake. He saw life on a cosmic scale. He suddenly made any kind of writing possible." Golding said of *Lord of the Flies*, "Its theme is grief, sheer grief, grief, grief, grief."

June. The Velvet Underground has resurfaced for a European tour.

June 15. Arnold Schwarzenegger's new adventure, "Last Action Hero."

June

1993

Su	Mo	Tu	We	Th	Fr	Sa
		1	2	3	4	5
6	7	8	9	10	11	12
13	14	15	16	17	18	19
20	21	22	23	24	25	26
27	28	29	30			

London, 20
A high-speed train makes a first trial run from France to England via the Channel Tunnel.

New York, 20
Billionaire Walter Annenberg announces the largest one-time gift to private education in U.S. history: $365 million.

Wimbledon, 21
The 107th Wimbledon tennis championships open with tight security, following the stabbing of Monica Seles by a spectator in Germany. (→ July 4)

Dundee, Scotland, 21
A study by doctors claims that instant coffee helps protect against heart disease.

Washington, D.C., 23
The House of Representatives approves further spending for the proposed U.S. space station *Freedom*.

Berlin, 23
The Stars and Stripes is lowered for the last time at Tempelhof Air Base, after 48 years of U.S. military presence.

Moscow, 24
Yeltsin warns Estonia about discrimination against Russian-speakers in the Baltic state.

Los Angeles, 24
The city imposes a total ban on smoking in indoor restaurants.

Jerusalem, 24
Israel announces plans to build a $13-million fence around the Occupied Territories to curb Palestinian attacks on Israelis.

London, 25
Jacques Attali resigns as president of the European Bank for Reconstruction and Development.

Ottawa, 25
Kim Campbell takes office as Canada's first woman premier. (→ Oct. 26)

London, 25
An appeals court bans a British soft-drink maker from using the word "Champagne" on its bottles.

Jakarta, 26
Indonesian businessmen who owe money to state banks are banned from traveling abroad.

Chicago Bulls outshine the Phoenix Suns

Phoenix, Sunday 20
The Chicago Bulls tonight became the third team in NBA history to win three national championships in a row, beating the Phoenix Suns in Game 6 of the finals, 99-98.

Michael Jordan set two records, becoming the first to be named the series' Most Valuable Player for three consecutive years and averaging an unprecedented 41 points per game.

The Bulls led the best-of-seven series 3-2 before tonight's game. The game went to the wire, with John Paxson sinking the winning three-pointer just 3.9 seconds before the buzzer.

A third MVP for Michael Jordan.

Basque bombers cause carnage in Madrid

The explosions were an hour apart.

Madrid, Monday 21
ETA, the Basque terror group, struck in the heart of Madrid today, killing five senior military officers with a car bomb which destroyed their mini-bus during the morning rush hour. The bomb was packed with shrapnel in the rear of a stolen car and detonated by remote control in the busy Salamanca district. Two other men died in the blast and 24 people were injured, including three children waiting for their school bus. Two of the wounded children are the daughters of a doctor who rushed to the scene. One may lose a leg, the other an eye. An hour later, a second, smaller bomb exploded in fashionable Serrano Street, injuring three people.

Minister resigns as scandal rocks Tories

London, Thursday 24
John Major stunned the House of Commons today by announcing the resignation of his security minister for Northern Ireland. The downfall of Michael Mates follows criticism of his defense of the fugitive tycoon Asil Nadir. Nadir's flight to Northern Cyprus last month has embroiled the Conservative Party in a scandal over £365,000 donated by Nadir to the party. Revelations that Mates and other Conservatives had intervened on behalf of Nadir, who has jumped bail after being charged with 13 counts of fraud and false accounting, are deeply embarrassing to the Tory hierarchy.

Asil Nadir, now safely in Cyprus.

Old parties routed in Italian elections

Rome, Sunday 20
The Communists – now the Democratic Party of the Left – and the federalist Northern league were confirmed tonight as the new dominant forces in Italian politics with the old parties, tarnished by corruption, taking a terrible hammering in the municipal elections. The Northern League has won Milan, Italy's economic capital, while the leftists won decisively in central Italy, taking Siena and trouncing the Christian Democrats and other middle-of-the-road parties who dominated the old regime but are now disgraced.

Nigerian election is voided by military

Lagos, Wednesday 23
General Ibrahim Babangida, the military ruler of Nigeria, put a stop today to this troubled country's transition to civilian rule by declaring void the presidential poll held June 12. Results released last Friday by a human-rights group showed that businessman Moshood K.O. Abiola had won in 19 of the country's 30 states.

Official election results were delayed by several lawsuits contesting the election, the most significant of which was brought by a group which openly supports Babangida's rule. Foreign observers had judged the elections fair. The court cases are Babangida's pretext for voiding the election. His decree makes no mention of a new vote. (→ July 1)

June 20. Manuel Benitez, "El Cordobes," returns to the bullring at the age of 57.

Kurds unleash wave of attacks in Europe

Turkey's Bern embassy was also hit.

London, Thursday 24
Radical members of the Marxist Kurdistan Workers Party mounted a series of coordinated attacks on Turkish institutions today. In London, some 20 demonstrators stormed a Turkish bank in the City and protested the treatment of Kurds by the Turkish government before being arrested. In Munich, armed men burst into the Turkish consulate and threatened to shoot 21 employees. There was an exchange of gunfire with Turkish diplomats in Bern. Kurds carrying grenades and handguns occupied the Turkish consulate in Marseilles, and there have been violent incidents in Hamburg, Frankfurt, Cologne, Bremen and Berlin. (→Nov. 4)

A Muslim plot to blow up U.N. is foiled

New York, Thursday 24
Eight followers of Sheikh Omar Abdul Rahman, the blind mullah, are under arrest tonight, accused of plotting a number of terrorist attacks, including a suicide bombing of the United Nations headquarters. The FBI had planted an informer in the group, who revealed that the plot was to drive a car filled with explosives into the U.N. complex, code-named "the Big House," and blow it up, Beirut style. Other targets were said to be the FBI building in New York and the Lincoln and Holland tunnels, which carry thousands of commuters to Manhattan under the Hudson River. FBI sources say the men were caught in the act of assembling bombs.

Security alert at U.N. headquarters.

Fermat's Theorem cracked by Briton

Cambridge, Wednesday 23
"The equation $x^n + y^n = z^n$, where n is an integer greater than 2, has no solution in positive integers." This rule was found in the margins of a book owned by the 17th-century French mathematician Pierre Fermat. He claimed to have the proof, but did not have the room to include it. Since then, mathematicians have been trying to work out what it could have been. Englishman Andrew Wiles, who works at Princeton University, stunned his audience at a Cambridge University lecture by casually presenting the solution.

AIDS czar is named by White House

Washington, D.C., Friday 25
Kristine Gebbie, a former nursing professor and a member of President Reagan's AIDS commission, was appointed today by President Clinton to fill the new position of AIDS policy coordinator. Gebbie has served as top health administrator to the states of Washington and Oregon. The AIDS czar will oversee the government's $2.7-billion fight against the disease, coordinating the research, prevention and education activities of the departments of Health and Human Services, Education and Justice.

June 23. A statue of General Charles de Gaulle is unveiled in London by the Queen Mother.

June 22. Former First Lady Pat Nixon (*March 16, 1912) dies of cancer in California.

French enact tough immigration law

Paris, Thursday 24
"Zero immigration" is the objective cited by French Interior Minister Charles Pasqua for a series of proposed laws that have been debated this month in the French parliament, dominated by a rightist coalition since the March elections. The National Assembly passed a law today making it more difficult for foreigners to become citizens. The major change is that children born to foreign parents in France do not automatically become citizens but must request French nationality on reaching majority.

Pentagon launches Cruise missile reprisal raid against Baghdad

A total of 23 Tomahawk missiles were fired at Saddam Hussein's capital.

Iraq, Saturday 26
American warships in the Persian Gulf and the Red Sea launched 23 Tomahawk cruise missiles against Iraq's intelligence headquarters in Baghdad in an attack starting just before midnight tonight. The raid was mounted after President Clinton decided there was "compelling evidence" of a "loathsome and cowardly" plot by Iraq to assassinate President Bush during his visit to Kuwait in April. First reports tell of the "near complete destruction" of the intelligence center, but it is known that four of the missiles fell in the surrounding area and caused civilian casualties. (→27)

June
1993

Su	Mo	Tu	We	Th	Fr	Sa
		1	2	3	4	5
6	7	8	9	10	11	12
13	14	15	16	17	18	19
20	21	22	23	24	25	26
27	28	29	30			

Athens, 27
Greece begins deporting 13,500 illegal Albanian immigrants in reprisal for the expulsion of a Greek Orthodox priest.

Washington, D.C., 27
Bill Clinton has a telephone conversation with a man who claims to be his half-brother, Henry Ritzenthaler.

Baghdad, 27
Iraqi officials say eight civilians were killed in the U.S. missile attack.

Rome, 27
Colin Jackson of Britain runs the world's best 110-meter hurdles race this year, clocking 13.10 seconds.

Kildare, Ireland, 27
Commander In Chief, ridden by Pat Eddery, wins the Irish Derby.

Paris, 27
American cyclist Greg LeMond drops out of this year's Tour de France. (→ July 25)

London, 28
Buckingham Palace says that the estranged Duke and Duchess of York "will continue to lead their own lives," thus ending speculation about a reconciliation.

Amsterdam, 29
The Police Complaints Commission says policemen should wear large numbers, like soccer players, so that victims of police brutality can identify the culprits.

Greenland, 29
Scientists drilling through the ice cap reach a record depth of 10,021 feet and extract an ice core deposited 250,000 years ago.

Washington, D.C., 30
The House of Representatives votes, 255 to 178, to maintain the government's 16-year-old ban on federal funding for abortion for poor women.

France, 30
The number of unemployed reaches a record 3.14 million.

London, 30
Michael Hunt, former deputy chairman of Nissan U.K., is jailed for eight years for his part in Britain's biggest tax fraud.

Serial killer caught by New York police

New York, Tuesday 29
A beige pickup with no license plates ran a stop sign on Long Island. When state troopers tried to pull the truck over, the driver led them on a four-mile chase. When they stopped him, the police noticed a foul odor coming from the truck. They found a body, a woman who had been dead for three days. Joel Rifkin, 34, was arrested, and police say he told them that he had killed 16 other women, prostitutes, over the last two or three years. If his claim is true, he is the worst serial killer in New York history. Rifkin pleaded not guilty to one count of murder today.

Joel Rifkin claims to have killed 17 New York City prostitutes.

Rebel leader is new premier of Azerbaijan

Colonel Surat Huseynov's rebel forces have been deployed around Baku.

Baku, Wednesday 30
The political situation in this oil-rich former Soviet state took another bizarre turn today with the appointment of the rebel leader, Colonel Surat Huseynov, as prime minister. It was Huseynov's advance on the capital which led to the flight to the mountains two weeks ago of the popularly elected President Abulfaz Elchibey. The nation's former Communist leader and member of the Soviet Union's ruling Politburo, Geidar Aliyev, then took over the presidency, and Huseynov, who funds his army from the millions he made from what his supporters call trade and his opponents call mafia dealings, got his reward. He has sworn allegiance to Aliyev, but for how long? (→ Aug. 14)

French soccer club in bribery scandal

Marseilles, Wednesday 30
Players from the Valenciennes soccer team have accused a player and an official of the European champions, Marseilles, of offering them bribes to lose a game. The judge investigating the case seized financial documents from the club's headquarters today. Bernard Tapie, the flamboyant president of Olympique Marseille, refused to comment. In Paris, Valenciennes supporters demonstrated outside the football league's HQ, calling for Marseilles' win over the team to be annulled. (→ Sept. 6)

June 30. Queen Elizabeth and Prince Philip lay a wreath at the Lockerbie memorial for the 270 people killed by the bombing of Pan Am Flight 103.

June 30. Royal Regatta opens at Henley, with women allowed to compete for the first time in the event's 154-year history.

July
1993

Su	Mo	Tu	We	Th	Fr	Sa
				1	2	3
4	5	6	7	8	9	10
11	12	13	14	15	16	17
18	19	20	21	22	23	24
25	26	27	28	29	30	31

Germany, 1
Refugees are turned away as a restrictive asylum law takes effect.

London, 1
Britain freezes new aid to Nigeria. (→ Aug. 26)

U.S., 2
Clinton says he will ask Congress for funds to aid farmers in four Midwest states who have suffered from days of torrential rains. (→ 8)

South Africa, 2
The country's first election in which blacks and whites will be able to vote is set for April 27, 1994.

London, 3
The City is sealed off with roadblocks to keep IRA bombers out.

Washington, D.C., 4
Clinton picks Sheila Widnall to be secretary of the Air Force, the first woman to head one of the military services.

Mount Julian, Ireland, 4
British golfer Nick Faldo wins the Irish Open.

Sicily, 5
Police seize $60 million of Mafia assets.

Washington, D.C., 7
The World Bank reports that life expectancy in developing countries has risen from 46 to 63 years since 1960.

Egypt, 8
Seven Muslim militants are executed for attacks on tourists.

U.S., 8
Thousands of people are evacuated in Iowa, Illinois and Missouri as the Mississippi and Missouri rivers flood. (→ 12)

London, 9
Scientists announce that bones found in 1991 in Russia are the remains of Czar Nicholas II and his family, murdered by the Bolsheviks in 1918.

DEATHS

3. Curly Joe DeRita, last of the Three Stooges comedy team (*1910).

6. Lady Ruth Fermoy, lady-in-waiting to the Queen Mother and grandmother of Princess Diana (*Oct. 2, 1908).

Independence Day victory for Pete Sampras at Wimbledon final

Sampras's second Grand Slam win.

Wimbledon, Sunday 4
Pete Sampras overpowered his friend Jim Courier today in an all-American final to win the Wimbledon men's championship 7-6, 7-6, 3-6, 6-3. It was a game of booming serves played in temperatures which rose to over 100 degrees.

Both men were exhausted, and Sampras, who overcame a shoulder injury to play, was threatened by a cramp but produced a barrage of powerful serves and volleys to win the game, with one of his volleys timed at 125 mph.

Yesterday, Steffi Graf brought off a remarkable turnaround after being 1-4 down in the final set against Jana Novotna to win the women's finals 7-6, 1-6, 6-4.

Steffi Graf confirms her supremacy.

U.K. to comply with halt on bomb tests

Washington, Saturday 3
Britain's plans to maintain the safety of its stockpile of nuclear weapons were set back tonight by President Clinton's announcement that the ban on nuclear tests in the Nevada desert will be extended for another year.

Britain, which had hoped to keep a two-year window open for three explosions to test the safety devices on existing weapons, has no option but to comply and must now rely on computer simulations to check the triggers of its ageing Polaris warheads. Making the announcement in his weekly radio program, President Clinton said he hoped the ban would discourage other nations from developing nuclear arsenals.

Haiti's coup leader accepts U.N. plan

New York, Saturday 3
Exiled Haitian President Jean-Bertrand Aristide signed an accord today with the man who ousted him, General Raoul Cedras. He is to return to power by October 30. Under the terms of the deal, brokered by the U.N., Cedras will resign and the coup leaders will be granted political amnesty, but this will not extend to criminal prosecutions.

It is hoped the accord will bring an end to the crisis which has paralysed Haiti for nearly two years, but the news was greeted with extreme caution in Port au Prince. Armed supporters of Cedras gathered in a show of force outside army headquarters chanting, "Aristide No, Democracy Yes." (→ Aug. 30)

Navy to bear brunt of U.K. force cuts

London, Monday 5
The Royal Navy is to suffer draconian cuts in a reassessment of the U.K.'s defense commitments following the collapse of the Soviet Union. The destroyer and frigate force will be cut from 40 to about 35, and the Upholder class of four diesel-electric submarines, which cost £900 million to build, will be sold, leased or moth-balled. The RAF will also suffer, with the loss of a Tornado F3 squadron.

The cuts, announced in a white paper, *Defending Our Future*, will meet Treasury demands for £1 billion in military savings. Tonight, angry Tory MPs said this was the real reason for the measures. They threatened to resist further cuts.

July 1. Tom Cruise stars in "The Firm," out in the U.S. this week.

July 1. The world's first electronic newspaper is presented at the PC Expo in New York.

Georgia crisis deepens

Georgian forces approach Sukhumi, capital of the rebel region of Abkhazia.

Tbilisi, Tuesday 6

Eduard Shevardnadze, the Georgian leader and former Soviet foreign minister, has been given sweeping powers in face of an onslaught by Abkhazian rebels against the Black Sea resort of Sukhumi, on what was known as the Soviet Riviera. Shevardnadze himself narrowly escaped being killed when his car came under fire while visiting Georgian troops fighting off Abkhazian attacks.

Russia has called on Georgia and the Abkhazians, Muslims seeking their own state, to sign a peace formula, but the Georgians refuse, accusing Moscow of supporting the separatists.

No quick fix at G7 talks

All together now: photo-op time for Group of Seven leaders and their aides.

Tokyo, Friday 9

The Group of Seven, the world's leading industrialized nations, delighted to have agreed to the "biggest tariff reduction in history," said at the end of their summit here today that they were determined to achieve economic recovery. They recognized, however, that it was going to be no easy matter and emphasized the need to control welfare spending. The summit's final communiqué declared that the success of the GATT negotiations were the G7's highest priority. The Seven also listened to President Yeltsin, gave him their moral support and promised him $3 billion in aid.

U.N. warns of a vast migration problem

London, Tuesday 6

The U.N. Population Fund's annual report warns that migration "could become the human crisis of our era." More people than ever before are leaving their homes and looking for better lives abroad. At least 100 million, about 2% of the world's population, have emigrated. Most are economic migrants, but 17 million are estimated to be refugees. The classic circular pattern of immigration, where people live and work for a while abroad, then return home, is breaking down. Most now stay in their adopted countries.

Royal commission calls for justice reforms

London, Friday 9

The government reacted cautiously today to fundamental changes in the legal system proposed by the Royal Commission on Criminal Justice. Among its most controversial proposals is the scrapping of the centuries-old right of defendants to choose trial by jury and their right to remain silent. Home Secretary Michael Howard said he wished to study the findings before bringing forward legislation. He is, however, expected to agree swiftly to setting up an independent body to investigate miscarriages of justice.

July 4. Heavy duty: U.S. wrestling star Lex Luther meets 450-pound sumo champ Akebono.

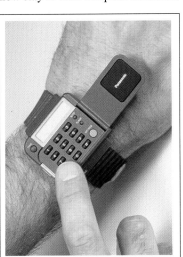

July 5. It's Dick Tracy time for Panasonic's new wristband cordless 30-channel telephone.

July 6. Michelangelo's "The Holy Family on the Flight to Egypt" is sold by Christie's for £4.18 million, a world record for an Old Master drawing.

July

1993

Su	Mo	Tu	We	Th	Fr	Sa
				1	2	3
4	5	6	7	8	9	10
11	12	13	14	15	16	17
18	19	20	21	22	23	24
25	26	27	28	29	30	31

Silverstone, England, 11
Alain Prost of France wins the British Grand Prix and becomes the first driver to win 50 Formula One races.

Cleveland, 11
Paul Tracy wins the IndyCar Cleveland Grand Prix, ahead of Britain's Nigel Mansell.

Somalia, 12
A mob kills three journalists after U.S. helicopters attack General Aidid's stronghold near Mogadishu. (→Aug. 8)

South Korea, 12
During a visit to Seoul by President Clinton, North Korea returns the remains of 17 Americans killed during the Korean War.

Brussels, 13
The EC Commission threatens to take Britain to court for flouting rules on drinking-water quality.

Moscow, 13
Rolls-Royce opens its first showroom in Russia.

London, 14
Armed robbers raid a diamond shop and escape with jewels valued at £7 million.

U.S., 14
Bill Clinton visits the flood-ravaged Midwest and promises $2.48 billion in federal disaster relief. (→16)

U.K., 14
The annual inflation rate fell to 1.2% in June, the lowest since 1964.

New York, 15
The consumer products firm Procter & Gamble cuts its workforce by 13,000.

London, 15
Princess Diana attends the premiere of *Jurassic Park*, which has taken advance bookings of £1 million in Britain.

Saint Louis, 16
The Missouri River breaks through a levee and merges with the Mississippi; up to 25 people have died in floods in Midwest states. (→18)

DEATH

14. Léo Ferré, French songwriter and singer (*Aug. 24, 1916).

Glittering premiere for 'Sunset Boulevard'

Sir Andrew Lloyd Webber's new musical takes the West End by storm.

London, Monday 12
All the stars in London turned out to shine at the premiere of Andrew Lloyd Webber's musical version of *Sunset Boulevard*. The Strand between the Aldelphi Theatre and the Savoy, where an after-show dinner for 700 was held, was a glittering parade of show-biz luminaries. The show itself, with Patti LuPone playing the part of ageing Hollywood goddess Norma Desmond, is said by *The Times* to be "often gorgeous to look at, sometimes enchanting to hear ... and merits the century-long run it may well achieve."

East Coast, Midwest hit by freak weather

U.S., Monday 12
A deadly heat wave has smothered the East Coast and killed 48 people since it began five days ago. New York City and Philadelphia had temperatures in the 100s from Friday to Saturday. The toll was heaviest in the Philadelphia area, where 47 people have died. Temperatures dropped somewhat today, and meteorologists predict the wave will break by the weekend.

The heat is caused by the same weather system that is linked to the flooding in the Mississippi basin. The winds of a high-pressure system in the Atlantic have been sending moisture from the Gulf of Mexico into the Midwest and warm air up the East Coast. (→14)

Conservatives lose a round to Yeltsin

Moscow, Monday 12
President Yeltsin won a major battle in the power struggle against his die-hard enemies today when the constitutional assembly approved his draft for changing Russia's Soviet-era basic law, or constitution. The draft, which will enable him to dissolve the Congress, the main seat of conservative power, passed by 433 votes to 153. It must now be approved by the 88 regional councils. Yeltsin may run into trouble with the councils demanding more autonomy and control of their resources in exchange for their support. (→Aug. 13)

U.S. forces join U.N. effort in Macedonia

Skopje, Monday 12
American soldiers arrived here today to join Scandinavian troops on U.N. peacekeeping duty in this former Yugoslav republic. The 300 soldiers will serve under the command of Danish Brigadier General Finn Saemark Thomsen. The troops will undergo a month of training to learn the rules of engagement that apply to a peacekeeping effort. General Thomsen says he will keep the troops here, miles away from the Serbian border, as a reserve unit but may later assign them to the border if he feels the Serbs need to be sent a tougher message.

July 11. The Princess of Wales visits a leprosy clinic during a four-day tour of Zimbabwe.

July 12. Miss Turkey, 20-year-old model Arzum Onan, is elected Miss Europe 93 in Istanbul.

July 12. Clint Eastwood is an ageing Secret Service agent in "In the Line of Fire."

Russian border guards slaughtered in cross-border Muslim raid

Tajikistan, Tuesday 13
Tajik rebels, operating out of Afghanistan and helped by Afghani guerrillas, swooped on Russian army posts guarding the border today, killing 25 soldiers. The Russians are in Tajikistan to support the government, which is clinging to power after a bloody six-month civil war between the old-style *apparatchiks* and Muslim fundamentalists. The Russians have reacted vigorously to the attacks, extra troops have been rushed to the area and their commander, General Bondarenko, says "they have the right to raid Afghan territory if violations of the border do not stop."

Muslim guerrillas set to cross Afghan border to attack Russians in Tajikistan.

Secretive MI5 lifts veil on operations

London, Friday 16
Stella Rimington, head of MI5, met the press today and for the first time revealed details of her organization's work. She issued a booklet, *The Security Service*, which gives its address, its structure, a partial history, its coat of arms and discusses its role in the post-Soviet world. Britain's first woman spy-master revealed herself as cheerful and relaxed with a liking for chunky jewellery. She said the aim of the disclosures was to dispel "some of the more fanciful allegations" about her once-secret service.

China sets up army for Hong Kong duty

Hong Kong, Friday 16
China's army sent a shiver of unease through the colony today by confirming that it intended to deploy troops throughout Hong Kong when the territory reverts to Chinese sovereignty in 1997. Xu Huizi, deputy head of the People's Liberation Army, said it would set up its headquarters at HMS Tamar, site of the British garrison command in the heart of the city's financial district. Xu said the troops would undergo special training and observe local laws, but he refused to guarantee they would wear civilian clothes in town as the English troops do.

Dennis Connor claims a yacht race record

Southampton, Friday 16
American skipper Dennis Connor has won the Gold Cup Trans-Atlantic Yacht Race, arriving here just after midnight. He piloted the *Winston* across the Atlantic in 12 days, 8 hours, 4 minutes and 12 seconds. He broke the 88-year-old record for a trans-Atlantic crossing by clocking a time of 11 days, 18 hours from Ambrose Lighthouse in New York harbor to Lizzard Point in the English Channel, the marks used for such records.

'Gay gene' evidence sparks a controversy

New York, Friday 16
The journal *Science* published a report today that suggests the presence of a "gay gene." Genetic material from 40 couples of homosexual brothers were studied, and it was found that 33 of them had identical pieces of the X chromosome. The odds of this happening randomly are less than half a percent. The reaction to the news was split among gay groups, some welcoming it as helpful in fighting discrimination, others worrying that the discovery may lead to experimentation on gays to eliminate homosexuality.

Covertly photographed: Britain's counterspy boss Stella Rimington.

July 13. Spain's new cabinet ministers include (from left) Angeles Millan (Health), Carmen Alborch (Culture) and Cristina Alberdi (Social Affairs).

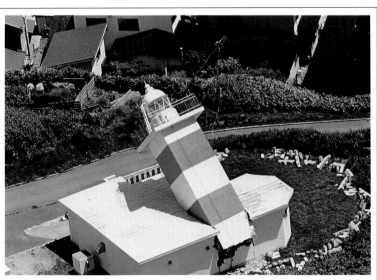
July 14. Japan's strongest earthquake in 25 years leaves more than 165 dead. Worst hit was the tiny island of Okushiri, off the Hokkaido coast.

July. A hitch in time: A drive-in wedding chapel is doing brisk business in Las Vegas.

July

1993

Su	Mo	Tu	We	Th	Fr	Sa
				1	2	3
4	5	6	7	8	9	10
11	12	13	14	15	16	17
18	19	20	21	22	23	24
25	26	27	28	29	30	31

Japan, 18
Voters deny a majority to the ruling Liberal Democratic Party for the first time in 38 years. (→22)

U.S., 18
The Mississippi River reaches a record crest of 47 feet; 11 airports and 15 million acres of farmland across eight Midwest states are under water. (→30)

U.K., 19
According to a poll, only 37% of Britons think Prince Charles is fit to be king.

London, 19
Policemen begin a six-month test of American-style billy clubs.

U.K., 19
The Trades Union Congress picks John Monks as its general secretary.

Washington, D.C., 19
Congress reports that arms sales to the Third World fell to $23.9 billion in 1992, the lowest level since 1985.

London, 19
American film director Sam Wanamaker is awarded an honorary CBE.

Washington, D.C., 20
Vincent Foster, a close Clinton friend and White House aide, commits suicide.

Bangkok, 20
Two British girls, Karyn Smith and Patricia Cahill, sentenced to long jail terms for heroin smuggling are pardoned.

Washington, D.C., 22
Clinton rejects suggestions that his administration has given up on the conflict in Bosnia. (→30)

Rio de Janeiro, 23
Hooded killers, believed to be policemen, gun down eight homeless boys.

Bordeaux, France, 23
Briton Chris Boardman breaks the world record for one-hour cycling, covering 32.48 miles.

DEATHS

18. Jean Negulesco, Romanian-born Hollywood film director (*Feb. 26, 1900).

24. Francis Bouygues, French businessman (*Dec. 5, 1922).

Clinton announces new policy on homosexuals in the military

The president says the complex new rules are "an honorable compromise."

Washington, D.C., Monday 19
Clinton and the Joint Chiefs have reached a compromise on gays in the armed forces. "Don't ask, don't tell, don't pursue" is the new rule. "Don't ask" means that although the ban on homosexual conduct is not removed, the military may not ask recruits if they are gay. "Don't tell" means that gays cannot declare their homosexuality, because showing "propensity or intent" to engage in homosexual acts is forbidden. "Don't pursue" means that only "credible" evidence of homosexual acts is cause for dismissal. Going to gay bars would not suffice to launch an investigation, for example.

Stylish Australian wins British Open

Norman plays his best round ever.

Sandwich, Kent, Sunday 18
Greg Norman, the "Great White Shark" from Australia, beat Nick Faldo by two shots to win the British Open at Royal Saint George's today. Often criticized for promising but rarely winning, he recorded one of the most outstanding last rounds in the 122-year history of the championship to silence his detractors. His 64 gave him a four-round total of 276, 13 under par, and he beat a field of brilliant golfers fair and square. "It was one of those days when I felt I never hit a shot other than out of the middle of the club," he said. "I am in awe of myself at the way I played. I have never gone round a golf course and hit every shot perfectly. I did so today."

Ian Botham, cricket great, to quit game

Durham, Sunday 18
Ian Botham, one of the greatest all-rounders of English cricket announced his retirement today. He will be sadly missed; his swashbuckling approach to the game entertained fans all over the world. When "Beefy" strode to the crease, swinging his heavyweight bat over his head, excitement ran round the ground. His was a career of heights and depths. Having resigned the captaincy of England in 1981, he beat the Australians almost single-handedly in the next match, with an innings of 149 not out. "All good things must come to an end," he said today. "The body has decided that enough is enough." (→26)

July 19. A Greenpeace ship sails past the U.N. to warn against the decline in global fish stocks.

Mafia-buster Freeh to be new FBI boss

Freeh, aged 43, is a New Yorker.

Washington, D.C., Tuesday 20
Louis J. Freeh, a federal judge and former FBI field agent, was named today to head the FBI. Freeh, whom President Clinton called a "law-enforcement legend," is well-known in international law-enforcement circles for his work in combatting the Mafia. He gained prominence in the 1980s when, as federal prosecutor in New York, he brought the "Pizza Connection" case to court. The trial ended with the conviction of Salvatore Catalano, the reputed boss of a Mafia operation that used pizzerias as fronts for their heroin business. Yesterday, Clinton dismissed the former director, William Sessions, who had been accused of financial impropriety in office.

apan politics in turmoil

Bank's ruble recall causes panic in Russia

A dejected Kiichi Miyazawa.

Tokyo, Thursday 22
Japan is without a prime minister today following the resignation of Kiichi Miyazawa as leader of the ruling Liberal Democratic Party, which lost control of the Lower House in last Sunday's elections. "We lost so many important comrades," said Miyazawa. "As party president, I am completely responsible, and to clarify my responsibility, I announce my intention to resign." His departure has added to the turmoil of Japanese politics as his colleagues not only try to restore their parliamentary majority by making alliances with small parties but wheel and deal to succeed him in an increasingly heated power struggle. Meanwhile, the opposition parties are trying to form a coalition to oust the Liberal Democrats. (→ 29)

Only banknotes printed prior to 1993 are to be withdrawn from circulation.

Moscow, Saturday 24
A surprise announcement today of draconian currency reforms to curb inflation and forgery has caused panic and utter confusion in Russia. The news that all pre-1993 banknotes are going out of circulation tomorrow brought crowds out to besiege the banks, demanding that their hoarded savings be changed into new notes. But many of the banks are closed, and at others staff said they had received no instructions on what to do. The government promised that "all money that has been earned will be exchanged," but cynics pointed out that the currency crooks deal in U.S. dollars.

Parent-killer trial opens in California

Los Angeles, Tuesday 20
Four years ago two brothers walked into the room where their parents were watching TV and fired shotguns, killing Kitty and Jose Mendez. The trial of Erik, 22, and Lyle, 25, began today. The prosecution hopes to convict them of murder, the motive being the inheritance from their wealthy parents. The brothers claim they acted in self-defense, that they were pushed to the act by years of physical and sexual abuse by their father.

New French scandal over hormone case

Paris, Tuesday 20
Growth hormones used to treat children suffering from dwarfism were contaminated with the infectious agent that causes Creutzfeldt-Jakob disease. Twenty-five children treated with the hormone, extracted from the pituitary gland, or hypophysis, have the disease. Today the president of the France-Hypophysis Association and the doctor in charge of extracting the hormone at the Pasteur Institute were placed under investigation for manslaughter.

House finally approves Maastricht treaty

London, Friday 23
Prime Minister John Major threatened a packed and often rowdy House of Commons today that if the government lost its vote of confidence over the Maastricht bill, he would seek the dissolution of parliament and call a general election. He said he was not prepared to let the stalemate over Europe poison the political atmosphere any longer. "The boil must be lanced, and it must be lanced today." The threat brought back into line the Tory Euro-rebels who had humiliated him yesterday by voting with the Labour Party. Forced to make a choice between a general election in which the Tories would have faced defeat or giving Major the authority to proceed with ratification of Maastricht, their resistance crumbled, and he won his vote of confidence. The vote, when it came, was an anti-climax, there was none of last night's high drama. The prime minister can now proceed with the ratification process and with uniting his party. "The matter is behind us. We have drawn a line in the sand," he said. "Everyone came back into the fold." (→ Aug. 2)

Italy's corruption fight takes grim toll

Raul Gardini was being investigated.

Milan, Saturday 24
Raul Gardini, former head of the Ferruzzi Group, shot himself in his palatial 17th-century home here today, the second suicide victim of the corruption scandals which are tearing at the heart of Italian social and political life. Three days ago Gabriele Cagliari, former chairman of the energy giant ENI, killed himself in his prison cell. Both were under investigation by the "Clean Hands" magistrates. Gardini, one of Italy's most flamboyant tycoons, spent $100 million in an attempt to win the America's Cup with his yacht *Il Moro di Venezia*. It lost.

July 24. Two Russian MIG-29s in a mid-air collision during an air show in Gloucestershire.

July 24. "Coneheads" stars Dan Aykroyd and Jane Curtin.

July

1993

Su	Mo	Tu	We	Th	Fr	Sa
				1	2	3
4	5	6	7	8	9	10
11	12	13	14	15	16	17
18	19	20	21	22	23	24
25	26	27	28	29	30	31

Cape Town, 25
Black gunmen burst into an Anglican church and kill nine whites. (→Aug. 25)

Lebanon, 25
Israeli warplanes launch an attack against pro-Iranian Hezbollah guerrillas. (→27)

Germany, 25
President Richard von Weizäcker calls for a memorial to be built in Berlin in honor of Jews killed by the Nazis.

Headingly, Yorkshire, 26
Graham Gooch resigns as England's cricket captain after the Australians win the Fourth Test.

Boston, 27
The Boston Celtics' star Reggie Lewis collapses and dies while shooting baskets.

England, 28
Thieves steal a 14-foot canvas replica of a police car used to deter drivers from speeding.

Japan, 28
Jews demand an apology after a leading paper publishes an ad for books alleging a Jewish plot to destroy Japan.

U.K., 29
The Tories lose a by-election in Christchurch, a Tory stronghold for 83 years, to the Liberal Democrats.

Tokyo, 29
Opposition parties pick Morihiro Hosokawa as their candidate for premier.
(→Aug. 6)

Washington, D.C., 29
The U.S. economy grew by just 1.6% in the second quarter.

Geneva, 30
Bosnia's warring factions agree to a plan to divide Bosnia-Herzegovina into three republics. (→Aug. 3)

U.S., 30
Only one bridge across the Missouri River is left open as flooding spreads throughout the Midwest. (→Aug. 1)

New York, 31
The pound is quoted at $1.48.

DEATH

25. Margaret Duchess of Argyll, British socialite (*Dec. 1, 1912).

Franco-British talks amid currency crisis

John Major is flanked by President Mitterrand and Premier Balladur.

London, Monday 26
Prime Minister Major got acquainted today with his French counterpart, the fledgling Premier Edouard Balladur, under the experienced eye of President Mitterrand; but the summit, overshadowed by France's fight to save the franc and with it the European Monetary System, achieved little else. Mitterrand did not help Major by reaffirming his commitment to monetary union and securing a single currency "within a few years." (→Aug. 2)

Castro OK's dollar

Santiago de Cuba, Monday 26
As Cuba celebrates the 40th anniversary of its revolution, another tremendous change is taking place. Cubans are openly using dollars in stores where previously only foreigners could shop. A few days earlier, officials announced the decision to end the ban on Cubans possessing foreign currency. The idea of allowing small private businesses is also being considered.

Gen. Ridgway dies

Fox Chapel, Penn., Monday 26
General Matthew Bunker Ridgway (*March 3, 1895), who pioneered the use of airborne troops in World War II, has died. He planned the first major night airborne assault in the invasion of Sicily in 1943 and parachuted with his men on D-Day. He served as commander-in-chief of the U.N. forces in Korea, supreme commander of allied forces in Europe and U.S. Army chief of staff.

Mystery bombings in Rome and Milan

Rome, Tuesday 27
Two car bombs exploded in Rome and another in Milan today, killing five people and severely damaging the Basilica of Saint John Lateran, one of Christendom's greatest churches and the spot where Romulus and Remus were found. The pope visited the basilica and condemned

Rome's San Giorgio church is hit.

the "vile attacks aimed at the heart of Rome." No one has admitted responsibility for the bombings, which are the latest manifestation of a wave of terrorism aimed at cultural treasures. Some blame the Mafia, some the anti-corruption campaign. Premier Ciampi says they are "attempts to create disorder and panic to slow progress."

July 25. Spain's Miguel Indurain (center) leads the pack on the way to his third victory in the Tour de France, which ended in Paris today.

July 26. A pensive Mick Jagger is 50 today, but is he satisfied?

Israeli raids prompt exodus in Lebanon

Lebanese civilians flee their villages for the relative safety of Beirut.

Southern Lebanon, Tuesday 27
The main road to Beirut is jammed with heavily laden vehicles as some 150,000 people flee the heaviest Israeli bombardment of southern Lebanon since 1985. Israeli guns and aircraft are pounding villages which the Israelis say are harboring Hezbollah guerrillas firing rockets into northern Israeli towns. Air force commander, Maj.-Gen. Herzl Bodinger, said the flight of civilians was deliberate, to create pressure on "Lebanese power brokers" to restrain Hezbollah. Prime Minister Rabin agrees: "If there is no quiet over here, there will be such disquiet in Lebanon that they will not be able to live there." The fighting has prompted U.S. Secretary of State Warren Christopher to end his Far East visit and return to Washington for consultations. (→ Aug. 6)

Jerusalem tribunal frees John Demjanjuk

Jerusalem, Thursday 29
The concentration camp guard John Demjanjuk had his conviction for Nazi war crimes and his sentence of death by hanging nullified by the Israeli Supreme Court today. The court said it had "gnawing doubts" that the retired American car worker was really the sadistic "Ivan the Terrible." Demjanjuk, who was extradited from the U.S. in 1986 and convicted two years later of running Treblinka's gas chamber in which 870,000 Jews died, will now be freed. Holocaust survivors are furious. "Gentlemen, now all the Nazis can celebrate," said Treblinka inmate Yosef Charni.

New Soviet evidence set him free.

King Baudouin of Belgium dies in Spain

Europe's longest-reigning monarch.

Motril, Saturday 31
King Baudouin of the Belgians died suddenly tonight while on holiday at this southern Spanish resort. Born on Sept. 7, 1930, the shy, bespectacled Baudouin died of a heart attack.

Baudouin succeeded to the throne in 1951 when his father, Leopold, wrongly villified for his conduct during the war, was forced to abdicate. Few reigns could have succeeded after starting in such dire circumstances, but he won the respect and affection of his people. He ruled impartially over a kingdom divided between the Flemish-speakers and the French-speaking Walloons. His brother, Prince Albert, is expected to succeed him. (→ Aug. 1)

July 30. In "Rising Sun" Sean Connery and Wesley Snipes are part of a cop team investigating a bizarre sex murder.

July 30. Torrential rains cause severe floods in Nepal, where up to 1,700 people are feared dead. India and Bangladesh also suffered flooding.

July 30. Britain's Linford Christie (center) outruns Americans Carl Lewis (left) and John Drummond over 100 meters at Gateshead, England.

August
1993

Su	Mo	Tu	We	Th	Fr	Sa
1	2	3	4	5	6	7
8	9	10	11	12	13	14
15	16	17	18	19	20	21
22	23	24	25	26	27	28
29	30	31				

U.S., 1
For the first time, NASA postpones a mission by a space shuttle, *Discovery*, because of a meteor shower.

London, 1
England's women's cricket team beat New Zealand to win the Women's World Cup.

Alexandria, Egypt, 2
U.S. Secretary of State Warren Christopher begins a Mideast tour aimed at speeding up the peace process. (→ 6)

U.K., 3
Suffolk-brewed Adnam's Extra Bitter is named Britain's best beer of 1993.

Rimini, Italy, 3
Film director Federico Fellini is hospitalized after suffering from a stroke. (→ Oct. 31)

Southampton, England, 3
Vandals daub anti-Semitic slogans on 150 Jewish graves.

Amsterdam, 3
The Dutch firm PolyGram says it will buy the U.S. record label Motown for $301 million.

Chad, 4
Security forces kill an estimated 100 anti-government demonstrators.

China, 4
The award-winning film *Farewell to my Concubine* is banned.

Germany, 6
Abbas Hammadi, a Lebanese guerrilla who kidnapped two Germans in Beirut, is released after serving half his 13-year sentence.

Italy, 6
A public outcry forces the government to drop a plan to make a $52 health tax apply to Italians who died this year.

Moscow, 6
Interior Ministry anti-terrorist troops are to be issued crossbows.

Washington, D.C., 6
The unemployment rate fell to 6.8% in July, its lowest level in two years.

New York, 7
Officials reveal that an 11-year-old girl who died on July 15 was the first person to die of rabies in New York state since 1954.

Midwest reeling after worst flooding

The region's businessmen, as well as its farmers, have suffered huge losses and will need help to get back on their feet.

Midwest, Sunday 1
The U.S. has seen the worst flooding in its recorded history. The Father of Waters, as Native Americans called the Mississippi River, and its tributaries overflowed their banks and the walls and levees built to protect Midwest farms and towns.

Since early spring, the region has had an abnormal amount of rain.

The trouble began in the northern reaches of the Mississippi basin, where farmers were unable to plant because the fields were sodden.

The first of many crests was recorded near Saint Paul on June 26. The upper Mississippi became unnavigable, with trees, dead animals and other detritus being rapidly swept along by the current, and a

500-mile stretch was closed to shipping. From June 27, the Mississippi has been above flood stage.

As President Clinton met with officials from the states suffering from the floods on July 17 in Saint Louis, the river was inching up the city's floodwalls. The next few days brought hope in the form of clear skies, but those hopes were dashed

Sandbagging saved a few towns.

The calamity brought out the best in people facing a common enemy.

in U.S. history leaves trail of death and destruction

It will take weeks, if not months, of hard work and a lot of federal aid for communities such as this one close to Saint Louis to get back to normal.

as new rains, and with them new record crests, came. The Midwest now resembled a great lake. Its raging rivers were a muddy brown, and the standing water stank and was dangerous, polluted with fertilizer, sewage, diesel fuel and other contaminants. Midwesterners were innoculated against water-borne diseases. The conditions seemed apocalyptic. Indeed, 18% of the 1,011 people responding to a CNN/*USA Today*/Gallup poll in mid-July said they believed the floods were "an indication of God's judgement on the people of the United States for their sinful ways."

The end of July saw the climax of the flooding. The Missouri and Kansas rivers, at their convergence near Kansas City, Mo., both set records on July 27. The Kansas reached 55 feet and the Missouri reached 49 feet. The Mississippi's largest crest came today, when it reached 49.5 feet at Saint Louis.

The flood's toll is monumental. The homes of 38,000 families have been damaged and 20 million acres of farmland are underwater. At least 50 people died due to the catastrophe and 70,000 were driven from their homes. The damage is estimated at $12 billion dollars.

The Great Flood of '93 seems to have come to an end, but much work remains to be done. The river will take at least a month to recede to its normal levels and the massive cleanup will take even longer. (→ 23)

Many fought every inch of the way.

Bill Clinton views the flooded ball park in Davenport, Iowa, on July 5.

The only plus: no lawns to mow.

Europe's monetary system in chaos

Brussels, Monday 2
Jacques Delors, president of the European Commission, rose from his sickbed today and summoned his commissioners back from holiday for crisis talks on Europe's monetary chaos. This move follows the decision by member governments effectively to suspend the Exchange Rate Mechanism by widening the ERM's trading bands to allow currencies to move by 15% on either side of their central rate.

This decision appears to have curbed the selling of the franc and other weak currencies by speculators which led to near-panic over the weekend, but it has called into question Delors's hopes of economic and monetary union by the end of the decade. Wim Kok, the Dutch finance minister, summed up EC feeling: "It is a sad day for Europe."

But John Major said Britain's decision to suspend sterling's membership of the ERM and his government's view that the timetable for union was impracticable had now been vindicated. (→ Sept. 24)

Allies warn Serbs of possible air strikes

Brussels, Tuesday 3
As the Bosnian Serbs continue their military drive to take control of the heights surrounding Sarajevo, the NATO allies have agreed to prepare for possible air strikes on Bosnian Serb troops. The U.S. pushed for the authorization, overcoming objections from other allies, especially Canada, in a meeting of officials from NATO countries which began yesterday and lasted until the early hours of this morning. (→ 15)

Japanese apologize for sex slave policy

Tokyo, Wednesday 4
Japan has admitted that its military forced tens of thousands of women into sexual slavery from the beginning of its invasion of China in 1932 until the end of World War II in 1945. An apology was offered for the enslavement of the "comfort women," mostly Korean but including other Asians and a few Europeans, but there was no mention of compensation. Some of the victims have sued the Japanese government.

Billionaire George Soros.

One of the most powerful players in the currency markets is American George Soros. He left his native Hungary during the Soviet repression of the 1956 uprising.

He is seen as one of the major factors in the pull-out of the pound from the European Monetary System last September. The funds he managed made nearly a billion dollars from speculation against the British currency. His recent speculation against the franc, after having implicitly supported it in June by saying that he expected the Deutsche mark to fall, is not the least of the causes of the current turmoil in European markets. His $7-billion investment power and his influence in the markets make him the guru of the speculators and the worst nightmare of the state banks.

Hungarian smashes world swim record

Sheffield, Tuesday 3
Karoly Guttler of Hungary proved himself the fastest swimmer in the world at the 100-meter breast stroke today when he stormed to a world record of 1 minute 00.95 seconds, taking 0.34 seconds off the record held by his compatriot, Norbert Rozsa.

Having broken the record in the heats, he could not do it again in the final, but took the gold medal, beating Britain's Nick Gillingham, who took second place. "This morning, I didn't think I could swim such a good race," said Guttler, "it was a surprise but perhaps I got lucky."

Maastricht treaty is ratified by U.K.

London, Monday 2
The United Kingdom today at last ratified the Maastricht treaty, 20 months after it was negotiated. The final obstacle was removed when Lord Rees-Mogg abandoned his court case against its legality. A four page instrument of ratification written on vellum and signed by the Queen, had already been flown to Rome – where the EC began – and as soon as the Rees-Mogg case ended it was deposited with the Foreign Ministry. The irony is that after its politically divisive progress through the British parliament, many Eurosceptics now regard the treaty, in the words of Norman Lamont, as "a bit of a fossil." (→ Sept. 24)

Aug. 1. The Belgian government announces that Prince Albert, aged 59, is to be the new king.

Aug. 1. Buganda's 36th Kabaka (king), Ronald Mutebi, begins to reign over his 4 million subjects.

Aug. 4. The Ocean Dome at the vast Seagaia resort complex, boasting perfect surfing waves, opens at Miyazaki, on Japan's Kyushu Island.

Clinton budget scrapes through Congress

It took a lot of presidential arm-twisting to get the budget package passed.

Washington, D.C., Friday 6

Congress has narrowly passed President Clinton's deficit-reduction program, after much heated debate and presidential lobbying.

The House passed the package yesterday by a vote of 218-216. With many representatives undecided, Clinton got on the phone, pointing out the advantages to the home districts of the wavering. The climax was when Pennsylvania's Marjorie Margolies-Mezvinsky voted for the plan. She had said earlier she would vote against it.

Today in the Senate, Vice President Al Gore broke a 50-50 tie. The key Senate "yea" vote was from Bob Kerrey of Nebraska, who had remained undecided right up to the wire. No Republican in either chamber voted for the president's plan.

Crossword addicts mourn their tormentor

Daytona Beach, Thursday 5

Those who have memorized the world's rivers and have learned that the "Nice" way to say yes is "oui" are heartbroken at the passing of Eugene Maleska (*1916), who had edited the *New York Times* crossword since 1977. He died of throat cancer on Tuesday.

Maleska edited 7,000 puzzles during his tenure and had contributed dozens as a free-lancer before taking the job. Previously he had worked for 30 years as an English teacher and school administrator. His first puzzle was written in 1933 when he was a student at Montclair State College in New Jersey.

Christopher is hopeful after Mideast tour

Pleased with the progress: Warren Christopher and Israel's Shimon Peres.

Jerusalem, Friday 6

U.S. Secretary of State Warren Christopher ended his five day round of shuttle diplomacy in the Middle East today on an upbeat note, telling reporters, "I leave full of hope that the peace process has been salvaged and that we can make progress over the next few months." Nobody will spell out the source of his hopefulness, but it is thought here that he has received assurances from the Syrians that they would keep the pro-Iranian Hezbollah under control on Israel's northern border. The well-informed *Jerusalem Post* reports Israel's prime minister, Yitzhak Rabin, is "convinced Damascus genuinely wants to reach a peace accord with Israel." However, even before Christopher left the country his hopes were overshadowed by a series of incidents which left four dead. (→ 30)

Aug. 7. Buckingham Palace has its first visitors, the most patriotic of whom queued all night for a chance to be among the first.

Hosokawa takes over as Japan's premier

Tokyo, Friday 6

Morihiro Hosokawa, heir to a clan of feudal lords, was elected prime minister today, taking power away from the Liberal Democrats after 38 years of one-party rule. Hosokawa, 55, has had a dizzying ride to power, having launched his Japan New Party only 15 months ago. He has a playboy reputation, but his promise to clear out the corruption rife in Japanese politics appealed to voters tired of the old gang. He will not have an easy task: His government is a coalition of eight groups with widely differing policies.

Enigmatic smile from the premier.

Aug. 6. Harrison Ford, aged 51, takes over from David Janssen as Dr. Kimble in "The Fugitive."

Aug. Nirvana on wheels: Los Angeles car buffs spare no effort to get that extra-special look.

August

1993

Su	Mo	Tu	We	Th	Fr	Sa
1	2	3	4	5	6	7
8	9	10	11	12	13	14
15	16	17	18	19	20	21
22	23	24	25	26	27	28
29	30	31				

Venezuela, 8
A tropical storm leaves more than 70 dead and 300 injured.

Somalia, 8
Four U.S. soldiers are killed when their vehicle hits a land mine in Mogadishu. (→ Sept. 9)

Prague, 8
Sergi Bruguera of Spain wins the Czech Open tennis championship.

London, 8
An American Bowl exhibition game between the Dallas Cowboys and the Detroit Lions ends in a 13-13 draw.

London, New Hampshire, 8
Nigel Mansell wins the New England 200 IndyCar race.

Georgia, 8
CIA agent Fred Woodruff is killed in an ambush near Tbilisi.

U.K., 9
A British couple is jailed, separately, for 14 days after a 13-hour domestic row caused neighbors to call the police.

Jamaica, 10
Pope John Paul II arrives in Kingston on the first leg of a tour that will take him to Mexico and the U.S. (→ 14)

Turkey, 10
Kurdish rebels free a Briton and an Australian taken hostage on July 5. (→ Nov. 4)

Ottawa, 11
Canada lifts its 15-year-old embargo on humanitarian aid to Cuba.

U.K., 11
The Department of Health says that the number of people awaiting hospital treatment has risen to more than a million for the first time.

U.S., 12
Officials announce the completion of the cleanup at Three Mile Island, scene in 1979 of the nation's worst commercial nuclear power plant accident.

Bournemouth, England, 13
Firebombs planted by the IRA cause damage but no casualties.

Zurich, 13
FIFA declares Germany the world's best soccer team; England is ranked 12th.

Irma, a frail symbol of Sarajevo's suffering, is flown to London

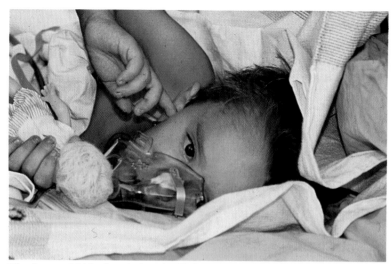

The 5-year-old Muslim victim of a Serbian mortar attack on July 30.

London, Monday 9
Irma Hadzimuratovic, the desperately ill Bosnian child whose pitiful appearance on television touched the heart of the nation, was flown from Sarajevo yesterday and is being treated at the Great Ormond Street children's hospital. Irma, 5, suffered severe injuries in a mortar attack which killed her mother. She then developed meningitis and faced certain death in Sarajevo's shattered hospital. Public outrage led Prime Minister Major to intervene, and she was flown out by the RAF in horrendous weather. She remains very ill, but her doctor says: "She is very brave and will not give in." All she can say is "pain everywhere."

Heidi Fleiss, 'Madam to the stars', has Hollywood in a tizzy

Los Angeles, Monday 9
Tinseltown's inhabitants waited, some fearful, some eagerly when Heidi Fleiss, alleged madam of the film industry's most profitable call-girl ring appeared in court to plead not guilty to five charges of cocaine trafficking and pandering "by procuring for prostitution."

The interest centers not so much on Fleiss, 27-year-old daughter of a prominent doctor, but on her "little black book," which she says contains her star-studded list of clients. So far she has revealed nothing, but the town is buzzing and film executives are running for cover.

Tinseltown's big players are hoping her black book will remain firmly shut.

Aug. 8. Soweto student Jacqui Mofokeng, aged 21, becomes the first black woman ever to be crowned Miss South Africa.

Helmut Kohl to cut welfare spending

Bonn, Wednesday 11
For the first time in the history of the postwar German state, welfare and unemployment compensation may be cut. The reunification of East and West Germany has been a great drain on the country's finances, and the recession has helped to push up the budget deficit. The cuts, which will add up to about 77 billion Deutsche marks ($45.2 billion) over the next three years, are meant to bring the deficit down. The plan must be approved by parliament, and Kohl's government faces opposition from the Social Democrats, as well as organized labor and the German Red Cross.

Aug. 10. Los Angeles FBI agents display masterpieces by Chagall, Degas and Picasso, worth more than $9 million, which had been stolen in February 1992. Two men have been arrested so far.

Discord over Clinton's abortion policy marks pope's U.S. visit

John Paul II, aged 73, arrives in Denver aboard the president's Marine One.

Denver, Saturday 14

Pope John Paul II was diplomatic, but made his point on abortion, a subject on which he disagrees with President Clinton. When he was welcomed Thursday by the president and a crowd of young people who had come for World Youth Day, the pope stressed the importance of the "right to life." After Clinton and some of his aides met with the pope, he said the subject of abortion had not come up. But the pope had again stressed "the right to life and the defense of life." Today the pope celebrated mass before the World Youth Day delegates and will hold another mass for 350,000 people tomorrow before returning to Rome.

Yeltsin calls for a parallel parliament

Moscow, Friday 13

President Yeltsin sought to outflank his hardline opponents in parliament today by proposing that local leaders form what would be a rival parliament.

Addressing the heads of the 88 areas of the Russian Federation in Petrozavodsk, near the Finnish border, Yeltsin said he wanted to ensure a fair redistribution of power from the capital to the provinces. He made it clear, however, that he would not tolerate any attempts to secede: "If any republics or regions have hopes of leaving Russia, then they are deeply mistaken." (→ 20)

Anti-crime plan is unveiled by Clinton

Washington, D.C., Wednesday 11

"The first duty of any government is to try to keep its citizens safe," President Clinton said today. He was announcing his anti-crime package, which includes $3.4 billion to put 50,000 more police on the streets, $475 million to help make public schools safer, a $100-million initiative to recruit and train college students for police work and a restoration of the death penalty for some federal crimes. His first step was to sign an executive order suspending importation of assault pistols.

German yachts win 1993 Admiral's Cup

Cowes, England, Wednesday 11

The Admiral's Cup, top prize in ocean racing, has been won this year by the unfancied three-yacht German team of *Container, Rubin* and *Pinta*, whose victory in the seven race series was as narrow as it was unexpected. At the end of the final race today, the gruelling 605-mile Fastnet Rock run, the Australian *Ragamuffin* came third, 12 minutes ahead of *Container*, but when the points were added up the Germans were just 0.25 of a point ahead of the Australian team.

Armenians launch a big new offensive

Azerbaijan, Saturday 14

Another round of Armenian offensives has taken 8 villages near the southern town of Dzhebrail near Azerbaijan's border with Iran. Armenians also have the advantage to the east of the disputed region of Nagorno-Karabakh, having occupied and razed the city of Agdam and taken many other towns. Thousands of Azeris are fleeing the fighting and heading toward Iran. The Azeri government is facing another separatist movement in Lenkoran, also near the Iranian border.

Aug. 11. Top NATO commander, General John M. Shalikashvili, born in Poland and known as "Shali," is nominated to be head of the Joint Chiefs of Staff.

Aug. 10. Veronica Blume, a 16-year-old from Barcelona, Spain, is named Supermodel of 1993.

Aug. 11. Salman Rushdie makes a surprise appearance during a rock concert at Wembley by the Irish group U2, attended by 72,000 fans.

Aug. 14. An estimated 112 people are killed when the Royal Plaza Hotel, north of Bangkok, collapses. The illegal addition of three top floors may be to blame.

August

1993

Su	Mo	Tu	We	Th	Fr	Sa
1	2	3	4	5	6	7
8	9	10	11	12	13	14
15	16	17	18	19	20	21
22	23	24	25	26	27	28
29	30	31				

Stuttgart, 15
Linford Christie of Britain wins the World Championship 100-meter race in 9.87 seconds. (→ 17)

Memphis, 16
More than 7,000 fans pay tribute to Elvis Presley on the 16th anniversary of his death.

Johannesburg, 16
South Africa agrees to return Walvis Bay, its last colonial possession in Africa, to Namibia.

London, 17
Health officials back a doctor who refused to treat a heavy smoker with heart problems; the patient later died.

New York, 17
General Colin Powell, outgoing chairman of the Joint Chiefs of Staff, signs a record $6-million deal for his memoirs.

Stuttgart, 17
Jackie Joyner-Kersee (U.S.) wins the heptathlon at the World Athletic Championships. (→ 19)

Cairo, 18
Four people are killed in a bomb attack by Islamic extremists.

Taipei, 18
The ruling Kuomintang re-elects President Lee Teng-hui of Taiwan as party leader.

New York, 18
Eastman Kodak Co. says it plans to cut 10,000 jobs.

Ulster, 19
Jean Kennedy Smith, the new U.S. ambassador to Dublin, makes her first visit to Northern Ireland.

Stuttgart, 19
Sally Gunnell (U.K.) wins the 400-meter hurdles and sets a world record time of 52.74 seconds; Sergei Bubka (Ukraine) clears 6 meters to win the pole vault event. (→ 22)

Beirut, 19
Eight Israeli soldiers are killed by bombs while on patrol in southern Lebanon.

Khartoum, 19
Sudan says a U.S. decision to place it on the list of nations that sponsor terrorism is "anti-Islamic."

Bosnian Serbs agree to withdraw from strategic mountain tops

Serb forces have shelled Sarajevo from atop Mounts Igman and Bjelasnica.

Sarajevo, Sunday 15
With NATO fighters wheeling overhead, Serb forces withdrew from the commanding heights of Mount Igman and Mount Bjelasnica today from which they have overlooked Sarajevo for the last three weeks. Their withdrawal was a condition for the resumption of the stalled peace talks in Geneva, and Bosnian President Izetbegovic announced that he would return to the talks tomorrow. The Serbs left the mountains in no spirit of peace, however. Before boarding their buses they burned and blew up the ski-lifts and chalets built on Mount Igman for the 1984 Olympics. (→ 31)

Damon Hill wins his first Grand Prix

Budapest, Sunday 15
Damon Hill claimed his first Formula One victory today when he won the Hungarian Grand Prix under a blazing sun at the Hungaroring. He had been denied victory after leading in both the British and German Grand Prix, but the son of double world champion Graham Hill had his share of luck today.

His teammate Alain Prost lost the pole position by stalling and then suffered a broken rear wing, while both Ayrton Senna and Michael Schumaker retired. The field left open, Hill brought his Canon Williams Renault home a comfortable 1 minute 11 seconds clear of second-placed Riccardo Patrese.

Hill's run of bad luck has broken.

Teenagers arrested for Jordan's murder

A grieving Michael Jordan.

Fayetteville, N.C., Sunday 15
Larry Demery and Andre Green, both 18, have been charged with the murder of James Jordan, father of basketball star Michael Jordan.

Jordan was shot with a .38-caliber gun at a rest-stop on Interstate 95 in North Carolina at about 3:30 a.m. on July 23. When the boys realized their victim was the sports great's father, having looked at his ID papers, they drove to South Carolina and dumped his body in a swamp.

Jordan was found Aug. 3, but was cremated after police were unable to identify him. When the car was found two days later, the connection was made and Jordan's dental records were matched against autopsy reports.

Screen idol Granger dies of cancer at 80

Santa Monica, Calif., Monday 16
Stewart Granger, as handsome, debonair and athletic an actor as ever swashbuckled his way through Hollywood, died here today. He was born James Lablanche Stewart in London on May 6, 1913. His career took off during the war when, released from the Black Watch after being injured, he made *The Man in Grey* with James Mason, Phyllis Calvert and Margaret Lockwood. The film was an enormous success and took Granger to Hollywood, where he changed his name to avoid being confused with Jimmy Stewart and became a U.S. citizen. He was married three times, and his life was as rumbustious off the screen as on.

Star of "King Solomon's Mines."

Moscow uneasy two years after coup bid

Pro-Communist militants demand President Boris Yeltsin's resignation.

Moscow, Friday 20
The second anniversary of the failed coup against former President Gorbachev was celebrated uneasily here today with rival groups of democrats and Communists holding meetings outside the White House, the scene of Yeltsin's triumph in 1991. There was none of the heady atmosphere of the dangerous days of the coup. The pouring rain dampened enthusiasm, and police kept the demonstrators apart. Yeltsin celebrated the anniversary by asking parliament to dissolve itself and face elections. His request was spurned by parliament's speaker, Ruslan Khasbulatov: "We are not going to reply to every militant statement by the president." (→ Sept. 1)

Reusable one-stage rocket test successful

White Sands, N.M., Wednesday 18
A revolutionary one-stage rocket made a successful first flight today. It is hoped that the development will usher in a new era of cheaper and more reliable space travel.

The multi-stage rockets used now shed their heavy fuel tanks and engines as they ascend in order to escape Earth's gravity. New electronics and lightweight materials – the *Delta Clipper* is made of epoxy and graphite fiber – make the one-stage rocket feasible.

The 42-foot-long prototype, one-third of the size of the proposed rocket, climbed to 150 feet, stopped and hovered, then move sideways about 350 feet before descending vertically and landing.

Aug. 18. Lucerne's 14th-century covered wooden bridge, which spans the Reuss River, is destroyed by fire. Only the old stone tower was saved.

Algeria's former premier is assassinated

Algiers, Saturday 21
Colonel Kasdi Merbah, former prime minister and security chief, was assassinated today, with one of his sons, a brother, his chauffeur and a bodyguard. Their two cars were raked with machine-gun bullets in an ambush at Alger Plage, a seaside resort east of the capital where Merbah had a holiday home.

There is little doubt that Merbah, a military hardliner, is the latest victim of the fundamentalist Islamic Salvation Front. The group has been fighting a guerrilla war since January last year, when the army scrapped elections which the fundamentalists seemed certain to win. (→ Oct. 11)

An opponent of fundamentalism.

Scotsman Obree cycles into record books

Smashes his own world record.

Hamar, Norway, Thursday 19
Graeme Obree, an unemployed Scot, riding a home-made bike using washing-machine bearings, broke the world record and became world pursuit champion over 4,000 meters tonight when he scorched to victory over Frenchman Philippe Ermenault. The crowd, which had laughed at Obree's bicycle and ungainly style at the start of the championships, cheered him home as he came from behind to win the 16-lap race by almost three seconds and break the world record he set yesterday in the semi-final, when he beat Olympic champion Chris Boardman. The record now stands at 4 minutes 20.894 seconds, and Obree, who turned professional for these championships, is a hot property.

First empire's fall caused by drought

U.S., Friday 20
The first imperial regime in world history, the Akkadian empire, was brought down by a drought that lasted for 300 years, according to an article published today in the journal *Science*. The dry period that led to the empire's collapse around 2200 B.C. followed a volcanic eruption in Mesopotamia. Archeologists and geologists found the evidence, deep layers of sand over the ash layer deposited after the eruption, near the ancient city of Tell Leilan in what is now Syria.

Aug. 21. The Clintons get away from it all with a round of golf on Martha's Vineyard, Mass.

August
1993

Su	Mo	Tu	We	Th	Fr	Sa
1	2	3	4	5	6	7
8	9	10	11	12	13	14
15	16	17	18	19	20	21
22	23	24	25	26	27	28
29	30	31				

Kwajalein, Marshall Is., 22
The island's 3,000 inhabitants wake up to find August 21 never happened: Kwajalein time was changed from one side of the international dateline to the other.

Indianapolis, 22
Jim Courier beats Boris Becker, 7-5, 6-3, thus reclaiming his No. 1 ranking from Pete Sampras. (→Sept. 12)

U.S., 23
The Mississippi River, closed to commercial shipping since July 11, reopens to traffic.

Washington, D.C., 23
The State Department posts its first-ever bounty on a terrorist suspect, offering $2 million for information about Ramzi Ahmed Yusef, indicted in the bombing of New York's World Trade Center.

London, 23
England's cricketers win their first match since July 1992, beating Australia by 161 runs to win the sixth Test.

Johannesburg, 25
South Africa's military announces the end of compulsory service for whites.

Lagos, 26
General Babangida, Nigeria's military ruler, resigns. (→27)

Prague, 26
President Yeltsin apologizes for the Soviet invasion of 1968 that crushed the Prague Spring reform movement.

Atlanta, 27
The number of deaths from cigarette smoking in the U.S. dropped from 434,000 in 1988 to 419,000 in 1990, the Centers for Disease Control say.

Washington, D.C., 30
Robert Malval is sworn in as Haiti's premier by deposed President Jean-Bertrand Aristide. (→Sept. 12)

New York, 30
Briton Mark Nyman clinches the World Scrabble Championship with the word "wet" (20 points).

U.S., 31
The Airbus A320 is the least safe narrow-bodied plane and the DC-10 the least safe widebody, according to a survey of commercial pilots.

World records fall at athletics meet

Californian Gail Devers wins the women's 100 meters in 10.82 seconds.

Stuttgart, Sunday 22
The U.S. was the big winner, with 1 gold, 7 silver and 6 bronze medal at the World Athletic Champio ships, which finished today. Russ was second with 3 gold, 8 silver an 5 bronze medals, followed by Bri ain with 3 gold, 3 silver and 4 bron medals. Today U.S. relay teams di more than their fair share, with th men winning the 4x100 and 4x40 and the women winning the 4x40

The big surprise was the perfo mance of the previously unexce tional Chinese women runners, wh took three gold medals. They swe the 3,000 meters and finished 1-2 i the 10,000. Many people suspect th use of steroids and point to the h ring of coaches from the forme East German and Soviet teams.

A world record 12.91 seconds in 110-meter hurdles for Colin Jackson (U.K.).

Cuba's Javier Sotomayor clears 2.4 meters to win the high jump final.

Merlene Ottey of Jamaica (right) wins the 200-meter final in 21.98 seconds.

U.S. track star Michael Johnson takes the men's 400-meter final.

NASA's costly 'Mars Observer' space probe has gone AWOL

The silent spacecraft was supposed to go into orbit around the Red Planet.

Pasadena, Calif., Tuesday 24
NASA engineers are frantically trying to re-establish contact with the *Observer*, the spacecraft on a mission to Mars. The $1-billion craft went missing last Sunday. Today it was due to start orbiting Mars, at the end of a space odyssey which has lasted 11 months and covered 450 million miles. No one knows what has happened. *Observer* may have fired its thrusters on schedule yesterday, it may have been destroyed in a space accident or it may have flown out of control into the depths of space. Glenn Cunningham, the project manager, said that if they failed to raise *Observer* it would be "a great blow to the planetary science community." It would also be a great embarrassment to NASA and provide its critics with another weapon.

Aug. 23. Leo Fender's famous Stratocaster, favored by such rock greats as Buddy Holly and Jimi Hendrix, is 40 today.

Killing of Yanomani Indians investigated

Rio de Janeiro, Monday 23
President Itamar Franco met today with the National Defense Council to plan a military effort to find gold miners who murdered Yanomani Indians on a reservation in the north of the Brazilian Amazon. The remains of five people were found at two lodges which had been razed by the attackers. Brazil's Indian protection agency interviewed survivors and reported that up to 73 people were killed. The investigation of the incident is difficult because the Yanomani avoid pronouncing the names of the dead and their counting system does not go beyond two.

Brazilian gold miners are said to have killed as many as 73 Yanomanis.

JFK assassination files released by U.S.

Washington, D.C., Monday 23
Nearly all of the files relating to the assassination of John F. Kennedy were made public by the National Archives today, in accordance with a law passed last year. The documents include FBI and CIA files on Lee Harvey Oswald, who had defected to the Soviet Union in 1959, returned to the U.S. in 1962, and made a visit to the Soviet embassy in 1963 before the assassination. Also to be found are files relating to investigations by the Warren Commission, which determined that Oswald was the lone killer, and the follow-up Rockefeller Commission.

800,000 pages of secrets to study.

Iraqi ambassadors slam Saddam's rule

London, Tuesday 24
Two senior Iraqi ambassadors denounced the "reign of terror" in Baghdad today and swore to work with Iraqi exiles to topple Saddam Hussein's regime. The two men, Hisham al-Shawi, former ambassador to Canada, and Hamed Alwan al-Jubouri, ambassador to Tunis, speaking at a press conference in London, said the time had come for open confrontation with a "police state" which was destroying the country. They have been granted political asylum in Britain.

World War II U-boat raised from the deep

Copenhagen, Monday 23
The dripping grey conning tower and anti-aircraft guns of U-534 broke the surface of the Kattegat off Denmark today, 48 years after she had been sunk by an RAF Liberator in the closing days of World War II. A long range U-boat, she was attempting to escape to Japan, and it was thought that she was carrying gold, jewels, looted art treasures and secret documents. She shot down one of the attacking Liberators, but the second sent her to the bottom. A Dutch consortium has financed the £2-million operation to salvage her. (→ Nov. 5)

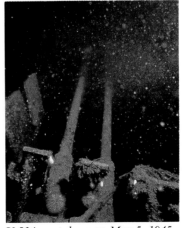

U-534 went down on May 5, 1945.

American student is slain by black mob

Capetown, Wednesday 25
Amy Biehl, a white American exchange student at the University of the Western Cape was stoned, stabbed and beaten to death by a mob of black youths tonight as she drove friends home to a black township outside Capetown. The 26-year-old Fulbright scholar, who was helping to prepare young black people for South Africa's first democratic election, was stopped by a barrage of bricks and stones from a mob chanting "one settler, one bullet." They dragged her out and killed her.

Michael Jackson facing child abuse case

The singer is currently in Bangkok on the latest leg of his world tour.

Los Angeles, Wednesday 25
Troubles piled up for Michael Jackson today as the Los Angeles police department's Sexually Exploited Child Unit continued its investigation into charges that the singer had sexually abused a 13-year-old boy. Photographs and videotapes seized in a raid on his ranch are being studied and a psychiatrist's report on an interview with the boy is said to contain graphic sexual details.

The singer, on a world tour with his "Dangerous" show has issued a statement saying that he is sure the investigation "will demonstrate there was no wrongdoing on my part." To add to his problems, dehydration forced him to cancel a Bangkok concert last night. (→ Nov. 12)

Jobs crisis for Germany's auto industry

Auto makers hope buyers will be attracted by small cars such as this BMW.

Frankfurt, Wednesday 25
Almost 100,000 jobs will be lost in Germany's automobile industry over the next few years, according to the annual report of the German Automobile Association. The report says the industry's retrenchment is a desperate attempt to cope with Germany's sagging international competitiveness. It argues that the cuts stem not only from the recession but also reflect efforts to increase efficiency and will therefore continue even when production takes of again. "Despite our warnings, politicians and labor have too long worshipped the illusion that Germany i an unassailable bastion of economic strength," says Erika Emmerich, the association's president.

Lord Kadoorie, Hong Kong taipan, dies

Hong Kong, Wednesday 25
Lord Kadoorie, who was born on June 2, 1899, died here today. He came from a family of Jewish merchants from Baghdad who arrived in Hong Kong in 1880. After reading for the Bar at Lincoln's Inn he joined his father's business and became one of the greatest of the Hong Kong "taipans," a founder of the modern economic miracle that will soon be inherited by Beijing. His fortune was based on China Light and Power, which took electricity to the villages and took part, controversially, in the building of China's first nuclear plant. He was a friend of Deng Xiaoping, a noted philanthropist and the first person born in Hong Kong to be ennobled.

Ozone layer threat abates, experts say

London, Thursday 26
The amount of ozone-destroying chemicals released into the atmosphere is decreasing, according to a report published today in the journal *Nature*.

Industry has been cutting the use of chlorofluorcarbons, or CFCs, since it has been shown that they destroy the ozone layer, which filters the sun's ultra-violet rays. But the good news does not mean that the problem is over. It will take another 10 years or so for the chemicals which have already been released to rise into the stratosphere, where they destroy the layer. It is expected that the ozone layer will then be able to start to repair itself, a process that could take another 50 to 100 years.

Aug. 25. A record 25,000 people attend this year's annual tomato fight, a ritual dating from the Middle Ages, in Bunyol, southeastern Spain.

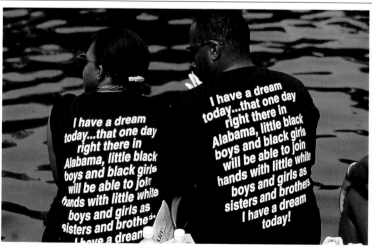

Aug. 28. Thousands gather in Washington, D.C., to mark the 30th anniversary of Martin Luther King's historic "I have a dream" speech.

Lance Armstrong takes world cycle title

First American to win since 1989.

Oslo, Sunday 29
Lance Armstrong, in his first full season as a professional, raced home in the rain 19 seconds ahead of Spain's Miguel Indurain to win the world road race championship here today. Armstrong, who fell twice in appalling conditions which reduced the field to twelve, is only the second American to win the world professional title. He has enjoyed an astonishing year, winning a million dollars in America, a stage in the Tour de France and now Norway's 160-mile championship. Indurain, winner of the Tour de France and the Tour of Italy this year, could not match him for strength.

Mideast breakthrough

Premier Rabin will have a hard time convincing some of his countrymen.

Soviets 'not guilty' in KAL 007 drama

Moscow, Monday 30
A Russian commission which investigated the downing of Korean Air Lines flight 007 on Sept. 1, 1983, said today that the incident, in which 269 people were killed, was not the Soviet Union's fault. Boris Yeltsin's chief of staff, Sergei Filatov, said that errors by the plane's crew were to blame. They set a faulty course from Alaska, and once over Soviet territory, failed to report their position and to respond to "friend or foe" queries from the attack fighter approaching the plane.

When asked about compensation for the victim's families, he said only that "the Soviet Union is not to blame for this incident."

Jerusalem, Monday 30
The Israeli Cabinet overwhelmingly approved the outline of a peace pact today which could see Palestinian rule established in the Gaza Strip and Jericho within three months. Amid uproar from opposition hardliners, Prime Minister Rabin told his colleagues: "Any change, any solution, entails risks. The time has come to take risks for peace."

This astonishing development stems from secret talks in Norway between Israeli ministers led by Foreign Minister Shimon Peres and Palestinian officials who met under the auspices of the Oslo government. There will be risks. Israeli right-wingers are opposed to ceding any land to the Palestinians, and Yasser Arafat has been threatened with death by Palestinian radicals who fear he has conceded too much to the Israelis. (→ Sept. 3)

Serbs and Muslims agree on a truce

Geneva, Tuesday 31
A small step towards peace was taken tonight when the Muslim-led Bosnian government and the Bosnian Serbs agreed to call an immediate cease-fire, set up a hotline and exchange prisoners. This agreement could ease the tension when the Muslims, Serbs and Croats resume their crucial talks here today on the proposed division of Bosnia into three ethnically based states. The reluctant Muslims are under intense pressure to accept their 30% share of the carve-up. Serb leader Radovan Karadzic is confident they will agree: "Negotiations are finished. We are expecting the Muslim side to sign the whole package." (→ Sept. 8)

Aug. 26. Princess Diana and her sons William and Harry enjoy a ride in Disney World, Florida.

Abiola rejects the new rulers in Lagos

London, Friday 27
Chief Moshood Abiola, the multimillionaire publisher who won Nigeria's presidential election in June but had his victory cancelled by the military leader, General Babangida, swore today to end his self-imposed exile in Britain and return home to form a government.

"By the end of next week, I'll be in Lagos – God willing," he said. He scoffed at the interim government set up by Babangida as a "non-event," but said he would not take up arms: "I am not a warrior."

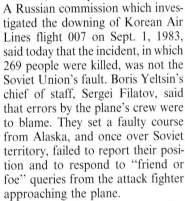

Aug. 30. The Grand Hassan II Mosque, in Casablanca, which boasts the world's tallest minaret (175 meters) and a laser beam aimed at the holy city of Mecca, Saudi Arabia, is dedicated by King Hassan II of Morocco.

September

Beaumont, Texas, 1
Bill Simpson, the last of eight blacks who tried to integrate the all-white town of Vidor, Texas, is murdered in an unrelated robbery hours after moving out.

Russia, 1
Yeltsin orders the suspension of his vice president and political foe Aleksander Rutskoi. (→21)

New York, 1
The Broadway hit *Angels in America* has donated $133,000, one dollar for every ticket sold, to Broadway Cares/Equity Fights AIDS.

Central African Republic, 1
Jean Bédel Bokassa, former self-proclaimed emperor, is released from prison by military decree, along with thousands of other prisoners. (→27)

Beijing, 2
Cardinal Roger Etchegaray meets with government officials in the highest-level diplomatic meeting between the Vatican and China since 1949.

New York, 2
Chrysler Corp. announces the retirement of Lee Iacocca as director and chairman of the board's executive committee.

Washington, D.C., 2
Police use a robot to subdue a murder suspect who was holding out in his apartment with a shotgun.

Buenos Aires, 2
Police arrest 12 members of the Family of Love, a cult with British and American members that advocates free sex and incest, on child-kidnapping charges.

London, 3
Jane's Information Group reports that Iraq has 300 combat aircraft, nearly double U.S. intelligence estimates.

Israel, 3
57% of Israelis back the Palestinian autonomy accord, a poll shows. (→9)

Atlanta, 4
George Bush is paid $100,000 for a speech to an Amway distributors convention.

London, 4
Sussex score a record 321 runs for six wickets but are beaten by Warwickshire with a single scored from the last ball.

Length of Africa trekked by Briton

Tangier, Wednesday 1
Ffyona Campbell soaked her blistered feet in the Mediterranean here today at the end of a 10,000-mile trek across Africa. She left from Cape Town, South Africa, in April 1991 and has been bedevilled by wars, riots, closed borders and, in the last few days, an attempted rape.

She has now walked across three continents. The 26-year-old Scot, who walked an average of 30 miles a day, said, "I am ecstatic but there is also the feeling I am leaving my home, Africa, which has been such an important part of my life."

Pentagon blueprint on force for future

Washington, D.C., Wednesday 1
The Pentagon has revealed its new strategy for the post-Soviet world. The five-year plan calls for a reduced, but more lethal and more highly mobile force. The objective is to be ready to fight two regional wars at the same time – for example, simultaneous invasions of Saudi Arabia or Kuwait by a reinvigorated Iraq and of South Korea by North Korea. The large U.S. presence in Europe will be reduced, but more equipment will be pre-positioned elsewhere and new "brilliant" weapons systems will be developed. The Marines will be the only force to remain at present levels.

Sihanouk to return as king of Cambodia

The ruler abdicated 38 years ago.

Phnom Penh, Friday 3
Prince Sihanouk will once again mount the throne in Cambodia. The announcement of his restoration made by his son, Prince Ranariddh co-chairman of the interim coalition government, has caused uproar in the constituent assembly, whose members claim they have not been properly consulted.

It has also surprised the United Nations mission, which in May supervised the country's first free elections in decades, despite the violent opposition of the Khmer Rouge. The fear is that Sihanouk's resumption of the crown will once again lead to civil disorder. (→24)

Roman artifacts declared treasure trove

This priceless gold body chain is the most impressive item in the hoard.

London, Friday 3
Last November, Eric Lawes was searching a field in Hoxne, Suffolk, for a lost hammer with a metal detector. He stumbled upon the greatest Roman hoard yet found in Britain: 14,780 coins and 200 gold and silver objects. Today, the collection was declared to be treasure trove. This means that Lawes is entitled to full-market value of the find, which could be up to £10 million.

Ukraine could sell fleet to Russians

Yalta, Friday 3
President Kravchuk of impoverished Ukraine finally gave in to Russian pressure here today after a summit meeting with Russian President Boris Yeltsin at the former czarist Massarene Palace.

Kravchuk agreed to allow Russia to buy Ukraine's share of the Black Sea Fleet and to dismantle the nuclear warheads left behind when the Soviet empire collapsed. In return, Ukraine will get enriched uranium for its nuclear power stations. The deal ends almost two years of acrimonious negotiations.

Sept. 2. Lenny Kravitz wins the Best Male Video prize with "Are You Gonna Go My Way" at the MTV Video Music Awards in LA.

Sept. 4. Hervé Villechaize, who played "Tattoo" in "Fantasy Island," dies at the age of 50.

September
1993

Su	Mo	Tu	We	Th	Fr	Sa
			1	2	3	4
5	6	7	8	9	10	11
12	13	14	15	16	17	18
19	20	21	22	23	24	25
26	27	28	29	30		

Rieti, Italy, 5
Algerian Noureddine Morceli runs a world-record mile at 3 minutes 44.39 seconds.

London, 6
The Times drops its price from 45 pence to 30 pence.

London, 6
Archbishop of Canterbury decries public flogging of Anglican bishop in Sudan; the bishop claimed innocence of adultery, for which he was found guilty in an Islamic court.

London, 6
Ministry of Defence says £5.2 billion in 1993 overseas orders for British arms has passed previous one-year record.

Washington, D.C., 7
Clinton says he will cut federal civilian work force by 12%, saving $108 billion over 5 years.

South Africa, 7
Multi-party negotiators agree on formation of Transitional Executive Committee, which will allow blacks to participate in governing the country for the first time. (→ 24)

Tokyo, 7
Japanese doctor says that army physicians used prisoners of war for medical experiments during World War II.

Moscow, 7
Uzbekistan, Armenia and Tajikstan will join Russia, Belarus and Ukraine in a ruble-based economic union.

Cincinnati, 7
St. Louis Cardinals' Mark Whiten ties two records, hitting four home runs and driving in four RBIs in the 15-2 victory over the Reds.

Washington, D.C., 8
Department of Education reports that 47% of Americans do not have the literacy skills necessary to function effectively at work.

London, 11
Lord Hesketh, government chief whip in House of Lords and close ally of John Major, announces his resignation.

DEATHS
9. Hellen O'Connell, American big band singer (*1920).

11. Erich Leinsdorf, American conductor (*Feb. 4, 1912).

Jack the Ripper diary withdrawn by publisher after hoax charge

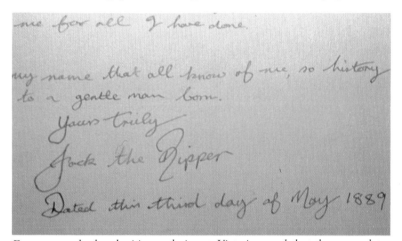

Experts say the handwriting style is not Victorian, and that the paper dates from the 1920s or early 1930s, decades after the killer stalked London's streets.

Washington, D.C., Tuesday 7
Warner Books Inc. has pulled what might have been its best nonfiction seller for the fall. *The Diary of Jack the Ripper* was scheduled to go on sale Oct. 7, but an investigation commissioned by the publisher into the authencity of the manuscript has found that it is a hoax. The handwriting does not match up to that of the 19th-century killer, and an analysis of the ink shows that the document dates from 1921, plus or minus 12 years. It is thought that the fake was written in the 1930s and hidden to be found at a later date. British publisher Smith Gryphon plans to go ahead with publication.

French champs out

Zurich, Monday 6
The UEFA, Europe's governing body for soccer, has barred the European champion team, Olympique Marseille, from defending their title in the 1993-1994 European Champions' Cup. Players from the club are accused of bribing members of another French team, Valenciennes, to throw a game. The UEFA has given the French Football Federation until Wednesday to choose a replacement team for the championship. Marseille was scheduled to take on the Greek champion, AEK Athens, on Sept. 15. The decision is controversial, to say the least, in France, where neither the police nor the French league have found enough proof to act against the team.

Bosnian leader gets little help from U.S.

Washington, D.C., Wednesday 8
Alija Izetbegovic, the embattled president of Bosnia, called on President Clinton at the White House to plead for American military intervention against his Serb and Croat enemies. It was a futile mission, for although Clinton spoke recently of possible NATO intervention being "very much alive," it is generally acknowledged here that air strikes are no longer on the agenda and that purely NATO intervention would not work. Izetbegovic had an equally discouraging experience last night when he addressed a closed session of the U.N. Security Council and urged it to enforce its resolutions against the Serbs. The council listened but took no action. (→ 29)

The first Clinton-Izetbegovic talks.

Kasparov wins first game in chess battle

Briton Nigel Short ran out of time.

London, Tuesday 7
Nigel Short refused the draw offered to him by Garry Kasparov and then lost by running out of time in the first game of *The Times* World Chess Championships at the Savoy Theatre today. The finish was exciting and chaotic, with the clock ticking away to deprive the Briton of his slight advantage over the Russian world champion. After the game, a rueful Short said, "I got some encouragement from this game. It was irritating, no more than that." Kasparov admitted that he had made what might have been a fatal mistake but pointed out, "I have just won a game." (→Oct. 21)

Sept. 5. The Dalai Lama attends the centennial celebration of the World's Parliament of Religions, first held in Chicago in 1893.

Israel recognizes Yasser Arafat's PLO

Israeli Foreign Minister Shimon Peres defends the accord in the Knesset.

Jerusalem, Thursday 9
Israel and the Palestine Liberation Organization have agreed to recognize each other after decades of terrorism, reprisals and a mutual hatred so deep it seemed there would never be peace between them.

That peace has now been made in an exchange of letters between Yitzhak Rabin, prime minister of Israel, and Yasser Arafat, chairman of the PLO. In his letter Rabin recognizes the PLO as the representative of the Palestinian people. In reply, Arafat renounces violence and hails a "new epoch of peaceful co-existence." The stage is set for an agreement on Palestinian self-rule, to be signed at the White House on Monday. (→ 13)

Marcos laid to rest on Philippine soil

A grieving Imelda at the funeral.

Batac, Philippines, Friday 10
Ferdinand Marcos was interred in a glass casket in a stone mausoleum beside his family's mansion here today. His widow, Imelda, told a crowd gathered outside the mausoleum, "I wanted him preserved so that you can see him again."

Tuesday, the body had been flown from Hawaii, where the former president of the Philippines died in exile in 1988. Thousands of cheering and sobbing supporters followed a procession to the cathedral of the town of Laoag, where a mass attended by 500 people was held.

President Fidel Ramos refused a burial in the capital, Manilla, and any state honors for Marcos. Imelda faces charges of plundering the Philippine economy of $5 billion during her husband's 20-year rule. (→ 24)

Sept. 10. Pope John Paul II visits the Hill of Crosses, a traditional place of pilgrimage in Lithuania, as part of an official week-long tour of the three Baltic states.

Aspin admits plan to fake Star Wars test

Washington, D.C., Thursday 9
The Pentagon had a secret plan to use trickery to make the Soviet Union believe the Star Wars program was more successful than it really was. The Army's Homing Overlay Experiment, conducted in 1984, was a test of a missile designed to blow up an incoming missile above the Earth's atmosphere. The plan was to put a charge on the target missile that could be set off to give the appearance that the interceptor was successful. Aspin admitted that the plan was kept secret from Congress but denied that it had been put into effect.

U.S. gunships fire on Somali civilians

Mogadishu, Thursday 9
There were heavy civilian casualties here today when American helicopter gunships opened fire on a mob of gunmen and civilians threatening to overrun United Nations soldiers. The gunships opened fire after Pakistani units which had been clearing barricades retreated from an attack by 300 Somali militiamen. Their way was blocked by a crowd of women and children, and they were forced to radio for help. A U.N. spokesman regretted the loss of life but said the women and children had become combattants when they attacked the U.N. troops. (→ Oct. 5)

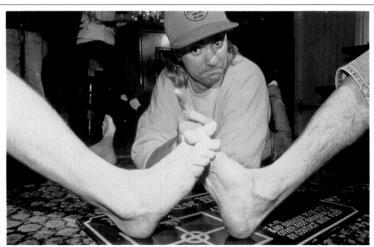

Sept. Something's afoot at the Royal Oak pub in Staffordshire: Clients prefer the esoteric sport of toe wrestling to more traditional activities.

Sept. The Folies Bergères, the Paris music-hall forced to shut down last year, reopens with a new revue directed by Argentinian Alfredo Arias.

September
1993

Su	Mo	Tu	We	Th	Fr	Sa
			1	2	3	4
5	6	7	8	9	10	11
12	13	14	15	16	17	18
19	20	21	22	23	24	25
26	27	28	29	30		

Haiti, 12
U.N. envoy says Port-au-Prince police chief, Michel François, is closely linked to murders of Jean-Bertrand Aristide's supporters. (→Oct. 15)

Monza, 12
Damon Hill wins third straight race, the Italian Grand Prix.

U.S., 14
A poll shows 80% of Americans favor the PLO-Israel peace pact; 65% oppose U.S. giving economic aid to Palestinians.

Washington, D.C., 14
Israel and Jordan sign an agreement to negotiate a peace treaty. (→Oct. 1)

Boston, 15
Katherine Ann Power, a fugitive radical wanted for murder in connection with a 1970 bank robbery, surrenders to police after a going-away party where she revealed her identity to friends. (→Oct. 6)

Florida, 15
Police begin 24-hour duty at highway rest stops after ninth killing of foreigners in a year. (→Oct. 22)

London, 15
British Aerospace announces a profit in first half of the year, after two years of heavy losses.

Sicily, 15
The Mafia assassinates Father Giuseppe Puglisi, a vehement opponent of organized crime.

Pittsburgh, 16
British girl Laura Davies, 5, has seven major organs replaced in 15-hour operation. (Nov. 11)

Key West, Florida, 17
Cuban Air Force pilot defects after flying a MIG-21 jet fighter to Key West Naval Air Station.

Brussels, 17
Government bans Ted Turner's TNT & Cartoon Network, which shows cartoons and old movies, because of its 100% American content.

Frankfurt, 17
Daimler-Benz AG announces its first loss, 949 million DM for first half of 1993, and a planned cut of 43,000 jobs.

DEATH
16. Willie Mosconi, American pocket billiards champion (*June 21, 1913)

British tourist is latest victim of spate of killings in Florida

Nine tourists died in the past year.

Monticello, Tuesday 14
Gary Colley, touring Florida with his girlfriend, Margaret Ann Jagger, was shot dead by muggers near here today. Colley, 34, from Bradford, was killed by a bullet in the neck and Jagger, 35, was grazed in the chest when they tried to escape from three black youths who demanded money after the tourists pulled into an un-manned rest stop. They were on their way back to Orlando from a visit to New Orleans. Colley is the ninth foreign tourist to be murdered in the state in less than a year, and tonight Florida state officials offered a $10,000 reward for the arrest of the killers. They also suspended tourist advertising with slogans such as: "C'mon, it'll be fun." (→15)

Rented cars are easy to identify.

Paramount, Viacom to form media giant

New York, Sunday 12
Paramount Communications Inc. will buy Viacom Inc. for $8.28 billion in cash and stock, the companies revealed in a statement today. The deal is the largest media merger since the marriage of Time and Warner in 1989. Paramount has produced hit movies and TV shows, including *Top Gun* and *Entertainment Tonight*. Viacom owns cable channels MTV, Nickelodeon and Showtime. Paramount Viacom will not only be a giant, but a healthy one as well, with a market capitalization of about $17 billion and debts of only about $2.4 billion. (→Oct. 13)

Sept. 12. Pete Sampras easily beats Cedric Pioline of France, 6-4, 6-4, 6-3, to win the U.S. Open final; Steffi Graf takes the women's final in straight sets, 6-3, 6-3, defeating Helena Sukova of the Czech Republic.

Your witness: Perry Mason rests his case

Dry Creek, Calif., Sunday 12
Raymond Burr (*May 21, 1917), died of cancer today, having just completed shooting for a new Perry Mason movie. The Canadian actor was synonymous with his roles as the defense lawyer and as Chief Ironside, and they brought him stardom and a considerable fortune. Before Erle Stanley Gardner, author of the Perry Mason books, chose him for the TV show, he had mostly played heavy-weight badmen. He was as natural as the crippled Ironside, having spent a year in a wheelchair after being wounded in the spine during World War II.

Sept. 12. "Short Cuts," directed by Robert Altman, wins a Golden Lion for best film at the 50th Venice Film Festival.

Shalom, salaam, peace: an historic handshake

Washington, D.C., Monday 13
History was made today at 11:47 a.m. on the South Lawn of the White House when two bitter enemies shook hands.

It was Yasser Arafat, chairman of the PLO, who extended his hand to Israeli Prime Minister Yitzhak Rabin, who briefly hesitated, then took it. Two minutes earlier, on the desk used for the signing of the 1979 Israel-Egypt peace treaty, Shimon Peres, Israel's foreign minister, and the PLO's Mahmoud Abbas signed an agreement providing for limited Palestinian autonomy in the Gaza Strip and the West Bank.

Bill Clinton, whose foreign policy on Somalia, Bosnia and Haiti has been criticized as unfocused, is reaping the political benefits of today's accord. In his speech, he hailed "the efforts of all who have labored before us," thanking Norway's government, which brokered the secret talks between Israel and the PLO.

The agreement gives Palestinians a measure of self-rule immediately in Gaza, Jericho and some parts of the West Bank. Israeli withdrawal from Gaza and Jericho is scheduled to begin by Dec. 13. The territories will be run by a Palestinian Council, which should be elected by July 13, 1994. The ultimate objective is a permanent peace accord, to become effective Dec. 13, 1998. But much work will be necessary to reach that goal – a Palestine shared by Jews and Arabs in peace. (→ 14)

May 14, 1948: David Ben Gurion proclaims the new state of Israel.

Terrorist leader George Habash has vowed to wreck the peace accord.

Israelis and Arabs take to the streets in Tel Aviv to celebrate the news.

A ray of hope at last for this young Palestinian girl in East Jerusalem.

U.N. condemns UNITA rebels in Angola

Jonas Savimbi's guerrilla fighters are now facing tough Western sanctions.

New York, Wednesday 15
Western countries, including Britain and the U.S., agreed today to propose U.N. sanctions on UNITA rebels who are waging a war in Angola with the highest fatality rate of any conflict in the world.

The rebels, led by Jonas Savimbi, were once armed by the West to prevent the spread of Soviet influence in Africa, but their rejection of U.N.-sponsored elections and resumption of the war against the formerly Marxist government of President Dos Santos has angered their one-time supporters. One western diplomat said: "This is a first step. It's a clear signal that everyone is fed up with Savimbi." The sanctions are expected to take the form of an oil and arms embargo designed to cripple Savimbi's forces and bring him to the negotiating table.

Polish hero Sikorski goes home at last

Cracow, Friday 17
The remains of General Wladislaw Sikorski, commander of Poland's wartime forces, were finally buried here today as he had stipulated, in a "free and independent Poland." He was laid to rest in Wawel Castle, ancient seat of Polish kings. He had been buried in a British military cemetery following his death in a plane crash at Gibraltar.

Sikorski was an inspirational leader and many of his soldiers, proudly wearing their medals, lined the route as his cortege wound its way to the castle. "For us," said one, "he was like the star of Bethlehem, and we realised our dream when we could fight for him."

Poland's wartime leader is reburied.

French afraid of 'Hollywood imperialists'

Paris, Tuesday 14
The French have erected another roadblock on the way to signing the General Agreement on Tariffs and Trade by Dec. 15.

France has been threatening to veto a U.S.-EC agreement on farm trade which is part of GATT, and today in an interview published in a leading French newspaper, Minister of Culture Jacques Toubon said that Edouard Balladur, the French premier, will not sign the accord if audio-visual trade is not excepted from GATT. Imports of American TV shows and films, such as *Jurassic Park*, are a threat to French culture, asserts Toubon. (→ Oct. 13)

Chinese free a leading political prisoner

Beijing, Tuesday 14
China announced today the release of the leading dissident Wei Jingsheng, who was a mere six months short of finishing a 15-year prison sentence for accusing Deng Xiaoping of being a dictator and arguing that democracy was essential for China's modernization. Observers suggest Wei's release is designed to help Beijing's chances in the competition to stage the Olympic Games in 2000 which will be decided in Monaco next week. (→ 23)

Berg not to blame for loss of 'Titanic'

New York, Thursday 16
A study conducted by naval architect William Garzke has concluded that if better-quality steel had been used in building the Titanic her loss "might have been averted or resulted in a slower rate of flooding," giving time for the passengers to be saved after she had plowed into an iceberg on her maiden voyage in 1912. An analysis of metal recovered from the wreck shows that she was built of low-grade steel, which became brittle in the icy Atlantic. Garzke told a meeting of naval architects here today that nobody knew about brittle fracture until after World War II.

Sept. 15. A rare nest of dinosaur eggs are auctioned at Sotheby's for £50,600. Steven Spielberg is reported to be the buyer.

Sept. 14. Flower power returns: The 1960s musical "Hair," starring Sinitta (left), begins a new run at the Old Vic in London.

Sept. 18. Kimberly Clarice, an 18-year-old from Columbia, South Carolina, is elected Miss America 1993 in Atlantic City.

Sept. 18. First President George Washington used a silver trowel to lay the cornerstone of the Capitol two centuries ago today.

September

1993

Su	Mo	Tu	We	Th	Fr	Sa
			1	2	3	4
5	6	7	8	9	10	11
12	13	14	15	16	17	18
19	20	21	22	23	24	25
26	27	28	29	30		

Pasadena, 19
HBO is the big winner at the Emmys, taking 17. Its *Barbarians at the Gate* and *Stalin* tie for best TV movie award; NBC's *Seinfeld* is best comedy series and CBS's *Picket Fences* is best dramatic series.

Baku, 20
Azerbaijan's parliament votes to rejoin the CIS.

London, 20
Salman Rushdie's 1981 book *Midnight's Children* is named the best book to have received the Booker Prize since its foundation in 1969. (→ Oct. 11)

Castel Gandolfo, 21
The chief rabbi of Israel's Ashkenazi Jews, Yisrael Lau, is received by Pope John Paul II, the first such meeting.

Russia, 21
Yeltsin dissolves parliament and calls for elections. (→ 24)

Seattle, 22
Nolan Ryan is relieved in the first inning of what is to be his last game, which his Texas Rangers lose 7-4 to the Mariners. He had torn a ligament in his pitching elbow.

Georgia, 22
Separatists shoot down a plane approaching Sukhumi, the second in two days. (→ 28)

New York, 22
Metropolitan Museum agrees to return a 2,500-year-old Lydian treasure, stolen just before the museum acquired it in 1960, to Turkey.

France, 23
The Crematoriums of Auschwitz, which uses German documents from previously unseen KGB archives to show how the "final solution" was carried out, is published.

Phnom Penh, 24
Norodom Sihanouk signs Cambodia's new constitution and becomes king. (→ Oct. 12)

Philippines, 24
Imelda Marcos is sentenced to 18 years in jail for corruption.

DEATHS

20. Cyrus Leo Sulzberger, U.S. journalist (*Oct. 27, 1912)

25. Bruno Pontecorvo, British nuclear scientist who defected to USSR (*Aug. 22, 1913)

Racist's election causes storm in U.K.

London police arrested 27 during clashes between pro- and anti-racists.

London, Sunday 19
Riot police broke up fighting between anti-racist demonstrators and members of the neo-Nazi British National Party in London's East End today in clashes reminiscent of the pre-war battles against Mosley's Fascists. The demonstration, in the heart of the Bengali community, follows Derek Beackon's election two days ago as the country's first BNP councilor, in a by-election at Millwall. Beackon, a fervent racist, benefitted from local belief that the Bengalis are given preferential treatment in housing and also from divisive tactics by his Labour and Liberal Democrat opponents. His success has fanned old flames.

Polish vote marked by swing to the left

Warsaw, Sunday 19
Two parties of former Communists, riding a wave of discontent caused by stringent economic reforms, emerged ahead of the field today in Poland's general elections. The Democratic Left Alliance, now wearing social democratic colors, won 18% of the vote, and the Polish Peasants' Party, once in the Communist stable, came second with 14%. With these results, former Communists are sure of playing a major role in the next government of the country which began the downfall of communism. (→ Oct. 18)

Welshman Ian Woosnam wins golf trophy

St.-Nom-la-Bretèche, Sunday 19
Wielding an orange-shafted driver flown in from Japan, Ian Woosnam struck the ball with all his old pugnacity today and then used his putter sweetly to roll in two birdies in his last three holes and win the Lancôme Trophy here. The little Welshman finished with a 65 for a 13-under-par 267 to win by two strokes from Sam Torrance, his teammate in this week's Ryder Cup.

The win brought him not only the elegant trophy but also a check for £91,500, which takes him into second place behind Nick Faldo in the order of merit, with winnings this year of more than £400,000.

Won after finishing 13 under par.

Sept. 19. Nigel Mansell becomes only the third driver, after Emerson Fittipaldi and Mario Andretti, to claim both a Formula One and an IndyCar title by winning the Grand Prix in Nazareth, Pennsylvania.

Sept. 23. Vicki Van Meter, aged 11, lands in San Diego and becomes the youngest girl to pilot an airplane across the U.S.

Alabama train disaster is deadliest in Amtrak's 23-year history

At least 44 people died when the train derailed and fell into a bayou.

Saraland, Alabama, Wednesday 22
The *Sunset Limited*, an Amtrak train with three engines and eight cars, jumped the tracks and plunged into a muddy bayou here at about 3:00 this morning. The train, which runs from Los Angeles to Miami, was crossing an 84-year-old bridge that had just been hit by a barge lost in the fog.

At least 44 of the 206 people aboard were killed, and a few are still missing. One car was completely submerged after the engines and four of the cars derailed. People were in the bayou, home to snakes and alligators, for up to 45 minutes before Brian McConnell of Scotland spotted them and shined a flashlight to help them find their way.

South Africans call for end of sanctions

Nelson Mandela appeals to the U.N.

New York, Friday 24
Nelson Mandela, president of the African National Congress, called for the repeal of economic sanctions against South Africa at the United Nations tonight and was met with an immediate response from the countries whose embargoes have played such a large part in forcing Pretoria to abandon apartheid.

The United States joined with the Commonwealth in abolishing the embargoes after Mandela's plea that "the time has come when the international community should lift all economic sanctions." U.S. Secretary of State Warren Christopher will now recommend that the most damaging sanction, the ban on aid from the International Monetary Fund, be lifted. (→ Oct. 8)

UNICEF faults care of children in U.S.

London, Wednesday 22
The United Nations Children's Fund has released "The Progess of Nations," a report on the efforts of the world's countries to provide care for children. The U.S. scored poorly, while Third World countries moved forward in child welfare. In the U.S., 20% of children live below the poverty line, compared with 5% or less in most European countries. The U.S. ranked 19th in survival rates for children under the age of 5, and the immunization rate for measles was 77%, compared with a world average of 80%.

Sydney gets the 2000 Olympic Games

Monaco, Thursday 23
In a night of high drama, the International Olympic Committee has awarded the 2000 Olympic Games to Sydney. The vote was 45 for Sydney and 43 for Beijing, which had led in the early voting. Manchester, eliminated in the third round, settled the issue with its votes going to Sydney instead of Beijing.

There is no doubt that the Australians, with their facilities and brilliant presentation, are worthy winners, but the issue was settled on political rather than athletic grounds. Those who condemn China's human rights record outweighed those who think the Olympics might foster reform.

A night to remember for Sydney.

Major decries folly of EC currency plan

London, Friday 24
John Major insists in an article in the *Economist* today that when the EC leaders gather for their summit meeting in Brussels next month they could not just endorse the "same old stale agenda" of Maastricht. He argues that the treaty's plan to achieve a common currency by the end of the decade is "folly" and "not relevant to our economic difficulties." His scorn was received coolly. A French official said the article was "a little excessive" but basically not much more than a reiteration of the prime minister's views. (→ Nov. 1)

Sept. 24. British model Naomi Campbell quits her New York agency amid talk of tantrums.

Moscow crisis worse

Moscow, Friday 24
Fears of civil war grew today as members of parliament ignored President Yeltsin's dissolution order and barricaded themselves inside the White House.

Hundreds of troops loyal to Yeltsin ringed the building and ordered the volunteer groups defending it to give up their weapons. Tension is fuelled by scuffles between the troops and demonstrators. Yeltsin dismissed rumors that he planned to storm the White House, saying that he would stand by his promise to win the conflict without bloodshed: "We have not used force and do not intend to use it." (→ 28)

Sept. 25. Fourteen yachts from 11 countries set off on the Whitbread Round the World Race. (→ Oct. 19)

September

1993

Su	Mo	Tu	We	Th	Fr	Sa
			1	2	3	4
5	6	7	8	9	10	11
12	13	14	15	16	17	18
19	20	21	22	23	24	25
26	27	28	29	30		

Sutton Coldfield, 26
America retains the Ryder Cup, defeating Europe 15-13.

New York, 27
In his first speech at the U.N., Clinton proposes a ban on production of weapons-grade plutonium and uranium.

China, 27
Eight financial workers are executed for embezzling.

Central African Republic, 27
Bokassa's former premier, Félix Patassé is elected president.

U.S., 28
National Safety Council reports 5% fewer Americans died in accidents in 1992 than in 1991.

London, 29
Buckingham Palace ends perks for the Queen's staff, who number about 400, such as free soap, suits and alcohol served at royal functions.

London, 30
The Queen approves honorary knighthood for General Colin Powell, who retired yesterday as chief of staff of the U.S. armed forces.

Tokyo, 30
Japan Tobacco Inc. pays 41 million yen ($370,000) to the family of a man who, the family claims, died of overwork.

Jakarta, Thursday 30
An Indonesian company that produces counterfeit products sues Levi Strauss & Co. and Pierre Cardin, claiming they registered their brand names in Indonesia first.

Washington, D.C., 30
Senate approves actress Jane Alexander as head of National Endowment for the Arts.

Nicosia, 30
Ian Davidson, a Briton who joined a Palestinian guerrilla group, is freed after serving eight years of a life sentence for killing three Israelis in Cyprus.

New York, 30
The pound is quoted at $1.50.

DEATHS

26. Nina Berberova, Russian novelist (*Aug. 8, 1901).

27. Lieutenant General James Doolittle, American World War II hero (*Dec. 14, 1896).

Biosphere 2 experiment ends after two years in Arizona desert

The eight "Biospherians," four men and four women, are aged 29 to 69.

Oracle, Arizona, Sunday 26
The team who spent two years in Biosphere 2, an enclosed, more-or-less self-sufficient environment, came out today and was greeted by a crowd of 2,500 supporters, curious onlookers and reporters.

The Biospherians proclaimed the experiment a magnificent success, even though the environment was not as independent of Biosphere 1, or Earth, as they had hoped. Oxygen had to be pumped into the great greenhouse twice, and a carbon-dioxide scrubber was brought in. When Jane Poynter, one of two Britons on the team, had her finger cut off in a threshing machine accident, she was taken out for surgery.

Pro-Yeltsin forces seal off parliament as stand-off continues

Moscow, Tuesday 28
President Yeltsin issued an ultimatum to the members of parliament barricaded in the White House today to surrender by tomorrow morning and hand over their weapons. He gave no indication of what he would do if they did not comply.

Ruslan Khasbulatov, the parliament's speaker and Yeltsin's leading opponent, said any attempt to storm the building would be met with armed force. "Blood spilled will fall on the heads of those who support this coup d'état," he said. "They are trying to turn us into a concentration camp. This is sheer fascism." He insisted they had sufficient supplies to last a month. (→ Oct. 4)

Militiamen take up positions around the besieged White House in Moscow.

Georgian leader slams Moscow as Abkhaz rebels take key city

Eduard Shevardnadze reaches Tbilisi after a narrow escape from Sukhumi.

Tbilisi, Tuesday 28
Eduard Shevardnadze, forced to flee from the Black Sea port of Sukhumi as it fell to Abkhazian rebels, accused Moscow tonight of empire-building and trying to humiliate a smaller nation. "The plan to occupy Sukhumi," he said, "was masterminded at Russian headquarters."

He feels betrayed because he persuaded the Georgian parliament to accept a cease-fire with the Abkhazians arranged by Moscow, which the Abkhazians promptly broke. The Georgian leader insists: "We must get Sukhumi back. If this generation is unable to do so, the next generation will." (→ Oct. 18)

Hillary a hit presenting health plan on Hill

Skeptical congressmen were very impressed by the First Lady's arguments.

Washington, D.C., Wednesday 29

Hillary Clinton has dazzled members of Congress with her performance as the White House's chief representative for its health-care reform plan, a ground-breaking role for a first lady. She has been on Capitol Hill for the last few days explaining the plan she was charged with developing. After a televised session with the House Ways and Means Committee, Democrat Dan Rostenkowski told her: "In the very near future, the president will be known as your husband." She said that the White House was open to compromise on methods for reform but insisted that the end result be a guarantee for every American of "a comprehensive package of benefits that can never be taken away under any circumstances."

Libya tries to avoid Lockerbie sanctions

Tripoli, Wednesday 29

In yet another seeming concession today, the Libyan Foreign Ministry announced that the two Lockerbie bombing suspects, Abdel Baset al-Megrahi and Al Amin Fhimah, can stand trial in Scotland if they agree to surrender. Previously, Tripoli insisted that a fair trial in Scotland was impossible. The British Foreign Office takes a jaundiced view of this latest move, pointing out that it has been made on the eve of the U.N. deadline for compliance. Libya faces sanctions if the suspects are not turned over. (→ Nov. 11)

French Communists' leader vows to quit

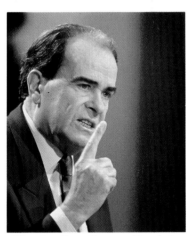

Ailing hardliner Georges Marchais.

Paris, Wednesday 29

The Stalinist head of the French Communist Party announced today his intention to retire because of ill health. Georges Marchais became party leader in 1970 and toed the Moscow line, maintaining close relations with the East European Communists. In 1979, he backed the Soviet invasion of Afghanistan. In 1981, he won 15% of the votes in the presidential election then entered into an alliance with President Mitterrand and the Socialists.

He was not favorable to Gorbachev's reforms and kept down his own party's reformers. During his tenure, the once-powerful Communists lost supporters and influence, winning only 9% of the popular vote in general elections last March.

Bosnia parliament rejects new peace plan

Sarajevo, Wednesday 29

The latest peace plan for Bosnia, which would divide the former Yugoslav republic into three ethnic mini-states, was accepted tonight by the Muslim-led parliament but then effectively strangled at birth by the addition of a proviso demanding that "territory seized by force" be returned. The Serbs and Croats have already made it plain that they will not return any more territory. Radovan Karadzic, leader of the Bosnian Serbs, argues that they have already made seven territorial concessions to the Muslims and that "enough is enough." He threatens to revoke all concessions if the peace plan is not signed. (→ Oct. 24)

More destruction is sure to follow.

Killer quake devastates India's heartland

Still in shock, the women of Maharashtra mourn their friends and relatives.

Some villages simply ceased to exist.

Bombay, Thursday 30

Some 16,000 people are feared to have died in an earthquake which destroyed their homes as they slept today. The quake has reduced two towns and thirty villages to rubble in Maharashtra state, southeast of Bombay. Lasting just ten seconds and measuring between 6.0 and 6.4 on the Richter scale, the violent tremor struck at about 4 a.m. Survivors said huge cracks opened in the ground, swallowing houses whole.

Many people are believed to be trapped in the ruins of their homes. Troops and police are being sent from all over India to this remote area to help with the rescue operation, and loads of firewood and kerosene are being sent to the villages for mass cremations. (→ Oct. 5)

October

1993

Su	Mo	Tu	We	Th	Fr	Sa
					1	2
3	4	5	6	7	8	9
10	11	12	13	14	15	16
17	18	19	20	21	22	23
24	25	26	27	28	29	30
31						

London, 1
Buckingham Palace closes after being open to the public for eight weeks; visits by about 400,000 people raised £2.2 million.

Washington, D.C., 1
A U.S. appeal for funds for the PLO results in pledges of $2 billion by 43 countries. (→ 10)

U.K., 1
Fifty people are injured when a rogue wave hits the liner *Queen Elizabeth II* off Cornwall.

Argentina, 3
President Carlos Menem's Peronist Party wins legislative elections.

Stuttgart, 3
British golfer Steven Richardson wins the German Masters.

Strasbourg, France, 4
Romania becomes a member of the Council of Europe.

Egypt, 4
President Mubarak is re-elected for a third six-year term.

Washington, D.C., 4
General George Joulwan is appointed commander of NATO forces in Europe.

India, 5
The official toll of last month's quake is set at 9,748 dead.

U.S., 5
Larry Johnson of the NBA's Charlotte Hornets, the 1992 rookie of the year, signs the biggest contract in U.S. professional team sports history: $84 million for 12 years.

New York, 8
The U.N. lifts economic sanctions against South Africa.

Palermo, Sicily, 8
Italy's top Mafia boss, Salvatore Riina, is sentenced to life in prison for murder.

Washington, D.C., 9
A congressional report says tuberculosis has increased by 20% in the nation since 1985.

DEATHS

7. Cyril Cusak, Irish actor (*Nov. 26, 1910).

7. Agnes de Mille, U.S. dancer and choreographer (*1905).

Dozens are killed as Yeltsin sends in

Moscow, Monday 4
The hardline rebellion against Boris Yeltsin was crushed today when the army swung its might behind the president and in a day-long battle reduced the besieged parliament building to a smouldering wreck, its white walls holed by tank shells and blackened by smoke pouring from shattered windows.

Dozens of people are feared dead in the hand-to-hand fighting that raged inside the building as Spetsnaz commandos took it over floor by floor. The end came when hundreds of the delegates who had barricaded themselves inside the White House emerged under the guns of the soldiers. Some waved white flags, others clasped their hands behind their heads as they walked dejectedly towards buses which carried them off to prison.

Among the last to surrender were the leaders of the rebellion, Aleksander Rutskoi, the vice president, and Ruslan Khasbulatov, the speaker, who were driven off to the infamous Lefortovo prison. But even after their capitulation, the sound of gunfire still echoes round Moscow as defiant snipers shoot from tall buildings and the tanks answer with their heavy machine guns.

Muscovites are shocked by this battle in their capital. Yeltsin has won, but he now finds himself perilously indebted to the army. (→ 9)

Defenders of the parliament surrender after the assault by elite paratroopers.

Khasbulatov, Rutskoi: two men who defied President Yeltsin

Parliament Speaker Khasbulatov.

Ruslan Khasbulatov and Aleksander Rutskoi, leaders of the failed rebellion, are united in only one thing: their hatred of Yeltsin.

Rutskoi is a gravel-voiced former fighter pilot, twice shot down in the Afghanistan war. Yeltsin trusted him so completely he made him vice president and sent him, Kalashnikov in hand, to rescue Mikhail Gorbachev from house arrest in the Crimea in the 1991 coup.

Khasbulatov is quite different. He is hugely ambitious, has none of Rutskoi's popularity or charisma, but acquired great power over parliament. He is also a Chechen, a Caucasian minority regarded as criminals by most Russians. Both men now face interrogation and a most uncertain future.

Vice President Aleksander Rutskoi.

tanks to quell rebellion by hardliners in Moscow

Tension rises as anti-Yeltsin fighters prepare to defend the White House.

The rebels included nationalists, elderly Stalinists and young anti-Semites.

Scores of soldiers, many of them young, turned and fled from angry crowds.

Pro-Yeltsin Muscovites celebrate the end of the bloody two-day uprising.

Oct. 6. The goose-stepping round-the-clock honor guard at Lenin's mausoleum on Red Square, in place since January 1924, is abolished.

Russia's leader tightens his grip on power

Moscow, Saturday 9

On the eve of his visit to Japan, Boris Yeltsin extended the state of emergency in Moscow for a further eight days and imposed a reform of local government which will bring the regional soviets under the control of administrators loyal to him. He has moved swiftly and audaciously to tighten his grip since winning the shoot-out at the White House. He has rounded up most of his opponents. A curfew keeps the streets clear after dark. Cars entering Moscow are checked and non-Muscovites are turned back. A purge is going on in the ministries and the army and has reached as far as Siberia. He has failed in an attempt to reimpose censorship. That was going too far. (→ 15)

Boris Yeltsin puts a brave face on it.

Bloody fiasco in Somalia

A raid gone badly wrong: debris of a U.S. helicopter downed by gunfire.

Mogadishu, Tuesday 5
About 650 American troops are on their way here to reinforce the U.S. presence after at least 12 U.S. soldiers were killed and 78 wounded in a failed raid to capture key aides of Mohammed Farah Aidid.

Army Rangers captured 19 of Aidid's men in a raid on a meeting Sunday, but when they were leaving they were attacked. Two helicopters were downed, and the soldiers prepared to defend themselves. Help was slow in coming, and the battle lasted on into Monday.

Today, Americans were shocked by TV-news images of a dead U.S. soldier being dragged through Mogadishu and of the bruised and cut face of Michael Durant, who was videotaped after his capture. (→ 7)

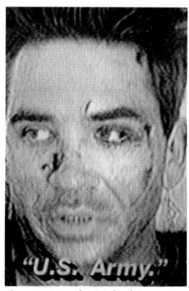

In captivity: pilot Michael Durant.

Woman to run Britain's security services

London, Friday 1
Pauline Neville-Jones, a career diplomat, has been appointed to chair the Joint Intelligence Committee. The JIC's task is to evaluate intelligence from MI5, MI6, Government Communications Headquarters and the Defence Ministry and to advise the prime minister of potential threats to British political, economic and military security.

As is becoming customary, she was introduced to the press and a booklet giving details of the JIC was issued. Neville-Jones, the second woman to fill a top intelligence job, will continue in her present post as head of the Defence and Overseas Secretariat in the Cabinet Office.

Pauline Neville-Jones is aged 53.

Lennox Lewis takes trophy in seventh

Cardiff, Wales, Sunday 3
Britain's favorite heavyweight, 31-year-old Frank Bruno, lost his attempt to take the World Boxing Council title from Lennox Lewis when the referee stopped the fight in the seventh round.

In order to accomodate U.S. television, the match started at 1 a.m. Bruno rocked his opponent with a right cross in the third round, but Lennox recovered to overwhelm Bruno with powerful punches. It was Bruno's third and probably last try at winning a world title. He is now expected to retire.

Number of U.S. poo hits a 30-year high

Washington, D.C., Monday 4
In 1992, there were 36.9 million poor in the United States, or 14.5% of the population, the Census Bureau reported today. A family of four was considered poor if its income was $14,335 or less. The number of poor is the largest since 1962 before Lyndon Johnson's War on Poverty program began. In 1962, 20% of Americans were poor, but the population was smaller. The rate was around 12% during the 1970s, but went up in the 1980s, only dropping below 13% once, in 1989. The rate in 1991 was 14.2%.

'60s radical gets jail for role in cop killing

Boston, Wednesday 6
Katherine Ann Power, a fugitive since taking part in a 1970 bank robbery, was sentenced to 8 to 12 years in jail on charges of manslaughter and armed robbery. When Power, who drove the getaway car, and three other anti-Vietnam War radicals robbed the bank, a Boston policeman was shot dead.

Power, now 44, is banned from making a profit from any movies or books about her story. On the FBI's most-wanted list for years, she initially hid in women's communes. Since 1977, she has lived in Oregon, calling herself Alice Metzinger.

Oct 1. Judges head for Westminster Abbey for a ceremony which dates back to the Middle Ages to mark the start of the legal term in England.

Oct. 5. Material Girl Madonna plays to an estimated 50,000 fans in Tel Aviv, which she mistakenly called Israel's "holy city."

ordan quits basketball

The 30-year-old star, sitting beside his wife Juanita, explains his decision.

Deerfield, Illinois, Wednesday 6

The world's greatest basketball player and perhaps its most famous sportsman announced his retirement from the game here today. "I have no more challenges," explained Michael "Air" Jordan. "I had achieved everything in basketball I could. And when that happened, I felt it was time to call it a career."

And what an achievement-filled career it was. Jordan, 30, led the Chicago Bulls to three straight NBA championships, being named MVP in all three series. He has the game's highest scoring average in the regular season, 32.3 points a game, and in the play-offs, 34.6 points.

When asked if he would really never grace the courts again, he responded: "I never say never."

A Nobel for U.S. author

Stockholm, Thursday 7

Toni Morrison has become the first black American to win the Nobel Prize for Literature. Describing her six novels as "finely wrought and cohesive, yet at the same time rich in variation," the Swedish academy praised the 62-year-old writer for her prose, "written with the luster of poetry."

She was the outsider in a field which included V.S. Naipaul, Seamus Heaney and Doris Lessing. When told of her success she said she was "unendurably happy" and "profoundly honored." Her latest novel, *Jazz*, tells the story of Harlem in its musical heyday. (→ 11)

Toni Morrison teaches at Princeton.

Elizabeth II attends 'wedding of the year'

London, Friday 8

Viscount Linley, son of Princess Margaret and the Earl of Snowdon, married Serena Stanhope, granddaughter of the Earl of Harrington, at St. Margaret's Westminster today in the most glittering event of the social calendar.

Mingling with the 650 guests, the Queen, dressed in dusty pink, chatted with the Princess of Wales; the Queen Mother was escorted by Prince Edward. The Prince of Wales was missing, abroad on royal business. The newlyweds left for a safari honeymoon in Zimbabwe, and it is hoped they will stay married longer than some of their royal cousins.

Conservatives unite behind John Major

Blackpool, England, Friday 8

The Tory faithful gave Prime Minister John Major a flag-waving demonstration of loyalty at the end of the Conservative Party Conference here today. He had promised to lead the country back to the basics of "common sense values," self-discipline and respect for the law. "We have allowed things to happen that we should never have tolerated," he said. His words and the reaction of the delegates came as sweet relief to the party, which had threatened to tear itself apart over the Maastricht treaty.

Oct. 7. Clinton and Ray Charles share a joke at the White House after the president gave the singer and 17 others the National Medal of Arts.

Oct. 7. As a soldier killed while serving in Somalia is buried at Arlington, President Clinton sets a six-month deadline for U.S. involvement in the war-torn country, saying forces will be withdrawn by March 31, 1994. (→ 14)

October
1993

Su	Mo	Tu	We	Th	Fr	Sa
					1	2
3	4	5	6	7	8	9
10	11	12	13	14	15	16
17	18	19	20	21	22	23
24	25	26	27	28	29	30
31						

Greece, 10
Socialist leader Andreas Papandreou, aged 74, is elected premier.

U.S., 10
A poll shows that 60% of Americans want U.S. troops to leave Somalia.

Tunis, 10
PLO officials reveal that assassins tried to blow up a plane carrying Yasser Arafat two weeks ago. (→ 20)

Stockholm, 11
Briton Richard Roberts and American Phillip Sharp share the Nobel Prize for Medicine. (→ 13)

Oslo, 11
A gunman seriously injures William Nygaard, the Norwegian publisher of Salman Rushdie's *The Satanic Verses*.

Algiers, 11
Thirteen Islamic militants are executed for terrorism.

France, 12
The maker of one of France's most prestigious wines, Château d'Yquem, says there will be no 1992 vintage due to its inferior quality.

Cambodia, 12
King Norodom Sihanouk reveals that he has cancer.

Stockholm, 13
Americans Robert Fogel and Douglas North are awarded the Nobel Prize for Economy; Michael Smith, a British-born Canadian, and American Kary Mullis share the Chemistry Nobel; the Physics Nobel goes to Americans Joseph Taylor and Russel Hulse. (→ 15)

Mogadishu, 14
Chief Warrant Officer Michael Durant, a U.S. helicopter pilot, is freed after 11 days of captivity. (→ 19)

Germany, 14
The Constitutional Court bans marriages between homosexual couples.

Moscow, 15
Yeltsin orders a referendum to be held on Dec. 12 on whether to accept a new constitution. (→ 22)

DEATH

13. Leo Salkin, American cartoon animator (*1913).

Cloning of human embryos by U.S. scientists sparks vast debate

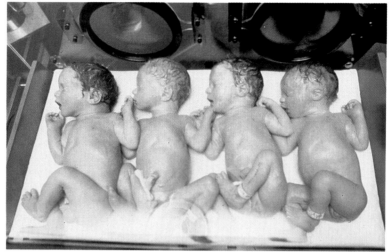

Doubts over the ethics of the creation of human organisms with identical genes.

Montreal, Wednesday 13
Jerry Hall of George Washington University presented a paper here today at a meeting of the American Fertility Society reporting the first instance of cloning human embryos.

Hall, who works for the university's in vitro fertilization program, cloned an embryo in an attempt to find a way to supply additional embryos to couples trying to have a child by the in vitro method. He used the technique which has been successful in cloning animal embryos but had not been used on human embryos. This first opens up a great debate on the morality of cloning people and on how the practice can be regulated.

Hundreds of British soccer hooligans cause havoc in Rotterdam

Rotterdam, Wednesday 13
England lost twice here tonight. Two-nil to Holland on the soccer field and by the hundreds on the streets, where drunken fans were rounded up by the Dutch police. The authorities made good on their threat to arrest anyone who turned up for the match without a ticket, and some 800 were herded into pens outside the stadium. The police and their dogs were not gentle. The first bloodied and bruised group of 88 fans were immediately flown home on a chartered plane. Dutch fans joined in the hooliganism. One of them filled a tennis ball with gunpowder and threw it at the English.

Dutch police arrest one of the 5,000 Britons who came to support their team.

Oct. 10. Edward Kennedy Jr., son of Senator Edward Kennedy, weds Katherine Anne Gershman, who arrived 20 minutes late.

Bell Atlantic signs $21-billion deal for TCI

New York, Wednesday 13
The "information superhighway" continues its development with the announcement today that Bell Atlantic Corp. intends to buy Tele-Communications Inc. for more than $21 billion in stock and assumed debt. This marriage of a telephone and cable-TV company will be the second-largest purchase in history if it is approved by the FCC and the Justice Department.

The deal threatens the Paramount-Viacom merger, announced Sept. 12. QVC Network Inc., partly owned by TCI, now has the backing of Bell Atlantic and is in better shape to win in its hostile takeover bid for Paramount, announced Sept. 20.

Marrying the telephone to cable.

ATT talks in crisis

Brussels, Wednesday 13

Leon Brittan, the EC trade commissioner, is locked in discussion with his U.S. counterpart, Mickey Kantor, in an increasingly desperate attempt to clear the way for a GATT world trade deal by the end of the year. As the negotiations reach a critical point, German officials point out that the Franco-German relationship, the basis of EC integration, could not survive a GATT failure due to French intransigence.

In Paris, Chancellor Kohl, in the first address by a foreign leader, told the Senate that Europe should "resist the temptation for protectionism. We should not close our markets." (→ Nov. 30)

Nelson Mandela, Frederik de Klerk are awarded Peace Nobel

Norway's Nobel committee praises their joint efforts to dismantle apartheid.

Oslo, Friday 15

This year's Nobel Peace Prize was awarded today to President de Klerk of South Africa and Nelson Mandela, president of the African National Congress. The five-man jury of the Norwegian parliament named them for "their work for the peaceful termination of the apartheid regime, and for laying the foundations for a new democratic South Africa." The award got a mixed reception in South Africa and the recipients seemed unsure how to react. De Klerk said he was "somewhat overwhelmed," while Mandela dedicated the prize to "the people, black and white, who have suffered and endured so much."

Mozart sonatas can make you smarter

London, Thursday 14

Students scored higher on IQ tests after listening to Mozart, researchers from University of California at Irvine reported in *Nature* today.

The average score of 36 students on nonverbal tests involving the geometry of paper objects shown as they would look after being folded or cut was higher after listening to Mozart's *Sonata for Two Pianos in D Major* than after a period of silence or after listening to a recorded message telling them to imagine themselves in a peaceful garden. The beneficial effect was only temporary.

Bill Clinton orders U.S. Navy ships to enforce blockade of Haiti

Washington, D.C., Friday 15

President Clinton has ordered six U.S. warships to Haiti to enforce a blockade, following the murder of Justice Minister Guy Mallary. The assassination of Mallary is seen here as a brutal answer to the U.N. Security Council's demand that Haiti's military rulers comply with a U.N.-brokered deal to restore democracy. If they refuse, the country faces renewal of the oil embargo and asset-freeze imposed in June. Under the deal, the democratically elected president, Jean-Bertrand Aristide, is due to return from exile this month. But General Raoul Cedras shows no sign of giving up power. (→ 28)

Opponents of the island's feared military rulers celebrate the U.S. move.

Seles's assailant is set free by court

Hamburg, Wednesday 13

Gunther Parche, the German tennis fan so besotted by Steffi Graf that he stabbed the World No. 1, Monica Seles, so that his idol could once again be the world's leading tennis player, was given a two-year suspended sentence here today and set free. Judge Elke Bosse said the evidence given by Parche was believable and honest. She described him as a "scared and lonely" man.

Seles said she was "shocked and horrified" by the light sentence: "He gets to go back to his life, but I can't because I am still recovering from his attack."

Oct. 16. These unique descendants of a 13th-century breed of shaggy-coated, red-eared cattle are raised by the Tankerville family on their estate at Chillingham, in northern England.

Oct. 15. Fit for King Tut: The huge Luxor hotel and casino in Las Vegas, which is large enough to accomodate nine Boeing 747s, opened today. Inside its glass walls, guests can sail down a replica of the Nile River.

October

1993

Su	Mo	Tu	We	Th	Fr	Sa
					1	2
3	4	5	6	7	8	9
10	11	12	13	14	15	16
17	18	19	20	21	22	23
24	25	26	27	28	29	30
31						

Saint Andrews, 17
The U.S. golf team defeats England, the holders, in the final of the Dunhill Cup.

Georgia, 18
Georgian leader Eduard Shevardnadze calls for Russian military aid to fight rebel forces. (→31)

Warsaw, 18
President Lech Walesa appoints Waldemar Pawlak as premier.

Washington, D.C., 19
Clinton ends the U.S. search for Somali warlord Aidid and pulls out the 750-member Ranger force sent to find him.

London, 19
Dublin-based fashion designer John Rocha is named British Designer of the Year.

Tokyo, 19
Empress Michiko, who has been the target of recent press criticism, collapses during a dinner celebrating her 59th birthday.

Uruguay, 19
The ketch *New Zealand Endeavour* arrives in Punta del Este and wins the first leg of the Whitbread Round the World Race.

The Hague, 20
The Dutch government says it will ban the sale of hashish and marijuana to foreign tourists.

London, 20
London Zoo announces the death at the age of 22 of Belinda, the tarantula who featured in James Bond and Indiana Jones films.

New York, 20
The U.N. reports that the U.S. was the largest exporter of combat aircraft and tanks in 1992.

London, 21
World chess champion Garry Kasparov beats British challenger Nigel Short by 12.5 to 7.5 matches.

Burundi, 21
President Melchior Ndadaye is killed during a military coup. (→29)

Florida, 22
Four youths are indicted for the Sept. 14 murder of British tourist Gary Colley.

Maggie's memoirs ruffle many a feather

London, Monday 18
Lady Thatcher's memoirs, *The Downing Street Years*, has sold 300,000 copies three days after publication. This news will give small pleasure to those statesmen she has "hand-bagged" in her book. John Major lacks "political instinct." President Reagan is praised for his "warmth, charm and complete lack of affectation." But with President Bush she felt "I could not rely as before on American co-operation." Giscard d'Estaing is "rather lofty and rather patronizing." And she has enraged the Germans with her description of their character: "Swerving unpredictably between aggression and self-doubt."

Lady Thatcher launches her book.

Benazir Bhutto back in power in Pakistan

Islamabad, Wednesday 20
Benazir Bhutto, ousted from power three years ago, was sworn in today as prime minister of Pakistan for the second time. She won a convincing vote of confidence in the national assembly over her rival, Nawaz Sharif, to end the uncertainty which followed the inconclusive result of the general election on Oct. 6. By what Sharif described as "horse trading," she gathered votes from the small parties and independents until she had 121 to Sharif's 72. Her Pakistan People's Party also seems set to win the key provinces of Punjab and Sind.

L.A. riot beating case ends in acquittal

Henry Watson listens to the verdict.

Los Angeles, Wednesday 20
Two black men who beat white truck driver Reginald Denny in the L.A. riots of last year have been acquitted of attempted murder.

The jury acquitted Henry Watson of the charge on Monday but deadlocked on Damian Williams. Both were found guilty of lesser counts, Williams of felony mayhem and Watson of misdemeanor assault. Denny was compassionate and said, referring to Watson, "They should let the guy go." His lawyer said that he would not seek further trials of the defendants. Williams was found not guilty of attempted murder today.

Premier again after an often bitter three-year political struggle.

Nuke waste outcry

Tokyo, Sunday 17
Russian officials confirmed reports by Greenpeace that the Russian Navy dumped liquid radioactive waste into the Sea of Japan today. The environmentalist group had a vessel following a navy ship towing a tanker containing the deadly waste.

Greenpeace estimates that 900 tonnes was dumped 295 nautical miles west of the island of Hokkaido. They also reported seeing the crew preparing to dump solid waste.

Tokyo, outraged, called for an immediate halt to the practice. Last week President Yeltsin met with Japanese Prime Minister Hosokawa; they signed a joint statement that such dumping was "a grave concern on a global scale." (→Nov. 12)

Commonwealth's leaders meet in Cyprus

Queen was targeted by protesters.

Cyprus, Thursday 21
The Queen opened the Commonwealth Conference of the 50-nation group of former possessions of Britain which recognize her as a symbol of their free association today. At the traditional state banquet on board the royal yacht *Britannia* she spoke of the future: "I am confident ... the Commonwealth and its ideals will have survived – changed, adapted, even weatherbeaten – but still there, a force for peace and good government." The royal visit has, however, revived anti-British anger stemming from the unrest in the 1950s when nine Eoka guerrillas were hanged by Britain. Protestors threw eggs at her and denounced her as the "Killer Queen."

Palestinians kill a moderate PLO official

Saftawi was a close Arafat aide.

Gaza Strip, Wednesday 20

Asaad Saftawi, a founder member with Yasser Arafat of the PLO, was gunned down outside his house here today by militants opposed to his moderate policies.

He took part in organizing the Palestinians' first guerrilla units but later became one of the very few Palestinian notables to campaign for the recognition of Israel as the only realistic way of winning back a portion of their homeland. He sealed his death warrant last April when he welcomed Yitzhak Rabin, the Israeli prime minister, to his home in a televised ceremony. He was born near Al Majdal, now the Israeli town of Ashkelon, in 1935. (→ 25)

Belfast bomb outrage

The blast devastated the Shankill Road offices used by the loyalist UFF.

Supercollider plan ended by Congress

Washington, D.C., Thursday 21

"The supercollider is dead," declared a House opponent of the $11-billion project. A Senate supporter was more dramatic, "The SSC has been lynched." The superconducting supercollider, being built to learn about the origin of matter by colliding beams of subatomic particles at nearly the speed of light, fell victim to the budget axe. Those who viewed the project as just too expensive to continue won out in a House vote, 282 votes to 143, Tuesday. Today, the House and Senate Appropriations Committees agreed on a shut-down plan allocating $640 million for an "orderly" termination.

U.S. aide in Moscow to support Yeltsin

Moscow, Friday 22

Secretary of State Warren Christopher announced tonight that President Clinton will hold a summit meeting with President Yeltsin here in January. This is seen as a move to underline Washington's support for Yeltsin in the wake of this month's failed parliamentary uprising.

Nevertheless, Washington is wary of Yeltsin. There are doubts in the administration about the prospects of speedy reform in Russia. It is also feared that the generals to whom Yeltsin is in debt for their decisive help during the attempted coup will insist that he defend Russia's "spheres of interest."

Belfast, Saturday 23

A bomb planted in a fish and chip shop in the Protestant Shankill Road killed nine people today, including two girls aged 9 and 13 and one of the bombers.

Acknowledging its responsibility, the IRA said the bomb was aimed at the leadership of the Ulster Freedom Fighters, who are conducting a vicious "eye for an eye" war with the republicans. The IRA statement said that a meeting of the UFF was in progress in the building next door to the fish shop. The death of one of the bombers – another is in hospital – indicates that the bomb went off prematurely.

The UFF has already sworn revenge, and Northern Ireland is waiting in fear for the inevitable retaliation. Any hopes for peace seem to have been blown away. (→ 27)

Oct. 23. Sixteen giant Fernando Botero sculptures, weighing up to 2.5 tons, are on display on New York's swank Park Avenue.

Oct. 23. French police move in as striking Air France workers paralyze Orly and Roissy airports, near Paris. The strike is seriously disrupting international flights, and many planes are avoiding French airspace. (→ Oct. 24)

Oct. 23. The Toronto Blue Jays take their second straight World Series by beating the Philadelphia Phillies, 8-6, giving them a 4-2 win in the series.

October

1993

Su	Mo	Tu	We	Th	Fr	Sa
					1	2
3	4	5	6	7	8	9
10	11	12	13	14	15	16
17	18	19	20	21	22	23
24	25	26	27	28	29	30
31						

Paris, 24
Air France president Bernard Attali resigns.

Wentworth, England, 24
U.S. golfer Corey Pavin beats Britain's Nick Faldo to win the World Matchplay Championship.

London, 26
Irish author Roddy Doyle wins the Booker Prize for his novel *Paddy Clarke Ha Ha Ha.*

Cairo, 26
A gunman kills two Americans and a Frenchman in a hotel.

Belfast, 27
Sinn Fein president Gerry Adams sparks widespread anger by helping to carry the coffin of Thomas Begley, the IRA bomber who killed himself and nine others in the Shankill Road attack. (→ 29)

Las Vegas, 27
The Dunes hotel and casino building, which opened in 1955, is destroyed by explosives to make way for a new resort complex.

Cyprus, 27
The Sultan of Brunei leaves a $170,000 tip after a five-day stay in a luxury hotel.

Pacific Ocean, 28
A disabled two-ton Chinese satellite crashes into the ocean.

New York, 28
Haiti's exiled leader, Jean-Bertrand Aristide, calls for a full-scale air and trade embargo against the island.

Brussels, 29
John Major and Irish Prime Minister Albert Reynolds agree to launch a new bid for peace in Ulster. (→ 30)

Lynnwood, Wash., 30
Dallas Malloy beats Heather Poyner in the first sanctioned boxing match between women in U.S. history.

DEATHS

24. Jiri Hajek, Czechoslovak politican (*June 6, 1913).

24. Lord (Joseph) Grimond, British politician (*July 29, 1913).

28. Doris Duke, American tobacco heiress (*1913).

31. River Phoenix, American actor (*Aug. 23, 1971).

Conservatives routed in Canadian election

Liberal Party leader Jean Chrétien.

Ottawa, Monday 25
Canadian voters demolished the Progressive Conservative majority in today's elections, putting Jean Chrétien's Liberal Party in power and boosting two smaller parties.

The Conservatives won only two seats; even Premier Kim Campbell lost hers. The Liberals won 178 of the 295 seats, a greater majority than held by the Tories before the vote. The separatist Bloc Québécois won 54 seats, and the Reform Party, which proposed a drastic deficit-reduction plan, won 52.

The desire for change also was shown by a rejection of incumbents: two thirds of those elected have never been in parliament before.

Hundreds of Palestinians freed by Israel

Jerusalem, Monday 25
Israel freed nearly 300 Palestinian prisoners in the first concrete move towards reconciliation since Prime Minister Yitzhak Rabin and Yasser Arafat shook hands last month.

The freed men and women are mostly "low-grade" prisoners – women, teenage stone-throwers, the sick and elderly – but they are seen as the forerunners of the release of most of the 10,000 now held in Israeli prisons and camps. They were met with celebrations in Gaza and the West Bank. But not everybody is happy. Militant Arabs demand the immediate release of all the prisoners, while Israelis fear terrorists will be freed to kill again. (→ Nov. 3)

A first result of the peace accord.

Croats rape and kill villagers in Bosnia

Vares, Bosnia, Sunday 24
In one of the worst atrocities in this appalling civil war, Croat militiamen slaughtered the Muslim inhabitants of the hillside hamlet of Stupni Do, several miles south of here.

The few survivors who managed to escape told of rape and murder and the hamlet's destruction by masked Croats. "It was like hell, fire everywhere. I saw many bodies; the Croats were throwing them into the fires," said one old man who escaped through the forest. The Croats are refusing to allow U.N. troops into Stupni Do. (→ Nov. 9)

Prince of ghouls die

A delightfully eerie Vincent Price.

Los Angeles, Monday 25
Vincent Price died of lung cance here today. His reputation as th suave master of the horror movi rests on compelling performances i films such as *The Pit and the Pendu lum* and *The Fall of the House o Usher*, but movie-goers were neve sure how far Price had his tongue i his cheek. Certainly *The Raven*, i which he appeared with Peter Lorr and Basil Rathbone, was a comi parody of the genre. In fact, horro accounted for only a quarter o Price's output of over 100 films. Tal and lean with a long handsome face and perfect enunciation, he playe roles from gangsters to noblemen He was also an art expert whose lectures earned him a small fortune He was born in St. Louis, Missour on May 27, 1911.

Oct. 28. Laguna Beach, 40 miles southeast of Los Angeles, is one of the many Southern California towns facing the fury of raging brush fires that have destroyed scores of homes and forced thousands to flee. (→ Nov. 3)

loodbath feared in Burundi after coup

iousands of refugees are fleeing.

Bujumbura, Friday 29
More than 500,000 people are fleeing the clan fighting between the majority Hutu and the Tutsi which broke out after last week's coup attempt. President Melchior Ndadaye was killed in the attempt, but it collapsed Monday when army generals disowned the plotters and called for government leaders to come out of hiding. The civilian government, which is dominated by the Hutu clan, has asked for protection from an international armed force. The prime ministers of Zaire, Tanzania and Rwanda issued a statement indicating their willingness to send in troops to protect the government and to stop the tribal war.

Addio, Federico Fellini

The Academy Award-winning Italian director was a perfectionist to the last.

even are killed in Ulster revenge attack

inn Fein's president, Gerry Adams.

Londonderry, Saturday 30
The Ulster Freedom Fighters took their revenge for the Shankill Road bombing tonight when two hooded gunmen sprayed people celebrating Halloween in the Rising Sun Bar in the village of Greysteel with automatic gunfire. "Trick or treat?" asked the gunmen, then opened fire. Seven people died in the hail of bullets and at least nine were wounded.

"At first we thought it was fireworks," said a survivor, "then there were bodies everywhere." Greysteel was a peaceful place with Protestants and Roman Catholics living alongside each other and drinking together in the bar. Tonight they died together. (→ Nov. 29)

Rome, Sunday 31
Federico Fellini, tempestuous genius of the Italian cinema, died here today, following a stroke he suffered in August. His films, drawn from his own life, were self-indulgent, something he would happily admit, but they were also innovative and ebullient. He directed 20 feature films of which the most successful were *La Strada, La Dolce Vita* and *8 1/2*. According to *The Times*, he had "a personal vision of mortal decadence which both fascinated and appalled him. He was also commercially successful and won five Oscars, a record for a European filmmaker. Born into a solid bourgeois family in Rimini on January 20, 1920, he is survived by his wife aged over 50, the actress Giulietta Masina, who starred in *La Strada*. (→ Nov. 4)

America's economy is out of doldrums

Washington, D.C., Thursday 28
Economic good news was the order of the day, as the Commerce Department reported that gross domestic product grew at a rate of 2.8% a year in the third quarter. Government economists say the rate would have been a half-point higher without the damage from the floods in the Midwest and the drought in the Southeast. The Treasury Department announced a drop in the budget deficit, down $35.39 billion from fiscal 1992 to $254.95 billion. And the Dow Jones industrial average closed at a record high today, 3,687.6 points, after active trading.

rench captives reed in Algeria

lgiers, Sunday 31
hree French consular officials kidapped a week ago have been freed fter raids by Algerian security orces. A group called the Islamic rmed Group claimed responsibiliy for the abductions in pamphlets istributed to news offices. At least ne gendarme and six of the kidnapers died in the raids. Jean-Claude hévenot and Alain Freissier were reed yesterday, and Michèle Thévenot was freed this evening as her usband and Freissier were on a light to Paris. She is expected to fly o France tomorrow.

Rebel forces suffer setbacks in Georgia

The war seems to be nearly over.

Tbilisi, Sunday 31
Eduard Shevardnadze, the Georgian leader, has struck back strongly against the rebels led by Zviad Gamsakhurdia, the ousted president.

Only three weeks ago, Gamsakhurdia seemed poised to topple the government, which had suffered humiliating losses in its separate conflict with Abkhazian separatists.

Now, Shevardnadze's forces are hammering the rebel base at Khobi and threatening their headquarters at Zugdidi. Shevardnadze's change of fortune is due to military help from Russia, given in exchange for his promise that Georgia will join the CIS. (→ Nov. 18)

Oct. 31. Designer Donna Karan of New York opens Spring 1994 collection shows in Bryant Park.

November

1993

Su	Mo	Tu	We	Th	Fr	Sa
	1	2	3	4	5	6
7	8	9	10	11	12	13
14	15	16	17	18	19	20
21	22	23	24	25	26	27
28	29	30				

Tokyo, 1
In the largest bankruptcy filed by a Japanese firm since 1945, the construction giant Osaka, with debts of $5 billion, asks for protection from creditors.

Preston, 1
The two 10-year-old Liverpool boys accused of killing a toddler go on trial for murder. (→ 24)

Australia, 2
Ireland's Vintage Crop, ridden by Michael Kinane, becomes the first European-trained horse to win the Melbourne Cup.

U.S., 2
A poll shows that NFL football is America's most popular sport and polo its least popular; soccer ranks 95th and rugby 122nd.

Beijing, 2
The U.S. and China resume high-level military contacts, frozen since 1989. (→ 20)

Moscow, 3
Russia's new military doctrine drops a long-standing Soviet pledge not to use nuclear weapons first.

Malibu, 3
British screenwriter Duncan Gibbins is killed while trying to rescue his cat from his blazing villa. (→ 5)

Europe, 4
Kurdish separatists attack 30 Turkish properties across Europe. One person was killed. (→ 18)

New York, 4
A jury decides that the Marquess of Northampton is the rightful owner of the Sevso treasure, a $100-million collection of Roman silver claimed by Croatia and Hungary.

Copenhagen, 5
Salvage experts who raised U-534 find no gold aboard the German U-boat.

Strasbourg, France, 5
Germany, France and Belgium inaugurate the Eurocorps, a military unit they hope will form the core of a future European army.

Arcadia, California, 6
The French horse Arcangues wins the Breeders' Cup Classic.

Republicans celebrate as Democrats suffer setbacks in U.S. vote

Giuliani with his wife, Donna (left).

U.S., Tuesday 2
Republicans are exuberant after winning the mayorship of New York City and the governorships of New Jersey and Virginia. They see today's election results as a rejection of President Clinton's policies. The president sees them as reflective of local issues and desire for change.

New York's first black mayor, Democrat David Dinkins, was defeated by Republican Rudolph Giuliani. New Jersey Governor Jim Florio, a Democrat, was ousted by Christine Todd Whitman. Republican George Allen won in Virginia, where Democrats have held the governorship for the last 12 years.

End of the road for David Dinkins.

Maastricht treaty goes into effect

Brussels, Monday 1
The European Union finally came into being at midnight with the implementation of the Maastricht treaty, but there were no celebrations, for this is All Souls Day, when families honor their dead.

Certainly, Jacques Delors did little to lift European spirits when he called on governments to pay for the creation of new jobs through giant infrastructure projects. The only fireworks came from Lady Thatcher, who accused Chancellor Kohl of "steamrollering everything in his path." He said the drive for monetary union was unstoppable. (→ 5)

Voters end Teddy Kollek's 28-year tenure

Jerusalem's ex-mayor is aged 82.

Jerusalem, Tuesday 2
Teddy Kollek, said by the Israelis to be the greatest builder of Jerusalem since Herod the Great, has been rejected by the voters after 28 years as mayor of the Holy City. The Viennese-born moderate was defeated by the right-wing Likud candidate, Ehud Olmert.

Olmert won 55% of the votes after making a votes-for-seats deal with the ultra-religious candidate, Meir Porush, who withdrew from the poll. Arabs are now regretting their boycott of the election, for they fear Kollek's respect for the rights of the city's 160,000 Arab minority will be replaced by a harsher, confrontational regime under Olmert.

Packwood ordered to hand over his diaries

He faces sexual harassment charges.

Washington, D.C., Tuesday 2
Oregon Senator Bob Packwood, accused of sexually harrassing women aides and lobbyists, was ordered by the Senate today to hand over his private diaries, as well as any other recorded or printed document relating to his professional activities, from the past five years. Packwood argued that the order infringed on his privacy and offered to hand over the material to a mediator, who would decide what was relevant to the investigation. The Senate rejected the compromise and voted, 94-6, that he turn over everything. Robert Byrd of West Virginia called for Packwood to resign, saying he had blackened the chamber's reputation.

A top Arafat aide was Mossad agent

Tunis, Wednesday 3
Adnan Yassin, one of the PLO's most trusted security officials, has been arrested here on charges of spying for Israel. It is alleged that Yassin bugged the luxurious Swedish orthopedic chairs favored by the PLO leaders and that their discussions were recorded by Mossad spies in a nearby hotel, thus enabling the Israelis to learn Yasser Arafat's game plan for the recent peace talks. Yassin's cover is said to have been blown by the French secret service because the activities of Mossad agents in France had overstepped "acceptable limits." (→ 30)

ontaminated blood scandal in Germany

uthorities fear that millions of patients may have to be tested for AIDS.

Bonn, Wednesday 3

Germans who have had surgery or blood transfusions in the past 12 years were urged by the health authorities of Lower Saxony today to take HIV tests. This move, which has done little to calm the AIDS scare sweeping the country, follows the arrest of senior officials of a company accused of supplying contaminated blood to 58 hospitals.

Many patients are refusing non-essential operations while the hospitals are searched for the contaminated blood. When this scandal first broke in August it was said that only hemophilic patients who needed frequent transfusions were at risk. But now, amid accusations of a cover-up, Horst Seehofer, the federal health minister, has set up a parliamentary investigation. (→9)

U.K.'s civil servants in massive walkout

London, Friday 5

Visitors were turned away from the Tower of London today when the Beefeaters joined other civil servants all round the country in the biggest one-day demonstration by the nation's officials in 12 years. The walkout was held to protest against "market-testing," the process by which central government functions are tested against private-sector competition. The civil servants fear that many jobs are at risk and union officials, who claimed the walkout was a great success, said, "It was a cry from the heart of the country's public servants."

Malibu reels following brush fire inferno

Hollywood stars fled as their million-dollar homes were engulfed in flames.

Malibu, Friday 5

The fires that have ravaged Southern California communities since Oct. 26 are finally under control.

Three deaths have resulted from the fires: Duncan Gibbins, a British screenwriter, died Wednesday, and two people, burned so badly it was impossible to identify them, were found yesterday in a burned-out car.

Police say the fire here, the most recent of 18 in the area, was started by an arsonist. A $250,000 reward has been offered for information leading to his arrest.

At least 1,000 homes have been destroyed in the fires, which covered an area of more than 200,000 acres. The property damage is more than $1 billion, and more than 200 people have been injured, most of them firefighters.

Nov. 6. Evander Holyfield (left) wins back his world heavyweight title after beating Riddick Bowe; the Las Vegas fight was interrupted for 21 minutes when a man parachuted into the ring.

Nov. 4. Feet wet: The 274 passengers and 22 crew members aboard this China Airlines Boeing 747-400 escaped safely when the airliner overshot the runway in a storm while landing at Hong Kong's Kai Tak Airport, known to pilots for its dangerous approach over the Kowloon Peninsula.

Nov. 4. Before his burial today, Federico Fellini's body lay in state in Studio 5 of Rome's Cinecittà studios, where he made many of his films.

November
1993

Su	Mo	Tu	We	Th	Fr	Sa
	1	2	3	4	5	6
7	8	9	10	11	12	13
14	15	16	17	18	19	20
21	22	23	24	25	26	27
28	29	30				

U.K., 7
Sunday Mirror publishes photos, taken with a hidden camera, of Princess Diana exercising in a gym. (→ 9)

Adelaide, Australia, 7
Brazil's Ayrton Senna wins the final race of the Formula One season; Alain Prost of France finishes second in the last race of his career.

Washington, D.C., 7
Clinton warns North Korea that the U.S. will respond militarily if it attacks South Korea or develops a nuclear weapon.

New Zealand, 7
The ruling National Party suffers a setback in elections that leave the House of Representatives without a clear majority.

Tampa, Florida, 7
Ross Perot says a pro-NAFTA group has hired Cubans to murder him. (→ 9)

Stockholm, 8
Eight works by Picasso and Braque worth $60 million are stolen from a museum.

Washington, D.C., 8
Supreme Court refuses to allow two Hawaii schools to hire only Protestants as teachers.

Germany, 9
AIDS tests are recommended for all U.S. soldiers who have received transfusions in Germany in the past 12 years.

New York, 9
U.N. says the number of refugees worldwide has risen from 2.5 million in 1973 to 19.7 million today.

New York, 11
U.N. imposes new sanctions on Libya for its refusal to hand over the two suspects in the downing of a Pan Am plane over Lockerbie.

Santiago, 12
Two policemen are jailed for the 1976 murder in the U.S. of a Chilean opposition leader, Orlando Letelier.

DEATHS

12. Harry R. Haldeman, former White House chief of staff (*Oct. 27, 1926).

12. Jill Tweedie, British columnist (*May 22, 1934).

Frankly, my dear ...

Los Angeles, Monday 8
Frankly, thousands of aspiring actresses do give a damn. They are green with envy of Joanne Whalley-Kilmer, who was revealed today as the successor to Vivian Leigh in the role of Scarlett O'Hara.

Whalley-Kilmer, who is married to movie star Val Kilmer, will star in the TV-movie adaption of *Scarlett*, the sequel to *Gone With the Wind* written by Alexandra Ripley. "It's an honor to play one of the great women's roles of all time – a dream come true," she said. A Briton, like Leigh, Whalley-Kilmer has been seen in *Scandal*, a film about the Profumo affair, and the BBC TV series *The Singing Detective*.

The Scarlett O'Hara of the 1990s.

Croats destroy Mostar's Ottoman bridge

The 16th-century Stari Most, or Old Bridge, built across the Neretva River.

Mostar, Bosnia, Tuesday 9
The elegant 16th-century bridge built by Sultan Suleiman to link east and west Mostar was sent crashing into the Neretva River by a barrage of shells from Croatian guns today. Muslims who had tried to protect its slender single span with a pathetic barricade of tires could only weep as the bridge, which has figured on a million postcards, was destroyed. Jerrie Hulme, a U.N. official, said the Croats pounded it until there was nothing left. "It was certainly targeted, there's no doubt about it," he said. "It was deliberate. It wasn't a symbol of the Muslims or the Croats. It was a symbol of the whole city." (→ 17)

New Diana scandal

London, Tuesday 9
The Princess of Wales today struck back at Bryce Taylor, the gym owner who took "Peeping-Tom" photographs of her exercising in a leotard and sold them to Mirror Group Newspapers. Her lawyers issued writs demanding the surrender of the photos and details of how much money has been made from them. This follows a High Court injunction banning publication of further pictures. David Banks, editor of the *Daily Mirror*, admitted he and Taylor were "ratbags" but remained unrepentant. (→ Dec. 3)

Al Gore wins on points after bitter debate on NAFTA with Perot

Washington, D.C., Tuesday 9
Fight strategy from Vice President Al Gore and once, and perhaps future, independent presidential candidate Ross Perot in tonight's debate on NAFTA was pretty much what was expected. Gore got in Perot's face with accusations of personal gain if NAFTA was defeated and generally tried to make him blow his cool. Perot said NAFTA would send American jobs south of the border and that Clinton was trying to buy votes in Congress. Most observers agree that Gore got the better of the Texan by keeping on the offensive without becoming overly aggressive. After the debate, Perot complained, "They sent poor little Al Gore out to try and destroy me personally." (→ 17)

CNN's Larry King (left) referees barbed exchanges between the two men.

Apocalypse postponed for sect in Ukraine

Michael Jackson quits tour and seeks help

Kiev, Thursday 11

The Ukrainian police would seem to have postponed Doomsday by arresting Marina Tsvygun, who prefers to be known as Maria Devi Khristos, self-proclaimed "Messiah" of a weird cult called the Great White Brotherhood.

She has promised that she would die outside St. Sofia's Cathedral, would rise again and lead her fanatical followers to salvation while the non-believers were consumed in the Apocalypse. When her cult zealots rioted in the cathedral today, the police, fearing mass suicides among the mainly young followers, arrested them all. The "Messiah" is now alive and well, behind bars.

Marina Tsvygun, alias the Messiah.

The star says he is unable to continue due to an addiction to painkillers.

Euro Disney posts massive first-year loss

Paris, Wednesday 10

Even Mickey Mouse was depressed today when squalls of icy rain swept across the Euro Disney theme park and the company announced losses of $900 million on its first year of business. Euro Disney's president, Philippe Bourguignon, blamed "Europe-wide recession, high interest rates and rising unemployment" for the losses.

The 10,000 staff now fear for their jobs – 950 have already been let go – and they were not reassured by the news that Euro Disney's survival has been guaranteed for a "limited period" by the parent Walt Disney Company with a deadline of next spring to restructure finances.

Visitors stayed away in droves.

U.S., Friday 12

Rumors abound about where singer Michael Jackson might be headed after an announcement that he was quitting his world concert tour to undergo treatment for addiction to painkillers. He is expected to seek treatment in Europe. Jackson faces a lawsuit and a criminal investigation in the U.S. on allegations of sexually molesting a 13-year-old boy.

Jackson released a videotape explaining that he began using the drugs after undergoing surgery because of the burns he suffered while filming a Pepsi ad in 1984. He said that the "great pain in my heart," resulting from the "extortion attempt," as he called the charges, combined with the stress of the concert tour made him increasingly dependent on the drugs. (→ Dec. 22)

Transplant girl loses long fight for life

Pittsburgh, Thursday 11

Laura Davies, the five-year-old British girl who has undergone two multiple transplant operations, was allowed to die at Children's Hospital here today.

It had become apparent that she was being killed by the drug used to prevent the rejection of her new liver, stomach, bowel, pancreas, kidneys and intestines. Her fight for life had stirred compassion around the world. Many, including King Fahd of Saudi Arabia, sent donations for her treatment but that treatment is now being questioned on ethical grounds. Was it all worthwhile?

Penis case husband is acquitted in U.S.

Manassas, Virginia, Wednesday 10

John Wayne Bobbitt was found innocent of marital sexual assault here today by a jury of nine women and three men.

On June 23, Bobbitt initiated sexual intercourse with his wife Lorena. She claimed that he raped her. After he fell asleep, she went to the kitchen, got a knife and cut off part of his penis. "I sat up in this silent scream," he testified.

The jury found that there was not enough evidence to convict John of sexual assault. Lorena will be tried for malicious wounding later.

Nov. 10. One Canadian and nine American tourists, as well as the British driver, were killed today when their bus, which was taking visitors on a trip to Canterbury Cathedral, careened off the road in rainy conditions.

U.K. rejects pact on dumping of N-waste

London, Friday 12

Britain has refused to join a worldwide ban on dumping nuclear waste at sea. Arguing at a meeting of the International Maritime Organization that there were good scientific reasons for having the option to resume dumping at sea rather than keeping the waste on land, British officials joined France, Belgium, Russia and China in abstaining on a proposal to replace a 10-year voluntary ban. Britain now has 100 days to reject the ban formally before being automatically bound by the majority vote.

November

New York, 14
60 Minutes, the granddaddy of U.S. news magazine TV shows, celebrates 25 years on the air with a two-hour special.

San Juan, 14
A narrow majority of Puerto Ricans votes in favor of maintaining the island's commonwealth status.

Paris, 15
American author Paul Auster wins France's Medicis prize for foreign literature for his novel *Leviathan*.

Lagos, 17
General Sani Abacha, a former defense minister, ousts Nigeria's civilian ruler, Ernest Shonekan, and bans all political parties.

Paris, 17
The government announces plans to curb "sex tours" to Asia by Frenchmen.

Warwick, England, 18
At least 11 children and their teacher are killed when their minibus crashes into the back of a truck.

France, 18
Police round up 110 suspected Kurdish militants. (→ 26)

Kiev, 18
The Ukrainian parliament votes to ratify the START-1 arms treaty.

Atlanta, 18
The Centers for Disease Control report that AIDS has become the leading killer for men aged 25 to 44 in the U.S.

Tbilisi, 18
Georgian leader Eduard Shevardnadze extends the state of emergency indefinitely. (→ Dec. 1)

Bhutan, 20
The kingdom's main political dissident, Tek Nath Rizal, is sentenced to life in prison for "anti-national activities."

Murrayfield, Scotland, 20
The New Zealand rugby team thrashes Scotland, 51-15. (→ 27)

DEATHS

14. Sanzo Nosaka, founder of Japan's Communist Party (*1892).

16. Lucia Popp, Austrian soprano (*Nov. 12, 1939).

Clinton boosted after winning crucial NAFTA vote in Congress

Many Americans are worried that the trade accord will mean lost jobs.

Washington, D.C., Wednesday 17
President Clinton has won his greatest legislative victory with the approval of NAFTA today by the House.

This summer, even Clinton's advisors figured it was a hopeless cause. NAFTA was backed by economists and Republicans – more of them voted for the pact than Democrats. Unions, environmental groups and Ross Perot lined up against it. Clinton sent Al Gore to take care of Perot and used the carrot and the stick to move representatives to his side. The victory will give the U.S. leverage in the GATT negotiations and in meetings with the Pacific Rim nations later this week. (→ 20)

War crimes tribunal opens in The Hague

The Hague, Wednesday 17
The inaugural session of the U.N. war crimes tribunal for the former Yugoslavia was held in the Peace Palace today with judges from 11 countries being sworn in. The tribunal, under Ramon Escovar Salom, the prosecutor-designate, will have a staff of 380 but does not yet have a permanent home. More importantly, it has no powers of arrest and cannot pass verdicts in the absence of the accused. As the main culprits in the Bosnian atrocities have no intention of surrendering themselves, the prospect of the tribunal actually holding trials seems remote. (→ 30)

Bishops crack down on pedophile priests

Washington, D.C., Wednesday 17
The National Conference of Catholic Bishops voted today to make it easier to dismiss priests who sexually abuse minors. They will ask the Vatican to raise the age at which a victim is considered a minor from 15 to 17, extend the church's five-year statute of limitations and speed up the adjudication process.

The bishops expressed their support for Cardinal Joseph Bernardin, 65, who has been accused by Steven Cook, 34, of using him as a "sex toy" between 1975-77 when he was a seminary student. Ironically, it was Bernardin who instituted significant measures last February to help victims of sexual abuse by priests.

Cardinal Bernardin of Chicago.

Nov. 14. Andres Espinosa of Mexico, aged 30, wins the 24th New York marathon in 2 hours, 10 minutes and 4 seconds.

Nov. 14. A monument to honor the casualties of past conflicts, bearing the inscription "To the Victims of War and Tyranny," is dedicated in Berlin. The ceremony is marred by protests from extreme rightists.

England's World Cup hopes dashed

England's 7-1 win was no help.

Bologna, Wednesday 17
England crashed out of the World Cup in utter ignominy tonight when the longed-for miracle – a Dutch defeat in Poland – failed to materialize. The frantic English players did manage to put seven goals past the amateurs of tiny San Marino, but that was only after the humiliation of allowing the worst team in European international football to score barely 10 seconds into the match.

England's manager, Graham Taylor, admitted afterwards that it was the worst moment of his career. It is a career which is not likely to be prolonged. (→ 23)

Teams qualified

Host country: U.S.
Defending champion: Germany
Europe: Belgium, Bulgaria, Greece, Holland, Ireland, Italy, Norway, Romania, Russia, Spain, Sweden, Switzerland
North America: Mexico
South America: Argentina, Bolivia, Brazil, Columbia
Asia: Saudia Arabia, South Korea
Africa: Cameroon, Morocco, Nigeria

Nov. 17. Pastels and earth tones dominate at Oscar de la Renta's Summer collection in New York.

President Clinton turns to Pacific Rim nations at Seattle summit

Seattle, Saturday 20
Just as the U.S. is clashing with Europe over trade in the GATT talks, Bill Clinton turned his attention to Asia today. He met leaders of the Asia-Pacific Economic Cooperation group on Blake Island in Puget Sound. Little of substance was decided; the chief objective was to get them together. As a Clinton aide said, "The meeting is the message." The talks showed the increasing tendency to ignore Europe and look to Asia's burgeoning economies.

The summit was the occasion for Clinton to meet with Jiang Zemin, China's president, the highest-level contact between the countries since the Tianamen massacre in 1989.

Pow-wow time: Clinton plays host in an Indian longhouse near Seattle.

White minority rule ends in South Africa

Johannesburg, Thursday 18
The "birth of a new nation" was proclaimed here today following the signing by President de Klerk and Nelson Mandela of the constitutional agreement designed to wipe out apartheid and bring democracy to this troubled land. The leaders shook hands to seal the end of white minority rule, and parliament will meet next week to pass the agreements into law.

When the transitional executive council begins work in two weeks, blacks will have access to executive power for the first time in the history of South Africa. (→ Dec. 7)

Nov. 18. Anti-Nazi militants destroy the memorial to Rudolph Hess, Hitler's deputy, just hours after its secret site at Eaglesham, near Glasgow, is revealed.

Large drop recorded in U.K. jobless rate

London, Thursday 18
There was more economic good news for the government today when it was announced that the number of unemployed in Britain had fallen by 49,000 – the biggest monthly drop in over four and a half years. The total is now 2,855,100.

Prime Minister Major hailed the fall as further evidence that Britain stands at the threshold of a "long period of growth with low inflation." Employment Secretary David Hunt attributed the improvement to Britain's "flexible and deregulated labor market." Tory backbenchers greeted the news with cheers.

Nov. 18. The Louvre Museum's Richelieu wing opens to the public after being entirely redesigned by American architect I.M. Pei, at a cost of more than $200 million. The wing's twin glass-covered courtyards house 12,000 paintings and sculptures, including Egyptian, Persian and French works.

November

1993

Su	Mo	Tu	We	Th	Fr	Sa
	1	2	3	4	5	6
7	8	9	10	11	12	13
14	15	16	17	18	19	20
21	22	23	24	25	26	27
28	29	30				

Italy, 21
The neo-fascist Italian Social Movement, the Democratic Party of the Left and the Northern League are the main winners of the first round of mayoral elections. (→ Dec. 6)

New York, 22
Britain wins six International Emmy Awards; the BBC's *Unnatural Pursuits* takes the drama category.

London, 23
Graham Taylor, manager of the England soccer squad, resigns following his team's elimination from the 1994 World Cup.

Europe, 23
Icy temperatures are blamed for 34 deaths.

U.K., 25
Police seize a huge consignment of arms and explosives destined for the Loyalist paramilitary group Ulster Volunteer Force.

Germany, 26
The Kurdish Workers Party, a leftist anti-Turkish group, is banned.

Hong Kong, 28
The latest round of Sino-British talks on the colony's future ends without agreement. (→ Dec. 16)

Mexico City, 29
Luis Murrieta is picked to succeed President Carlos Salinas de Gortari.

U.K., 29
Eton College appoints its first foreign headmaster since its founding in 1440: New Zealander John Lewis.

Geneva, 30
A new round of peace talks on Bosnia stalls as Bosnian Serbs and Croats reject Muslim demands. (→ Dec. 3)

London, 30
Former President George Bush is made an honorary Knight of the Order of the Bath.

U.K., 30
The Budget calls for £1.75 billion in new taxes next year.

Washington, D.C., 30
Mickey Kantor, the U.S. trade representative, says he is confident there will be an accord in the GATT talks within two weeks. (→ Dec. 15)

Boys found guilty of toddler's murder

Preston, Wednesday 24
At the end of a harrowing trial, two 11-year-old boys, the youngest murderers in modern British legal history, were found guilty of killing two-year-old James Bulger and ordered to be detained for "very, very many years."

The boys lured the toddler away from his mother during a shopping trip. They proceeded to drag him through Liverpool before beating and stoning him to death on a railway line. It emerged during the trial that a number of people saw the weeping, bruised boy but took no effective action.

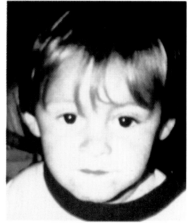
James Bulger was battered to death.

Throughout the trial, the boys had been known as Child A and Child B, but the judge, Michael Morland, today gave permission for their names, Jon Venables and Robert Thompson, to be revealed.

The judge put forward his theory on this "act of unparalleled evil and barbarity" that shocked and confounded the nation: "How it came about that two mentally normal boys committed this terrible crime is hard to comprehend. It isn't for me to pass judgment on their upbringings, but I suspect that exposure to violent video films may in part be an explanation."

Pete Sampras aced out by Michael Stich

Frankfurt, Sunday 21
Michael Stich won the ATP Tour World Championship with an ace to Pete Sampras. In fact, the ace that won the final point was one of 27 he served in his 7-6 (7-3), 2-6, 7-6 (9-7), 6-2 victory. Sampras began badly, making unforced errors. He came back in the second set, but after the end of the third, there was little hope for him. "When I lost that third set tie-breaker, the air kind of went out of the balloon," he said. "And then he probably aced me eight or nine times in that last set." In fact, it was 12. Stich's victory pushed him up in the ATP rankings past Jim Courier to take the number two spot.

1993 ATP rankings

1.	Pete Sampras (USA)	4,126
2.	Michael Stich (GER)	3,445
3.	Jim Courier (USA)	3,390
4.	Sergi Bruguera (SPA)	2,590
5.	Stefan Edberg (SWE)	2,571
6.	A. Medvedev (UKR)	2,415
7.	Goran Ivanisevic (CRO)	2,186
8.	Michael Chang (USA)	2,154
9.	Thomas Muster (AUT)	2,033
10.	Cedric Pioline (FRA)	2,012
11.	Boris Becker (GER)	1,958
12.	Petr Korda (CZE)	1,742
13.	Todd Martin (USA)	1,695
14.	M. Gustafsson (SWE)	1,586
15.	R. Krajicek (NET)	1,572

Uproar in Germany over car crash tests

Germany, Wednesday 24
"Professor Horror. He Did Car Tests Using Dead Children" screamed the front page of today's *Bild*, a tabloid newspaper. The German Automobile Club and the Vatican condemned using cadavers in crash tests as unethical. Heidelberg University admits that dead bodies were used in tests but insists that relatives gave permission. Cadavers are used in the U.S., too, and one scientist said the practice has been going on for 50 years. Researchers insist the tests are necessary to save lives. "At what point in a crash do ribs break?" asked one. "There is no way to know that except to test ribs."

Nov. 22. Americans today mark the 30th anniversary of President John F. Kennedy's assassination in Dallas, Texas.

Brady bill passes

The bill is named after James Brady.

Washington, D.C., Wednesday 24
Concern about violent crime has reached a point where the influence of the powerful National Rifle Association could no longer prevent passage of gun-control legislation. Filibusters by opponents to the Brady bill ended Saturday, when 16 Republicans added their votes to the Democrats' 47, enough to get the 60 votes needed to end debate on the bill.

"How sweet it is," said James Brady, the Reagan aide who was wounded in a 1981 assassination attempt on the president and for whom the bill is named, after it was enacted by the Senate today. The bill imposes a five-day waiting period during which background checks will be made on handgun purchasers and authorizes spending $200 million a year to set up a computerized system to perform the checks.

Author Burgess dies

London, Thursday 25
The death of an author of fierce intellect, a gifted composer and a remarkable linguist was announced today. Anthony Burgess (*Feb. 25, 1917) died of cancer on Monday.

He will be remembered best for his prophetic novel, *A Clockwork Orange* (1962), but it only became a best-seller after the successful and highly controversial film by Stanley Kubrick was released nine years later. His attitude towards Britain was one of contempt, accusing it of philistinism and corruption, but he had grudgingly assumed the mantle of the grand old man of English letters. Though he won neither the Nobel nor Booker prize, he was more highly regarded than many more fashionable prize-winners.

Outcry over secret contacts with IRA

London, Monday 29
Sir Patrick Mayhew, the Northern Ireland Secretary, easily fought off demands for his resignation and responded defiantly to the furor over his secret contacts with the IRA. These long-running discussions were revealed by *The Observer* yesterday.

Sir Patrick met fierce opposition from hardline Unionists when he explained his position to the House of Commons. Ian Paisley was suspended from the House for calling him a liar. Sir Patrick received a sympathetic hearing from most members, who are only too anxious to find a way out of the Ulster

Tensions remain high in Belfast.

quagmire. They agreed that the government had a duty to respond to peace overtures, but they were startled to learn that Major's peace proposals had moved so far and that he was ready for exploratory talks with the IRA's political wing, Sinn Fein. Talks could be held as early as January if the IRA renounces violence.

In Belfast, Sinn Fein bitterly denied the contacts had started with a message from the IRA which said that the "conflict is over." Gerry Adams of Sinn Fein accused Sir Patrick of squandering the best chance for peace in 25 years and said he told repeated lies. (→ Dec. 3)

Kohl's presidential nominee quits race

Bonn, Thursday 25
Chancellor Kohl's nominee for president has dropped out of the race after critics said his views were too close to those of extremist groups. A furious Kohl said, "The intolerable campaign of personal attacks and slander against Steffen Heitmann in recent months disgraced all who took part in it." Heitmann, whose bid was backed by neo-Nazis, has said that women should spend more time at home, that Germany was being overrun by foreigners and that it was time that Germans put the holocaust "in perspective."

Gaza Strip rocked by new wave of violence

Gaza Strip, Tuesday 30
Two weeks before Israeli troops are scheduled to begin withdrawal from Gaza and Jericho, fighting here recalls the violent days of the *intifada*. Palestinian youths throwing stones at Israeli soldiers were fired upon. Dozens were wounded and a teenage boy died. The fighting springs from the army's hunt for members of the Fatah Hawks, a PLO armed group; Palestinians see the manhunt as a violation of a cease-fire agreed in September. Fatah officials said tonight that an agreement has been reached with the army – the hunt will be called off and the Hawks will abide by the cease-fire. (→ Dec. 10)

Militants vow to continue intifada.

Dr. Death in jail, will go on hunger strike

Royal Oak, Michigan, Tuesday 30
Jack Kevorkian says he doesn't want anyone to pay his bail and that he will starve himself in jail unless the $50,000 bond is not dismissed. The retired pathologist, who has helped 19 terminally ill people commit suicide since 1990, was jailed today on a third charge of breaking Michigan's assisted suicide law. A Michigan judge has struck down the law, but it remains in effect until the Court of Appeals reviews it.

Kevorkian was jailed earlier this month and started a hunger strike in protest of the bail in that arrest. He was released after an opponent put up $2,000 to get him out.

Nov. 27. New Zealand's mighty All Blacks are humbled by the England XV, 15-9, at Twickenham for the first time in 10 years.

Nov. 28. Actor Ruben Blades, who starred in "The Two Jakes," is the presidential candidate of Panama's Mother Earth party.

Nov. 28. Jamaica's Lisa Hanna, aged 18, is elected Miss World 1993, beating South African beauty Jacqueline Mokofeng.

December
1993

Su	Mo	Tu	We	Th	Fr	Sa
			1	2	3	4
5	6	7	8	9	10	11
12	13	14	15	16	17	18
19	20	21	22	23	24	25
26	27	28	29	30	31	

Washington, D.C., 1
Following yesterday's lifting of the ban on women serving on U.S. Navy ships, the Pentagon says it plans to deploy up to 500 women aboard carriers next year; slacks, not skirts, will be standard attire.

Haiti, 1
Prime Minister Robert Malval says he will resign by the end of the year. (→ 22)

Geneva, 1
Georgian and Abkhaz representatives sign an accord aimed at ending the conflict in Georgia.

Isle of Wight, 1
A 12-year-old boy becomes the youngest person in British legal history to be charged with rape.

U.S., 1
Mother Teresa and Billy Graham top the annual *Good Housekeeping* list of most admired people, ahead of Hillary and Bill Clinton.

Sweden, 2
A planned merger between the auto firms Volvo (Sweden) and Renault (France) falls through.

Cape Canaveral, 2
The space shuttle *Endeavour* blasts off on a mission to repair the Hubble Space Telescope. (→ 10)

U.S., 3
The jobless rate fell to 6.4% in November, a three-year low.

Sarajevo, 3
At least three civilians are killed and 16 injured by artillery shells. (→ 9)

Vatican, 4
Pope John Paul II condemns "persistent racism" in the U.S., calling it an "intolerable injustice."

Manila, 4
Chinese athletes win a total of 23 gold medals, well ahead of second-placed South Korea (3 golds) at the Asian Games.

Monte Carlo, 4
Furniture and objects belonging to couturier Hubert de Givenchy are auctioned for a record $26 million.

DEATH

2. Pyotr Grushin, Soviet rocket expert (*Jan. 15, 1906).

Colombian drug lord Pablo Escobar dies in a hail of gunfire

Medellin, Thursday 2
The short, violent life of one of the world's most wanted men ended brutally today, as crack Colombian police units pumped round after round into 44-year-old drug lord Pablo Escobar.

The boss of the notorious Medellin drug cartel, who had been on the run since July 1992, died with a gun in each hand. He was wanted for scores of murders and cocaine trafficking. Police were able to trace him to a house in his hometown through phone taps. Escobar's end may however have little effect on the drug problem – the rival Cali cartel is sure to take up any slack.

The cocaine boss died in a Medellin rooftop shootout with security forces.

Unhappy Princess of Wales stuns Britons

Diana sadly announces her decision.

London, Friday 3
Princess Diana arrived at the London Hilton today for what was billed as a routine charity luncheon. By the time she left, Britain was in a state of shock. The 32-year-old estranged wife of the Prince of Wales had announced her decision to drastically curtail her public life.

"I hope you can find it in your hearts to understand and give me the time and space that has been lacking in recent years," Diana, close to tears, said.

She has been the target of increasingly intrusive media attention, culminating in last month's publication of photos of her working out at a private gym. (→16)

U.K., Irish premiers discuss Ulster peace

Dublin, Friday 3
The search for peace in Ulster failed to make progress today, despite seven hours of talks between British Prime Minister John Major and his Irish counterpart, Albert Reynolds.

The two men, who met at Dublin Castle, clashed repeatedly over recent disclosures about secret contacts between Britain and the IRA. Reynolds told Major that he resented having been kept in the dark about these talks.

The two leaders however agreed to continue their efforts to establish what they termed a "framework for peace" in Northern Ireland. (→15)

Dec. 1. A 22-meter condom is draped over the obelisk in Paris's Place de la Concorde early today to mark World AIDS Day.

Rocker Zappa dies

Los Angeles, Saturday 4
When Frank Zappa (*Dec. 21, 1940) was asked by his mom what he would like for his 15th birthday, he chose to make a long-distance phone call to Edgard Varèse in New York City. He had fallen in love with a record of the composer's work – the fact that he looked like a "mad scientist" in the picture on the sleeve was an added attraction. Zappa's first love was rhythm and blues, and those two musical influences informed his work ever after. Complexity, perverse (and often scatalogical) humor, intelligence and sarcasm were the primary ingredients. In addition to his 60-odd rock albums, including *Freak Out!* and *Jazz from Hell*, he composed orchestral works, such as *Yellow Shark* and *Naval Aviation in Art?*

Su	Mo	Tu	We	Th	Fr	Sa
			1	2	3	4
5	6	7	8	9	10	11
12	13	14	15	16	17	18
19	20	21	22	23	24	25
26	27	28	29	30	31	

Vienna, 5
Mayor Helmut Zilk, a critic of extreme rightists, is injured by a letter bomb, the fifth such attack in three days.

Dusseldorf, 5
Germany defeats Australia in the Davis Cup final.

Venezuela, 5
Rafael Rodriguez, aged 77, is elected president.

Paris, 6
American animal rights activists call for an end to France's foie gras trade.

South Africa, 7
The Transitional Executive Council, a multiracial body that will prepare the country's first universal-suffrage elections, is installed. (→ 22)

Twickenham, England, 7
Oxford beat Cambridge, 20-8, in the 112th annual university rugby match.

Washington, D.C., 7
Energy Department reveals that the U.S. carried out 204 previously unannounced nuclear tests between 1945 and 1990.

Washington, D.C., 8
Residents are told to boil drinking water because of a dangerous parasite.

Algeria, 9
A growing number of foreigners, who are facing death threats from Islamic militants, are fleeing the country. (→ 14)

Sarajevo, 9
Eight civilians are killed by sniper fire and shelling. (→ 17)

Sangatte, France, 10
Builders of the Channel Tunnel officially hand over its keys to the operators, Eurotunnel.

Tunis, 10
U.S. Secretary of State Warren Christopher meets Yasser Arafat to discuss the planned Israeli withdrawal from Jericho and the Gaza Strip. (→ 13)

DEATHS

7. Félix Houphouët-Boigny, president of Ivory Coast (*Oct. 18, 1905).

8. Daisy Adams, Britain's oldest person (*1880).

Italian voters give former Communists a boost in five major cities

Rome's mayor, Francesco Rutelli.

Rome, Monday 6
Italy turned its back on neo-fascism in yesterday's local elections. Alessandra Mussolini, granddaughter of Il Duce, was defeated in the race for mayor of Naples by Antonio Bassolini of the former Communist Democratic Party of the Left. In Rome, thousands of supporters of the Green activist Francesco Rutelli, the "Bill Clinton of Rome," danced in the streets in celebration of his victory over Gianfranco Fini of the neo-fascist Italian Social Movement.

The routed Mussolini was defiant: "The reds have won. But I have not renounced my ambitions. I am going to try again next time."

Duce's granddaughter lost in Naples.

Dec. 6. From the Berlin Wall to cell walls for Communist East Germany's celebrated spymaster, Markus Wolf, aged 70, who was sentenced to six years in prison.

Life is made easier for Sunday shoppers

London, Wednesday 8
The muddle over Sunday-shopping laws, which has lasted for 40 years, ended today when the Commons voted to permit large stores to open for six hours every Sunday. Small shops will be able to stay open all day. MPs were allowed to vote according to their consciences and not their parties, and despite the determined efforts of the Keep Sunday Special campaign, the measure to legalize what has become common practice was passed by a comfortable 75-vote majority. High street traders are now preparing themselves for a Sunday price war.

Danny Blanchflower dies at the age of 67

London, Thursday 9
Danny Blanchflower (*Feb. 10, 1926), the inspirational captain of Tottenham Hotspurs who was capped 56 times for Northern Ireland, died today of Alzheimer's disease.

He always seemed too frail for the hurly burly of the football field, but he was a player of intellect and marshalled Spurs to become the first club this century to win the League and Cup double. His team talks were sometimes not fully understood by all of his players, though. His playing days over, he became a much respected and fearless sports columnist.

Pro golf rankings

Professional Golf Association rankings as of Dec. 5 (by average points earned per game):

1.	Nick Faldo (GBR)	21.51
2.	Greg Norman (AUS)	19.45
3.	Bernhard Langer (GER)	17.11
4.	Nick Price (ZIM)	15.89
5.	Paul Azinger (USA)	14.87
6.	Fred Couples (USA)	14.81
7.	Ian Woosnam (GBR)	11.69
8.	Tom Kite (USA)	10.39
9.	Davis Love III (USA)	9.91
10.	Corey Pavin (USA)	9.64
11.	David Frost (SAF)	9.51
12.	Masashi Ozaki (JAP)	9.28
13.	Payne Stewart (USA)	9.25
14.	Jose Olazabal (SPA)	8.91
15.	C. Montgomerie (GBR)	8.80

Dec. 6. Don Ameche (*May 31, 1908), who won an Oscar for his role in the 1985 fantasy movie "Cocoon," dies of cancer.

Top sports earnings

Incomes (in millions of dollars) of the world's highest paid athletes according to *Forbes* magazine:

1.	Michael Jordan, basketball	36
2.	Riddick Bowe, boxing	25
3.	Ayrton Senna, Formula 1	18.5
4.	Alain Prost, Formula 1	16
5.	George Foreman, boxing	15.8
6.	S. O'Neal, basketball	15.2
7.	Lennox Lewis, boxing	15
8.	Cecil Fielder, baseball	12.7
9.	Jim Courier, tennis	12.6
10.	Joe Montana, football	11.5
11.	Arnold Palmer, golf	11.1
12.	E. Holyfield, boxing	10.7
13.	Jack Nicklaus, golf	10.2
14.	E. Fittipaldi, Formula 1	10
15.	Steffi Graf, tennis	9.8

Gunman kills five on Long Island Express

Garden City, N.Y., Tuesday 7
A man filled with hate and frustration boarded a Long Island Rail Road evening commuter train in Jamaica, Queens. As the train approached Merillon Station here, he began firing at passengers with a 9mm semi-automatic Ruger. Five people were killed and 18 wounded.

Colin Ferguson, 35, a black man from Jamaica, carried with him four pages of rambling grievances blaming many of his troubles on whites, Asians and "Uncle Tom Negroes." When he stopped firing to reload, three men tackled him. They held him until the train pulled into the station and he was arrested.

NASA's space mechanics fix Hubble

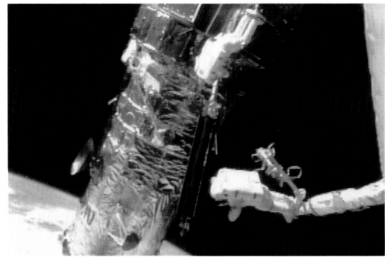

"Endeavour" astronauts replace the crippled telescope's faulty equipment.

Houston, Friday 10
As *Endeavour* passed 370 miles over the southern tip of Africa, the astronauts aboard commanded the robotic arm holding the Hubble Space Telescope to let it go. "Houston, we have a good release," announced Flight Commander Richard Covey.

His team had made five space walks, a NASA record, over the last few days. They replaced solar-power panels, added tiny mirrors to correct the focus of Hubble's faulty primary mirror and repaired the telescope's pointing system and main computer. The 43-foot-long, 24,000-pound telescope was launched in 1990 in order to study the origins of the universe. (→ 13)

Neo-Nazi arsonists get tough sentences

Schleswig, Germany, Wednesday 8
Two neo-Nazis were given the heaviest possible sentences here today for the murder of two Turkish girls and a grandmother in a firebomb attack on their hostel at Mölln, near Hamburg, in November 1992.

Michael Peters, 26, leader of a neo-Nazi gang, was jailed for life and Lars Christiansen, who is 20 and thus a juvenile offender, got 10 years. It was their firebomb which finally led the authorities to take firm action against the neo-Nazis. Now the extremists are threatening to exact vengeance.

Princeton physicists report fusion first

Plainsborough, N.J., Thursday 9
Science has moved a step closer to harnessing the power that drives the Sun. The Princeton University Plasma Physics Laboratory achieved a breakthrough in the complex field of controlled nuclear fusion. The giant Tokamak Fusion Test Reactor, as large as a five-story building, produced 3 million watts of power, almost twice as much as ever before. But six times as much energy was necessary to run the reactor. Scientists predict that fusion, safer than fission, could be a cheap supply of electric energy by the year 2040.

Three Britons freed by Saddam Hussein

Baghdad, Friday 10
Saddam Hussein has released three Britons held in the notorious Abu Gharib prison after former Prime Minister Edward Heath intervened on their behalf.

There is little doubt that the three men, Simon Dunn, Michael Wainwright and Paul Ride, given long sentences for illegally entering Iraq, were political hostages. The British government insists that no deal was made to secure their release. Ride and Wainwright flew to London tonight and Dunn, 24 today, was flying to his parents' home in Dubai.

Dec. Kevin Costner plays an escaped convict who kidnaps a boy in a film directed by Clint Eastwood, "A Perfect World."

Dec. 8. Fans of the late rock great Jim Morrison gather in Paris's Père Lachaise cemetery to mark the 50th anniversary of their idol's birth.

Dec. A new, neo-Classical look for the family quarters at the White House following a $396,429 facelift entirely financed by private donations.

December
1993

Su	Mo	Tu	We	Th	Fr	Sa
			1	2	3	4
5	6	7	8	9	10	11
12	13	14	15	16	17	18
19	20	21	22	23	24	25
26	27	28	29	30	31	

Portugal, 12
The opposition Socialist Party defeats the governing Social Democratic Party in local elections.

China, 12
For the fifth time in a month, an airliner is hijacked to Taiwan.

London, 12
Olympic 100-meter champion Linford Christie is voted BBC Sports Personality of 1993.

Addis Ababa, 12
Peace talks between rival Somali factions break down. (→ 17)

Palermo, Sicily, 12
FBI director Louis Freeh vows to root out Mafia criminals "from the dark places where they hide."

Cape Canaveral, 13
Endeavour lands after a successful mission.

London, 14
Yasser Arafat makes his first official visit to Britain.

Algeria, 14
Islamic militants kill 12 Croatian and Bosnian workers. (→ 17)

London, 15
The government approves plans for a nuclear-fuel reprocessing plant.

South Korea, 16
Lee Hoi Chang is appointed prime minister.

China, 17
Beijing slams a BBC documentary about Mao Zedong that includes revelations about the late Chinese leader's preference for sex with young girls. (→ 26)

Bosnia, 17
Warring factions agree on a cease-fire from Dec. 23 to Jan. 3. (→ 19)

DEATHS

12. Jozsef Antall, Hungarian premier (*April 8, 1932).

15. Ratu Sir Penaia Ganilau, president of Fiji (*Jul. 28, 1918).

16. Kakuei Tanaka, Japanese politician (*May 4, 1918).

18. Sam Wanamaker, U.S. actor-director (*June 14, 1919).

Russia's electorate stuns the world

Moscow, Sunday 12
The threat of fascism looms over Russia with the triumph of the misnamed Liberal Democratic Party in the elections for the new parliament.

Led by the ranting demagogue Vladimir Zhirinovsky, the LDP is fascist in everything but name. "Mad Vlad," derided as a buffoon, won support from the working class and the frustrated military, who have gained nothing from Yeltsin's economic reforms. Tonight, he is parading triumphantly round a post-election party, sneering at his ene-

Zhirinovsky is an ultra-nationalist.

mies. His election program was so outlandish that most foreign observers ignored him. He promised free vodka, prosperity and an expansion of Russia so that its soldiers would fulfill the old czarist dream of washing their boots in the warm waters of the Indian Ocean. Although he is reputed to be of Jewish origin, he is violently anti-Semitic.

There is the taint of the Weimar Republic and Adolph Hitler about these events. The only comfort for Yeltsin is that the voters approved his new constitution. (→ 21)

Chile's new president calls for civilian rule

Eduardo Frei's father was president of the nation from 1964 to 1970.

Santiago, Sunday 12
Christian Democrat Eduardo Frei has won a landslide victory in the Chilean presidential election. Standing as the candidate of the ruling center-left coalition, he won 58% of the vote, more than twice that won by his nearest rival, conservative Arturo Alessandri.

The new president appealed for national unity tonight, telling his celebrating supporters, "I will be a president for all Chileans, with no exception." Frei, 51, son of the late President Eduardo Frei, has promised to amend the constitutional rule which bars the president from sacking the former dictator, General Augusto Pinochet, from his post as army commander.

Dec. 14. Myrna Loy (*Aug. 2, 1905), who died in New York today, achieved stardom with the 1934 movie "The Thin Man."

Mideast accord stalls as violence continues

Israel, Monday 13
Record numbers of Israeli troops are deployed in the Occupied Territories on the day the soldiers were to begin withdrawing as provided by the accord signed by Israel and the PLO in September. The two parties were not able to come to an agreement on the boundaries of a Palestinian-ruled Jericho, on control of border crossings nor on security arrangements for Jewish settlers.

The delay of the pull-out was announced late last night by Yitzhak Rabin and Yasser Arafat after their meeting in Cairo. Despite their fears of a repeat of the violence that shook the country two weeks ago, the two leaders decided that these issues should be settled first. (→ 24)

On the Gaza Strip, young Palestinians harass Israeli security forces.

Pentagon post goes to Bobby Ray Inman

Washington, D.C., Thursday 16
Defense Secretary Les Aspin announced yesterday that he will step down, saying that he had decided it was "time for a break." Washington insiders believe the resignation came at Clinton's request, but the president said that it was Aspin who asked to go. Aspin has been criticized for his handling of military policy, especially in Somalia, and for a lack of organization. Today, Clinton picked intelligence expert Bobby Ray Inman, 62, to succeed Aspin in the post. The new Pentagon boss, who described himself as an "operator," is not expected to bring major changes to current military policy.

Ulster peace agreement

Premiers John Major and Albert Reynolds appeal to the men of violence.

London, Wednesday 15

John Major and Albert Reynolds, the prime ministers of Britain and Ireland, today signed an historic declaration designed to bring peace to Northern Ireland. Standing in front of a Christmas tree in Downing Street, they urged the terrorists to grasp the opportunity for peace, saying another may not come their way. The declaration, agreed after much hard bargaining, holds out the prospect of Sinn Fein joining talks on the future of the province, if the IRA renounces violence forever. It was generally welcomed in Westminster, although the unionist firebrand Ian Paisley denounced it out of hand. The question of war or peace is now in the unpredictable hands of the men of violence, republican and unionist. (→ 19)

GATT deal signed at last

Trade negotiators worked for seven long years to hammer out today's accord.

Geneva, Wednesday 15

Seven years of grinding, sometimes ferocious, negotiations ended here today with the bang of a mahogany gavel. The 117 nations involved in the Uruguay Round of the General Agreement on Tariffs and Trade came to an agreement on the most ambitious commitments on open trade ever made. The director-general of GATT, Peter Sutherland, said the treaty would mean "more trade, more investment, more jobs and larger income growth for all."

The negotiations have been marked by wrangling over French attempts to keep their agricultural subsidies and American attempts to increase U.S. access to French movie screens and television stations.

Algerian extremists make their demands

Bonn, Friday 17

The Islamic Salvation Front today laid down its terms for ending the civil strife in Algeria. More than 2,000 people, including President Mohammed Boudiaf, have been killed since 1992, when the military-backed ruling council took power and annulled elections which the Islamists seemed sure to win.

Rabah Kebir, spokesman in exile for the outlawed organization, demanded at a press conference that all political prisoners be freed and all laws passed since the council took power be repealed. He denied that the ISF was behind the recent killings of foreigners in Algeria but failed to condemn those responsible.

Anti-terrorist forces are on red alert.

Beijing gets tough over Hong Kong bill

Hong Kong, Thursday 16

China, furious at Governor Chris Patten's presentation of a political-reform bill for the colony, is threatening to act against the burgeoning trade between China and Britain.

Beijing's foreign ministry spokesman today blamed Britain for "clinging obstinately to its own course" and "sabotaging talks," thus souring bilateral ties to an extent that "will certainly affect Sino-British relations, including economic and trade ties." The threat is thought to refer to multi-million dollar projects for subways and power stations. (→ 17)

Time to go home for U.S. units in Somalia

Mogadishu, Friday 17

"It's hard when you come here to feed people and you wind up fighting for your life," said the commander of the U.S forces in Somalia, Maj. Gen. Thomas Montgomery.

U.S. combat troops began their withdrawal from the country today; some support units and the aircraft carrier *America* have already left. The deaths of 18 soldiers in a failed October raid to capture some of General Aidid's top aides was one of the major factors which led to President Clinton's decision to pull out. The withdrawal is scheduled to be completed by next March. (→ 20)

Dec. 15. A Paris appeals court rules that the fashion czar Yves Saint-Laurent can no longer use the name "Champagne" in France on his $120-a-bottle perfume.

Dec. 16. Princess Diana attends her last official public appearance; she has vowed to dedicate her time to her family.

December

1993

Su	Mo	Tu	We	Th	Fr	Sa
			1	2	3	4
5	6	7	8	9	10	11
12	13	14	15	16	17	18
19	20	21	22	23	24	25
26	27	28	29	30	31	

Altlandsberg, Germany, 19
Ravindra Gujjula, an Indian-born immigrant, is elected mayor.

Londonderry, 19
Several people are injured by an IRA bomb attack. (→ 21)

Bonn, 20
The government says all German troops are to be pulled out of Somalia by March 31, 1994.

Moscow, 21
President Yeltsin abolishes the Security Ministry, successor to the KGB. (→ 25)

Belfast, 21
Sinn Fein leader Gerry Adams calls for "direct and unconditional" talks with Britain and Ireland. (→ 27)

U.S., 22
Wal-Mart, the nation's largest retailer, says it will stop selling handguns over the counter. (→ 31)

Washington, D.C., 22
Exiled President Jean-Bertrand Aristide rejects a bid by the U.S. to open talks with Haiti's military regime.

London, 23
The Stock Exchange index closes at a record high of 3,396.50 points.

Europe, 25
At least seven people die as heavy rain causes flooding in much of northern France, Germany and Belgium.

Russia, 25
Final results of the Dec. 12 elections give Yegor Gaidar's Russia's Choice Party 96 seats in the 450-seat Duma, the parliament's lower house, while Vladimir Zhirinovsky's Liberal Democratic Party won 70 seats and the Communists 65. (→ 28)

London, 25
In her Christmas message, the Queen hopes 1994 will bring peace to Northern Ireland.

Sarajevo, 25
Despite a cease-fire, Serb forces fire more than 1,300 artillery rounds at the city, killing six civilians. (→ 29)

DEATH

24. Norman Vincent Peale, American preacher and author (*May 31, 1898).

Serbia's Milosevic tightens grip on power

Now less likely to seek compromise.

Belgrade, Sunday 19
Serbia's ruling Socialist Party, led by President Slobodan Milosevic, has won a stunning victory in today's general election. Early returns indicated the four main opposition parties would outnumber the Socialists, but as the results came in it became obvious that Milosevic will command a comfortable majority in parliament. His victory, won in the teeth of 250,000% inflation and economic hardship caused by international sanctions, has shocked his foes. Opposition leader Vuk Draskovic commented: "There is no rational explanation. It is in the sphere of the irrational." (→ 25)

Killer of gays sentenced to life in prison

London, Monday 20
Colin Ireland, a failed petty criminal who brought terror to London's gay community, was given five life sentences at the Old Bailey today after admitting the murder of five homosexual men. He picked up his victims in pubs, then strangled and suffocated them after tying, beating and, at times, torturing them. Ireland, six feet tall and heavily built, made taunting telephone calls to the police in which he said he wanted to be a serial killer and threatened to "kill one a week." The judge told him, "You are an exceptionally frightening and dangerous man. To take one human life is outrageous. To take five is carnage."

Colin Ireland admits five killings.

Bill Clinton rejects allegations of infidelity

The First Lady stands by her man.

Washington, D.C., Wednesday 22
The Clintons are again in the position of denying stories that the president has had numerous extramarital affairs. Two Arkansas state troopers say Clinton offered them jobs to keep quiet about what they know. They say that they arranged liaisons for Bill and helped hide the truth from Hillary. Yesterday, Hillary said the men were after financial gain, and today the president said: "That absolutely did not happen."

The president is also under scrutiny for his ties to James McDougal, owner of a failed Arkansas savings and loan association. He is accused of using funds from the S&L to help Clinton pay off old campaign debts.

'I'm innocent ...'

"Don't treat me like a criminal."

Santa Ynez, Calif., Wednesday 22
Michael Jackson, fighting back tears, denied that he had sexually molested a 13-year-old boy in a four-minute speech broadcast live on television throughout the world.

He described an examination by criminal investigators, in which photographs were taken of his genitals, as a "horrifying nightmare." The results of the examination could be used to verify the boy's description of discoloring spots on Jackson's skin. He had said that he suffers from a skin disease that causes such effects in a TV interview with Oprah Winfrey earlier in the year.

The singer also decried the treatment of the story by the "terrible mass media" and said, "I ask all of you to wait to hear the truth before you label or condemn me."

'Mad Vlad': Russia has a superweapon

Reichenfels, Austria, Wednesday 22
Vladimir Zhirinovsky, leader of Russia's neo-fascists, today claimed that Russia had a secret weapon called the Elipton which had "the capacity to annihilate the whole world." He claimed that only Russia has the weapon, which cannot be detected and against which there is "no defense." On his first trip abroad since his success in the parliamentary elections, "Mad Vlad" is staying with a former Waffen SS elite Nazi soldier. Western experts are skeptical of his claims but think Elipton may have been part of Russia's "Star Wars" research. (→ 28)

Centuries of white rule end in South Africa

Extremist Afrikaner groups see the new constitution as a mortal threat.

Johannesburg, Wednesday 22
The South African parliament voted itself out of existence by 237 to 45 today in a move certain to lead to black majority rule after the first all-race election next April. President de Klerk, architect of the reforms, said: "We have embarked on a new Great Trek. By accepting a new constitution, we took South Africa over the threshold of history into a new era, with all its dangers." He said the next parliament would remove "the albatross of injustice, exclusion and discrimination." The move was bitterly opposed by white suprema-cists, and there are threats of violence from the Afrikaner Volks-front, who had hoped their demand for a white homeland would be written into the constitution. (→ 30)

Dec. 25. Barely a week after his wedding to Barbara Feltus, Boris Becker causes a storm when he claims that drug use is rampant in world-class tennis; the charge is vehemently denied by the ATP.

Australia's aborigines get land rights back

Aboriginal land rights were abolished by colonists more than 200 years ago.

Fidel Castro's daughter, Alina, flees to U.S.

Washington, D.C., Wednesday 22
The day after her daughter's 16th-birthday party, Alina Fernandez Revuelta disguised herself, took a faked Spanish passport and left Cuba for Spain. On her arrival yesterday, she asked for political asylum in the U.S. and flew to Atlanta. The State Department confirmed today that Fernandez, Fidel Castro's daughter, had defected. She had stopped using her father's name as a teenager and has described him as a tyrant. The Cuban government had turned down a request from the former fashion model in the 1980s to emigrate with her Mexican husband to his country. (→ 27)

The Lider Maximo's daughter is 38.

Palestinian group murders Israeli officer

Gaza Strip, Friday 24
One of Israel's highest-ranking officers in the Gaza Strip, Lt. Col. Meir Mintz, was killed in an ambush today. The three or four armed men who staged the attack escaped. An Israeli army commander and two soldiers were wounded, and a Palestinian bystander was killed in the cross-fire that followed.

The Islamic fundamentalist group Hamas claimed responsibility for the ambush in a tract distributed later. The text said the attack was carried out by "Special Unit No. 12, of the martyr Imad Akel." Imad Akel was a member of Hamas who had been killed by the special forces coordinated by Mintz.

Israeli troops on alert in Gaza Strip.

Canberra, Wednesday 22
Aborigines celebrated tonight after the Australian government voted to enshrine their rights to land lost when Europeans colonized Australia more than 200 years ago.

The decision, fiercely opposed by mining companies, came when two members of the Green Party, who hold the balance of power in the Senate, voted for the Native Title Bill, which will allow Australia's original inhabitants to press claims to as much as a tenth of the huge country. Prime Minister Paul Keating said the bill recognized the right of the indigenous people to their own soil, but opposition leader John Hewson warned him that foreign investment would be endangered: "In doing this deal, you sold out all Australians."

U.N.'s chief on first visit to North Korea

Pyongyang, Saturday 25
Butros Butros Ghali became the first U.N. leader to pass from South to North Korea, crossing the border on Christmas eve. The United Nations secretary-general told reporters, "Merry Christmas is about peace. Peace is the purpose of my goodwill visit."

More to the point, he is making the visit to try to convince the "Great Leader," Kim Il Sung, to stop refusing International Atomic Energy Agency inspections at sites where the U.S. believes nuclear material is being processed. He offered U.N. mediation in the dispute.

December

1993

Su	Mo	Tu	We	Th	Fr	Sa
			1	2	3	4
5	6	7	8	9	10	11
12	13	14	15	16	17	18
19	20	21	22	23	24	25
26	27	28	29	30	31	

France, 26
Authorities ban walking on hundreds of miles of Atlantic and Channel beaches after a Cypriot cargo ship spills thousands of detonators.

London, 26
Experts question the wisdom of fertility treatments for older women after a 59-year-old Briton gives birth to twins.

Berlin, 26
Marlene Dietrich's grave is desecrated by neo-Nazis.

Seattle, 26
An 11-year-old Angora cat inherits a $500,000 estate.

Havana, 27
President Castro says his granddaughter is free to join her mother, Alina Fernandez Revuelta, in the U.S.

Cairo, 27
Muslim militants open fire on a tourist bus wounding 16, including eight Austrians.

Northern Ireland, 27
The IRA launches a mortar attack on a police post just minutes after a 72-hour Christmas truce ends. (→ 29)

U.S., 27
Time magazine names Yasser Arafat, Yitzhak Rabin, Nelson Mandela and Frederik de Klerk 1993 Men of the Year.

Moscow, 28
The government says that nearly 50% of Russia's economy has been privatized.

Sofia, 28
Russian nationalist leader Vladimir Zhirinovsky is expelled from Bulgaria.

Khartoum, 30
Britain's ambassador is ordered to leave as the Archbishop of Canterbury begins a visit to southern Sudan.

Cape Town, 30
Black gunmen kill four whites in a restaurant.

London, 31
French premier Edouard Balladur is named Man of the Year by the *Financial Times*.

New York, 31
The pound is quoted at $1.48.

DEATH

28. William Shirer, U.S. author and journalist (*Feb. 23, 1904).

Bosnia's agony continues as 1993 ends

A few more refugees flee Sarajevo.

Sarajevo, Wednesday 29
Bosnia is undergoing its second bitter winter of fighting; a holiday cease-fire agreed last week between Muslims, Croats and Serbs has not been observed. Seven people were killed Monday in Serb shelling of Sarajevo. Hundreds have died in recent fighting between Muslims and Serbs, the Serbs being particularly hard hit, near the central Bosnian towns of Olovo and Teocak.

The evacuation begun yesterday of about 1,000 people, mainly women, children and elderly men, from Sarajevo was completed early this morning. For the most part, the refugees are headed for the Adriatic port of Split, Croatia.

IRA vows to fight on

Northern Ireland, Wednesday 29
The IRA has defiantly vowed to continue its armed struggle against the British presence in Ulster, thus rejecting the olive branch held out earlier this month by London.

In an end-of-year message, the IRA said that the British government "holds the key to peace," adding ominously that its struggle "has outlasted one British offensive after another." Yesterday, some 400 republican supporters met secretly to discuss the Dec. 15 joint Anglo-Irish declaration on peace in Ulster. Sources close to the IRA stressed that none of those present backed the accord in its current form.

Vatican-Israel pact

Jerusalem, Thursday 30
Representatives of the Holy See and Israel met here today to sign an historic accord aimed at ending centuries of often bitter animosity between Catholics and Jews.

The 14-point accord was painstakingly hammered out over the past 18 months. It paves the way for full diplomatic relations between the two states and was signed by Israeli Deputy Foreign Minister Yossi Beilin and his Vatican counterpart, Claudio Celli. Today's ceremony has also removed remaining obstacles to a visit to Jerusalem by Pope John Paul II, probably after Israel and the Vatican establish full ties next April.

America seeks solution to gun madness

12,489 handgun homicides last year.

U.S., Friday 31
Tonight, Times Square revellers are watching the giant ball descend to mark a new year. From tomorrow, they can follow a different, sobering count: the number of people shot dead in America. A "death clock" will show death-from-gunfire figures reported by federal agencies.

Another response to gun violence is the "Toys for Guns" operation begun by a New York businessman. He swapped $100 gift certificates from Toys R Us bought with his own money for each gun handed in. The toy retailer began to contribute to the program, and the idea is now spreading across the U.S.

Dec. 26. The cult of Mao is alive and well as millions of Chinese celebrate the 100th anniversary of the revolutionary's birth.

Dec. 31. The final countdown is on for next February's Winter Olympic Games in Lillehammer, Norway, the most northern site yet for a winter Olympiad. The overall cost of the stadiums and sports sites, which include a hollowed-out mountain housing an ice rink, stands at over $1.5 billion.

Jan. 15, Sammy Cahn

Born in New York, Cahn (*June 18, 1913) was a disappointment to his mother, who wanted him to be a doctor or lawyer. Instead, he played truant and became a violinist in Bowery burlesque houses, a career which led to four Academy Awards for writing a string of memorable songs such as "Come Fly with Me" and "Three Coins in the Fountain."

Jan. 30, Queen Alexandra

Alexandra (*March 25, 1921), born princess of Greece and Denmark, was a great-great-granddaughter of Queen Victoria. She married King Peter II of Yugoslavia in 1944 in London after the German occupation of Yugoslavia and spent the whole of her reign in exile.

Feb. 18, Leslie Norman

One of Britain's finest filmmakers, Norman (*Feb. 23, 1911) left school at 14 and swept floors at the Ealing Studios, where he learned his trade. After the war, in which he served in a secret sound unit, he directed a series of films, among them *The Cruel Sea* and *Dunkirk*. He had a remarkable visual memory.

March 3, Albert Sabin

Albert Sabin (*Aug. 26, 1906) became one of the world's great medical pioneers with his development of the oral vaccine for poliomyelitis. His cherry-flavored sweets, much easier to administer than the Salk injections, ended the scourge of polio. He was born in Bialystok – then in Russian Poland. His family emigrated to the U.S. in 1921.

March 4, Lord (Nicholas) Ridley

Nicholas Ridley (*Feb. 17, 1929) was an uncompromising Thatcherite who served in all three of her governments. In the House he was often abrasive, and it was his tendency towards indiscretion which destroyed his political career when he revealed his fears about a resurgent Germany to a journalist.

March 10, C. Northcote Parkinson

The multi-talented Professor Parkinson (*July 30, 1909), who was an author, historian and popular philosopher, achieved instant and lasting fame with his "Parkinson's Law" which stipulates that: "Work expands so as to fill the time available for its completion."

April 8, Marian Anderson

A true, vibrant contralto, Marian Anderson (*Feb. 17, 1902) struggled against poverty and racial prejudice to become the first black singer to appear at the Metropolitan Opera, opening the way for later generations of black singers. Her Lincoln Memorial concert in 1939, set up by Eleanor Roosevelt, is a landmark in the fight for equal rights.

April 20, Henry Brandon

Henry Brandon (*March 9, 1916), a Czech-born refugee, became a uniquely influential British correspondent in the U.S. Working for the *Sunday Times*, he was a confidante of President John F. Kennedy and many other U.S. leaders. Richard Nixon complimented him by tapping his telephone.

May 6, Ian Mikardo

Ian Mikardo (*July 9, 1908), an uncompromising socialist, was a Labour MP for 37 years and chairman of the party in 1970-71. He combined his socialism with a successful business career, specializing in East-West trade. A genial man who served as the House of Commons bookmaker, he was born in Portsmouth to a Polish father and a Ukrainian mother.

May 9, Penelope Gilliat

An accomplished writer – she scripted *Sunday, Bloody Sunday* – Gilliat (*March 25, 1932) is possibly better-known for the drama of her own life. She was the wife of Professor Roger Gilliat, best man at Princess Margaret's wedding, but soon after ran away with the playwright John Osborne. She then gained more notoriety by attacking the gossip columnists who hounded her.

May 13, Wolfgang Lotz

Lotz, born in Mannheim (*1921), was known as the "champagne spy." Posing as a former Afrika Korps officer, he infiltrated Egyptian military and government circles on behalf of Israeli intelligence. He led a rich life but was eventually caught and sentenced to life. He was freed in a prisoner exchange in 1968, but his champagne days were over. He died, penniless, in Munich.

May 26, Joseph Pulitzer, Jr.

Newspaper magnate, grandson of the founder of the Pulitzer Prize and son of the publisher of the *St. Louis Post Dispatch*, Joseph, Jr. (*May 13, 1913) was a professional journalist who maintained his family's determination to "illuminate dark places." He also had a passion for modern art and built an important collection.

May 27, Lord (Joseph) Gormley

Blunt-speaking Joe Gormley (*July 5, 1917) was a moderate but, as president of the National Union of Mineworkers, was forced by circumstances to lead the miners in two strikes which led to the downfall of the Heath government and, ultimately, to the crushing of the miners' power by Margaret Thatcher. Born into a mining family, he followed his father down the pit at the age of 14.

May 30, Sun Ra

This bandleader, arranger and keyboard wizard was born Herman Blount in Birmingham, Alabama (*ca. 1914). His claims that he was an angel, sometimes archangel, from outer space and his outlandish costumes set up a facade hiding what *The Times* called "one of the boldest, most innovatory and influential musicians in jazz history."

June 10, Les Dawson

Lugubrious, hated by feminists for his jokes about mothers-in-law, Les Dawson (*Feb. 2, 1933) was recognized as a genuine comic after failing as a writer in Paris, playing the piano in a brothel and serving a tough apprenticeship in the clubs of Northern England.

June 13, Donald K. Slayton

Deke Slayton (*March 1, 1924) was a World War II combat pilot who was chosen as one of the original Mercury Seven astronauts. A heart problem kept him from going into space on that project, but he recovered and participated in the 1975 joint U.S.-Soviet Apollo-Soyuz mission.

June 15, John Connally

"Big John" Connally (*Feb. 27, 1917), then governor of Texas, was seriously wounded when riding with Jack Kennedy on that fateful day in Dallas. He later became Nixon's treasury secretary in a career which took him from small town poverty to wealth and then bankruptcy, with debts of $93 million.

he many who died in 1993

June 22, Patricia Nixon
Born Thelma Catherine Ryan (*March 16, 1912), Pat was given her nickname by her father because she was born the eve of St. Patrick's Day. She chose the role of a tradi-ional wife and won respect for the toic way she remained smiling by Richard Nixon's side during good imes and bad, notably the Water-gate debacle. In poor health since the late '70s, she died of lung cancer.

July 6, Ruth Lady Fermoy

Lady Fermoy (*Oct. 2, 1908) was one of the Queen Mother's oldest and closest friends. When the Prince of Wales and her granddaughter, Lady Diana, became engaged, it was said that the grandmothers had a hand in the match. Ruth Sylvia Gill married the fourth Lord Fermoy in 1931. A music-lover, she founded he King's Lynn Festival in 1950.

July 18, Jean Negulesco
Jean Negulesco (*Feb. 26, 1900) left his native Romania at 14 to study painting in Paris. He went to the U.S. in 1927 and began working as an editor, decorator and assistant director in Hollywood. *Singapore Woman*, his first feature, was made in 1941. His other films include *How to Marry a Millionaire*, *Titanic* and *Three Coins in the Fountain*.

July 25, Margaret Duchess of Argyll
Ethel Margaret Whigham (*Dec. 1, 1912) was presented to London so-ciety in 1930, and her beauty quickly attracted the cameras of the press. Her second marriage, to the 11th Duke of Argyll, ended in scandal. Her fortunes declined afterward, and she ended her days living on an allowance from her first husband, U.S. businessman Charles Sweeny.

Sept. 16, Willie Mosconi
Mosconi (*June 21, 1913), the king of billiards (he never called it pool), combined astonishing skill with an image of refinement. His goal was to lift the game out of seedy dives and make it a respectable sport. He set many records, including sinking 526 straight balls in exhibition play in 1954 and 150 in a row in a perfect game in 1956. He was world champ-ion 13 times from 1941 to 1956.

Sept. 20, C.L. Sulzberger
Sulzberger (*Oct. 27, 1912), born into a famous publishing family, made his name travelling the globe, gaining access to the most influen-tial leaders of the post-war era. He joined *The New York Times* in 1939, was its chief foreign correspondant from 1944 to 1954 and wrote edit-orials until his retirement in 1978. He was the author of some two do-zen books, including memoirs and books on foreign policy and history.

Sept. 25, Bruno Pontecorvo
This Italian-born nuclear scientist (*Aug. 22, 1913) became a British citizen in 1948. Having disappeared in Italy in 1950, he surfaced in Mos-cow five years later and said that he had defected and was working on peaceful uses of atomic energy. He worked in a physics lab near Mos-cow from 1950 until his death.

Sept. 26, Nina Berberova
Berberova (*Aug. 8, 1901) was not well known, despite her immense tal-ent, until the 1980s. She left Russia in 1922 with the poet Vladislav Kho-dasevich, settling in France. She came to the U.S. in 1951 and taught at Yale and Princeton. *The Italics are Mine*, her memoirs, is probably her most read work, but her talent was best revealed in her *povesti*, or long stories, of the early 1990s.

Sept. 27, Jimmy Doolittle
Lt. Gen. James H. Doolittle (*Dec. 14, 1896) led the first air raid on Japan, less than five months after Pearl Harbor. The raid helped to lift spirits in the U.S. after Japanese victories in the early part of the war. Franklin Roosevelt awarded him the Medal of Honor on his return. After leaving the military, Doolittle was a vice president at Shell Oil and president of an aerospace company.

Oct. 7, Agnes de Mille
Agnes de Mille was a pioneer in Broadway choreography, raising dance in musicals to an art. She won Tonys for *Brigadoon* and *Kwamina* and worked on *Oklahoma!* She also worked often with the American Ballet Theater. Her father, William, and her famous uncle, Cecil, were filmmakers. She was guarded about her age, but a book about her family said she was born Sept. 18, 1905.

Oct. 7, Cyril Cusack
Cusak (*Nov. 26, 1910) devoted his life to the Irish stage but also acted in films and on TV. As a child, he acted in his family's touring com-pany. He joined the Abbey Theatre in 1932 and ran his own company from 1946 to 1961. Himself head of an acting family, he and his daugh-ters starred in *The Three Sisters* at the Gate Theatre in 1990.

Oct. 24, Lord (Joseph) Grimond
Jo Grimond (*July 29, 1913) re-vived the Liberal Party under his leadership from 1957 to 1967. His politics were based on his belief in the need to decentralize government and give more power to individuals and communities. He campaigned for proportional representation in parliament, to give smaller parties such as his a greater voice.

Oct. 31, River Phoenix

Phoenix (*Aug. 23, 1971) was just beginning to make a reputation as an exciting and versatile actor when he died from a drug overdose out-side Hollywood's Viper Room. His first acclaim came for *Stand by Me* in 1986. He showed a desire to go beyond typical Hollywood fare by playing a narcoleptic male prostitute in 1991's *My Own Private Idaho*.

Nov. 12, Harry Robbins Haldeman
Bob Haldeman (*Oct. 27, 1926) was Richard Nixon's chief of staff du-ring the 1968 campaign and until 1973, when he resigned during the furor over the Watergate scandal. Sentenced to 2 1/2 to 8 years for perjury, conspiracy and obstruction of justice in the affair, he served 18 months. In his 1978 book, *The Ends of Power*, he insisted that Nixon was behind the break-in and coverup.

Nov. 12, Jill Tweedie
Guardian columnist for 22 years, Tweedie (*May 22, 1934) was in the vanguard of the feminist movement. Her columns were impassioned but always elegantly written and ration-al. She learned of the motor neuron disease from which she died just after her autobiography, *Eating Children*, was published this year.

Dec. 7, Félix Houphouët-Boigny

Houphouët-Boigny (*Oct. 18, 1905) was the longest-serving head of state in Africa. He became his country's first president after leading Ivory Coast to independence from France in 1960. Though long revered as the father of his country, criticism of the leader had increased recently, especi-ally after he built an enormously ex-pensive basilica, Our Lady of Peace, in Yamoussoukro, his birthplace.

Dec. 15, Ratu Sir Penaia Ganilau
When two coups d'état took Fiji out of the Commonwealth in 1987, Ratu Sir Penaia Ganilau (*July 28, 1918), governor-general since 1983, at first refused to recognize the new regime and resigned his post. But in order to restore stability, he later accepted to become the republic's first presi-dent and remained in office until his death in Washington, D.C.

General Index

Page numbers in roman refer to texts. The ones in italic refer to chronology pannels.

117

Picture Index

The position of the illustrations is indicated by letters: t = top, b = bottom, r = right, l = left, m = middle, x = middle left, y = middle right. SP stands for Sipa Press, Rex for Rex Features Ltd.

Jacket
from top to bottom, left to right:
SP, Chesnot/SP, Iso Press/SP, Labat/Tavernier/SS, Dewitt/SP, Crane, Villard/SP, Alpha Diffusion/SP, Andrews/SP, Mantel/SP, L.R.C./SP, Sunshine/SP, Sichov/SS.